The Python/C API

Release 3.6.4

**Guido van Rossum
and the Python development team**

February 03, 2018

Python Software Foundation
Email: docs@python.org

CONTENTS

This manual documents the API used by C and C++ programmers who want to write extension modules or embed Python. It is a companion to extending-index, which describes the general principles of extension writing but does not document the API functions in detail.

CONTENTS

INTRODUCTION

The Application Programmer's Interface to Python gives C and C++ programmers access to the Python interpreter at a variety of levels. The API is equally usable from C++, but for brevity it is generally referred to as the Python/C API. There are two fundamentally different reasons for using the Python/C API. The first reason is to write *extension modules* for specific purposes; these are C modules that extend the Python interpreter. This is probably the most common use. The second reason is to use Python as a component in a larger application; this technique is generally referred to as *embedding* Python in an application.

Writing an extension module is a relatively well-understood process, where a "cookbook" approach works well. There are several tools that automate the process to some extent. While people have embedded Python in other applications since its early existence, the process of embedding Python is less straightforward than writing an extension.

Many API functions are useful independent of whether you're embedding or extending Python; moreover, most applications that embed Python will need to provide a custom extension as well, so it's probably a good idea to become familiar with writing an extension before attempting to embed Python in a real application.

1.1 Include Files

All function, type and macro definitions needed to use the Python/C API are included in your code by the following line:

```
#include "Python.h"
```

This implies inclusion of the following standard headers: `<stdio.h>`, `<string.h>`, `<errno.h>`, `<limits.h>`, `<assert.h>` and `<stdlib.h>` (if available).

Note: Since Python may define some pre-processor definitions which affect the standard headers on some systems, you *must* include `Python.h` before any standard headers are included.

All user visible names defined by Python.h (except those defined by the included standard headers) have one of the prefixes `Py` or `_Py`. Names beginning with `_Py` are for internal use by the Python implementation and should not be used by extension writers. Structure member names do not have a reserved prefix.

Important: user code should never define names that begin with `Py` or `_Py`. This confuses the reader, and jeopardizes the portability of the user code to future Python versions, which may define additional names beginning with one of these prefixes.

The header files are typically installed with Python. On Unix, these are located in the directories *prefix/*`include/pythonversion/` and *exec_prefix/*`include/pythonversion/`, where `prefix` and `exec_prefix` are defined by the corresponding parameters to Python's **configure** script and *version* is `'%d.%d' % sys.version_info[:2]`. On Windows, the headers are installed in *prefix/*`include`, where `prefix` is the installation directory specified to the installer.

To include the headers, place both directories (if different) on your compiler's search path for includes. Do *not* place the parent directories on the search path and then use `#include <pythonX.Y/Python.h>`; this will break on multi-platform builds since the platform independent headers under `prefix` include the platform specific headers from `exec_prefix`.

C++ users should note that though the API is defined entirely using C, the header files do properly declare the entry points to be `extern "C"`, so there is no need to do anything special to use the API from C++.

1.2 Objects, Types and Reference Counts

Most Python/C API functions have one or more arguments as well as a return value of type *PyObject**. This type is a pointer to an opaque data type representing an arbitrary Python object. Since all Python object types are treated the same way by the Python language in most situations (e.g., assignments, scope rules, and argument passing), it is only fitting that they should be represented by a single C type. Almost all Python objects live on the heap: you never declare an automatic or static variable of type *PyObject*, only pointer variables of type *PyObject** can be declared. The sole exception are the type objects; since these must never be deallocated, they are typically static *PyTypeObject* objects.

All Python objects (even Python integers) have a *type* and a *reference count*. An object's type determines what kind of object it is (e.g., an integer, a list, or a user-defined function; there are many more as explained in types). For each of the well-known types there is a macro to check whether an object is of that type; for instance, `PyList_Check(a)` is true if (and only if) the object pointed to by *a* is a Python list.

1.2.1 Reference Counts

The reference count is important because today's computers have a finite (and often severely limited) memory size; it counts how many different places there are that have a reference to an object. Such a place could be another object, or a global (or static) C variable, or a local variable in some C function. When an object's reference count becomes zero, the object is deallocated. If it contains references to other objects, their reference count is decremented. Those other objects may be deallocated in turn, if this decrement makes their reference count become zero, and so on. (There's an obvious problem with objects that reference each other here; for now, the solution is "don't do that.")

Reference counts are always manipulated explicitly. The normal way is to use the macro *Py_INCREF()* to increment an object's reference count by one, and *Py_DECREF()* to decrement it by one. The *Py_DECREF()* macro is considerably more complex than the incref one, since it must check whether the reference count becomes zero and then cause the object's deallocator to be called. The deallocator is a function pointer contained in the object's type structure. The type-specific deallocator takes care of decrementing the reference counts for other objects contained in the object if this is a compound object type, such as a list, as well as performing any additional finalization that's needed. There's no chance that the reference count can overflow; at least as many bits are used to hold the reference count as there are distinct memory locations in virtual memory (assuming `sizeof(Py_ssize_t) >= sizeof(void*)`). Thus, the reference count increment is a simple operation.

It is not necessary to increment an object's reference count for every local variable that contains a pointer to an object. In theory, the object's reference count goes up by one when the variable is made to point to it and it goes down by one when the variable goes out of scope. However, these two cancel each other out, so at the end the reference count hasn't changed. The only real reason to use the reference count is to prevent the object from being deallocated as long as our variable is pointing to it. If we know that there is at least one other reference to the object that lives at least as long as our variable, there is no need to increment the reference count temporarily. An important situation where this arises is in objects that are passed as arguments to C functions in an extension module that are called from Python; the call mechanism guarantees to hold a reference to every argument for the duration of the call.

However, a common pitfall is to extract an object from a list and hold on to it for a while without incrementing its reference count. Some other operation might conceivably remove the object from the list, decrementing its reference count and possible deallocating it. The real danger is that innocent-looking operations may invoke arbitrary Python code which could do this; there is a code path which allows control to flow back to the user from a *Py_DECREF()*, so almost any operation is potentially dangerous.

A safe approach is to always use the generic operations (functions whose name begins with `PyObject_`, `PyNumber_`, `PySequence_` or `PyMapping_`). These operations always increment the reference count of the object they return. This leaves the caller with the responsibility to call *Py_DECREF()* when they are done with the result; this soon becomes second nature.

Reference Count Details

The reference count behavior of functions in the Python/C API is best explained in terms of *ownership of references*. Ownership pertains to references, never to objects (objects are not owned: they are always shared). "Owning a reference" means being responsible for calling Py_DECREF on it when the reference is no longer needed. Ownership can also be transferred, meaning that the code that receives ownership of the reference then becomes responsible for eventually decref'ing it by calling *Py_DECREF()* or *Py_XDECREF()* when it's no longer needed—or passing on this responsibility (usually to its caller). When a function passes ownership of a reference on to its caller, the caller is said to receive a *new* reference. When no ownership is transferred, the caller is said to *borrow* the reference. Nothing needs to be done for a borrowed reference.

Conversely, when a calling function passes in a reference to an object, there are two possibilities: the function *steals* a reference to the object, or it does not. *Stealing a reference* means that when you pass a reference to a function, that function assumes that it now owns that reference, and you are not responsible for it any longer.

Few functions steal references; the two notable exceptions are *PyList_SetItem()* and *PyTuple_SetItem()*, which steal a reference to the item (but not to the tuple or list into which the item is put!). These functions were designed to steal a reference because of a common idiom for populating a tuple or list with newly created objects; for example, the code to create the tuple (1, 2, "three") could look like this (forgetting about error handling for the moment; a better way to code this is shown below):

```
PyObject *t;

t = PyTuple_New(3);
PyTuple_SetItem(t, 0, PyLong_FromLong(1L));
PyTuple_SetItem(t, 1, PyLong_FromLong(2L));
PyTuple_SetItem(t, 2, PyUnicode_FromString("three"));
```

Here, *PyLong_FromLong()* returns a new reference which is immediately stolen by *PyTuple_SetItem()*. When you want to keep using an object although the reference to it will be stolen, use *Py_INCREF()* to grab another reference before calling the reference-stealing function.

Incidentally, *PyTuple_SetItem()* is the *only* way to set tuple items; *PySequence_SetItem()* and *PyObject_SetItem()* refuse to do this since tuples are an immutable data type. You should only use *PyTuple_SetItem()* for tuples that you are creating yourself.

Equivalent code for populating a list can be written using *PyList_New()* and *PyList_SetItem()*.

However, in practice, you will rarely use these ways of creating and populating a tuple or list. There's a generic function, *Py_BuildValue()*, that can create most common objects from C values, directed by a *format string*. For example, the above two blocks of code could be replaced by the following (which also takes care of the error checking):

```
PyObject *tuple, *list;
```

```
tuple = Py_BuildValue("(iis)", 1, 2, "three");
list = Py_BuildValue("[iis]", 1, 2, "three");
```

It is much more common to use *PyObject_SetItem()* and friends with items whose references you are only borrowing, like arguments that were passed in to the function you are writing. In that case, their behaviour regarding reference counts is much saner, since you don't have to increment a reference count so you can give a reference away ("have it be stolen"). For example, this function sets all items of a list (actually, any mutable sequence) to a given item:

```
int
set_all(PyObject *target, PyObject *item)
{
    Py_ssize_t i, n;

    n = PyObject_Length(target);
    if (n < 0)
        return -1;
    for (i = 0; i < n; i++) {
        PyObject *index = PyLong_FromSsize_t(i);
        if (!index)
            return -1;
        if (PyObject_SetItem(target, index, item) < 0) {
            Py_DECREF(index);
            return -1;
        }
        Py_DECREF(index);
    }
    return 0;
}
```

The situation is slightly different for function return values. While passing a reference to most functions does not change your ownership responsibilities for that reference, many functions that return a reference to an object give you ownership of the reference. The reason is simple: in many cases, the returned object is created on the fly, and the reference you get is the only reference to the object. Therefore, the generic functions that return object references, like *PyObject_GetItem()* and *PySequence_GetItem()*, always return a new reference (the caller becomes the owner of the reference).

It is important to realize that whether you own a reference returned by a function depends on which function you call only — *the plumage* (the type of the object passed as an argument to the function) *doesn't enter into it!* Thus, if you extract an item from a list using *PyList_GetItem()*, you don't own the reference — but if you obtain the same item from the same list using *PySequence_GetItem()* (which happens to take exactly the same arguments), you do own a reference to the returned object.

Here is an example of how you could write a function that computes the sum of the items in a list of integers; once using *PyList_GetItem()*, and once using *PySequence_GetItem()*.

```
long
sum_list(PyObject *list)
{
    Py_ssize_t i, n;
    long total = 0, value;
    PyObject *item;

    n = PyList_Size(list);
    if (n < 0)
        return -1; /* Not a list */
    for (i = 0; i < n; i++) {
        item = PyList_GetItem(list, i); /* Can't fail */
```

```
        if (!PyLong_Check(item)) continue; /* Skip non-integers */
        value = PyLong_AsLong(item);
        if (value == -1 && PyErr_Occurred())
            /* Integer too big to fit in a C long, bail out */
            return -1;
        total += value;
    }
    return total;
}
```

```
long
sum_sequence(PyObject *sequence)
{
    Py_ssize_t i, n;
    long total = 0, value;
    PyObject *item;
    n = PySequence_Length(sequence);
    if (n < 0)
        return -1; /* Has no length */
    for (i = 0; i < n; i++) {
        item = PySequence_GetItem(sequence, i);
        if (item == NULL)
            return -1; /* Not a sequence, or other failure */
        if (PyLong_Check(item)) {
            value = PyLong_AsLong(item);
            Py_DECREF(item);
            if (value == -1 && PyErr_Occurred())
                /* Integer too big to fit in a C long, bail out */
                return -1;
            total += value;
        }
        else {
            Py_DECREF(item); /* Discard reference ownership */
        }
    }
    return total;
}
```

1.2.2 Types

There are few other data types that play a significant role in the Python/C API; most are simple C types such as int, long, double and char*. A few structure types are used to describe static tables used to list the functions exported by a module or the data attributes of a new object type, and another is used to describe the value of a complex number. These will be discussed together with the functions that use them.

1.3 Exceptions

The Python programmer only needs to deal with exceptions if specific error handling is required; unhandled exceptions are automatically propagated to the caller, then to the caller's caller, and so on, until they reach the top-level interpreter, where they are reported to the user accompanied by a stack traceback.

For C programmers, however, error checking always has to be explicit. All functions in the Python/C API can raise exceptions, unless an explicit claim is made otherwise in a function's documentation. In general, when a function encounters an error, it sets an exception, discards any object references that it owns, and returns an error indicator. If not documented otherwise, this indicator is either *NULL* or -1, depending on the function's return type. A few functions return a Boolean true/false result, with false indicating an error. Very few functions return no explicit error indicator or have an ambiguous return value, and require explicit testing for errors with *PyErr_Occurred()*. These exceptions are always explicitly documented.

Exception state is maintained in per-thread storage (this is equivalent to using global storage in an unthreaded application). A thread can be in one of two states: an exception has occurred, or not. The function *PyErr_Occurred()* can be used to check for this: it returns a borrowed reference to the exception type object when an exception has occurred, and *NULL* otherwise. There are a number of functions to set the exception state: *PyErr_SetString()* is the most common (though not the most general) function to set the exception state, and *PyErr_Clear()* clears the exception state.

The full exception state consists of three objects (all of which can be *NULL*): the exception type, the corresponding exception value, and the traceback. These have the same meanings as the Python result of **sys.exc_info()**; however, they are not the same: the Python objects represent the last exception being handled by a Python **try … except** statement, while the C level exception state only exists while an exception is being passed on between C functions until it reaches the Python bytecode interpreter's main loop, which takes care of transferring it to **sys.exc_info()** and friends.

Note that starting with Python 1.5, the preferred, thread-safe way to access the exception state from Python code is to call the function **sys.exc_info()**, which returns the per-thread exception state for Python code. Also, the semantics of both ways to access the exception state have changed so that a function which catches an exception will save and restore its thread's exception state so as to preserve the exception state of its caller. This prevents common bugs in exception handling code caused by an innocent-looking function overwriting the exception being handled; it also reduces the often unwanted lifetime extension for objects that are referenced by the stack frames in the traceback.

As a general principle, a function that calls another function to perform some task should check whether the called function raised an exception, and if so, pass the exception state on to its caller. It should discard any object references that it owns, and return an error indicator, but it should *not* set another exception — that would overwrite the exception that was just raised, and lose important information about the exact cause of the error.

A simple example of detecting exceptions and passing them on is shown in the **sum_sequence()** example above. It so happens that this example doesn't need to clean up any owned references when it detects an error. The following example function shows some error cleanup. First, to remind you why you like Python, we show the equivalent Python code:

```
def incr_item(dict, key):
    try:
        item = dict[key]
    except KeyError:
        item = 0
    dict[key] = item + 1
```

Here is the corresponding C code, in all its glory:

```
int
incr_item(PyObject *dict, PyObject *key)
{
    /* Objects all initialized to NULL for Py_XDECREF */
    PyObject *item = NULL, *const_one = NULL, *incremented_item = NULL;
    int rv = -1; /* Return value initialized to -1 (failure) */

    item = PyObject_GetItem(dict, key);
    if (item == NULL) {
        /* Handle KeyError only: */
        if (!PyErr_ExceptionMatches(PyExc_KeyError))
            goto error;
```

```
        /* Clear the error and use zero: */
        PyErr_Clear();
        item = PyLong_FromLong(0L);
        if (item == NULL)
            goto error;
    }
    const_one = PyLong_FromLong(1L);
    if (const_one == NULL)
        goto error;

    incremented_item = PyNumber_Add(item, const_one);
    if (incremented_item == NULL)
        goto error;

    if (PyObject_SetItem(dict, key, incremented_item) < 0)
        goto error;
    rv = 0; /* Success */
    /* Continue with cleanup code */

 error:
    /* Cleanup code, shared by success and failure path */

    /* Use Py_XDECREF() to ignore NULL references */
    Py_XDECREF(item);
    Py_XDECREF(const_one);
    Py_XDECREF(incremented_item);

    return rv; /* -1 for error, 0 for success */
}
```

This example represents an endorsed use of the `goto` statement in C! It illustrates the use of *PyErr_ExceptionMatches()* and *PyErr_Clear()* to handle specific exceptions, and the use of *Py_XDECREF()* to dispose of owned references that may be *NULL* (note the 'X' in the name; *Py_DECREF()* would crash when confronted with a *NULL* reference). It is important that the variables used to hold owned references are initialized to *NULL* for this to work; likewise, the proposed return value is initialized to -1 (failure) and only set to success after the final call made is successful.

1.4 Embedding Python

The one important task that only embedders (as opposed to extension writers) of the Python interpreter have to worry about is the initialization, and possibly the finalization, of the Python interpreter. Most functionality of the interpreter can only be used after the interpreter has been initialized.

The basic initialization function is *Py_Initialize()*. This initializes the table of loaded modules, and creates the fundamental modules `builtins`, `__main__`, and `sys`. It also initializes the module search path (`sys.path`).

Py_Initialize() does not set the "script argument list" (`sys.argv`). If this variable is needed by Python code that will be executed later, it must be set explicitly with a call to `PySys_SetArgvEx(argc, argv, updatepath)` after the call to *Py_Initialize()*.

On most systems (in particular, on Unix and Windows, although the details are slightly different), *Py_Initialize()* calculates the module search path based upon its best guess for the location of the standard Python interpreter executable, assuming that the Python library is found in a fixed location relative to the Python interpreter executable. In particular, it looks for a directory named `lib/pythonX.Y` relative to the parent directory where the executable named `python` is found on the shell command search path (the environment variable `PATH`).

For instance, if the Python executable is found in `/usr/local/bin/python`, it will assume that the libraries are in `/usr/local/lib/pythonX.Y`. (In fact, this particular path is also the "fallback" location, used when no executable file named `python` is found along `PATH`.) The user can override this behavior by setting the environment variable `PYTHONHOME`, or insert additional directories in front of the standard path by setting `PYTHONPATH`.

The embedding application can steer the search by calling `Py_SetProgramName(file)` *before* calling `Py_Initialize()`. Note that `PYTHONHOME` still overrides this and `PYTHONPATH` is still inserted in front of the standard path. An application that requires total control has to provide its own implementation of `Py_GetPath()`, `Py_GetPrefix()`, `Py_GetExecPrefix()`, and `Py_GetProgramFullPath()` (all defined in `Modules/getpath.c`).

Sometimes, it is desirable to "uninitialize" Python. For instance, the application may want to start over (make another call to `Py_Initialize()`) or the application is simply done with its use of Python and wants to free memory allocated by Python. This can be accomplished by calling `Py_FinalizeEx()`. The function `Py_IsInitialized()` returns true if Python is currently in the initialized state. More information about these functions is given in a later chapter. Notice that `Py_FinalizeEx()` does *not* free all memory allocated by the Python interpreter, e.g. memory allocated by extension modules currently cannot be released.

1.5 Debugging Builds

Python can be built with several macros to enable extra checks of the interpreter and extension modules. These checks tend to add a large amount of overhead to the runtime so they are not enabled by default.

A full list of the various types of debugging builds is in the file `Misc/SpecialBuilds.txt` in the Python source distribution. Builds are available that support tracing of reference counts, debugging the memory allocator, or low-level profiling of the main interpreter loop. Only the most frequently-used builds will be described in the remainder of this section.

Compiling the interpreter with the `Py_DEBUG` macro defined produces what is generally meant by "a debug build" of Python. `Py_DEBUG` is enabled in the Unix build by adding `--with-pydebug` to the `./configure` command. It is also implied by the presence of the not-Python-specific `_DEBUG` macro. When `Py_DEBUG` is enabled in the Unix build, compiler optimization is disabled.

In addition to the reference count debugging described below, the following extra checks are performed:

- Extra checks are added to the object allocator.
- Extra checks are added to the parser and compiler.
- Downcasts from wide types to narrow types are checked for loss of information.
- A number of assertions are added to the dictionary and set implementations. In addition, the set object acquires a `test_c_api()` method.
- Sanity checks of the input arguments are added to frame creation.
- The storage for ints is initialized with a known invalid pattern to catch reference to uninitialized digits.
- Low-level tracing and extra exception checking are added to the runtime virtual machine.
- Extra checks are added to the memory arena implementation.
- Extra debugging is added to the thread module.

There may be additional checks not mentioned here.

Defining `Py_TRACE_REFS` enables reference tracing. When defined, a circular doubly linked list of active objects is maintained by adding two extra fields to every `PyObject`. Total allocations are tracked as well.

Upon exit, all existing references are printed. (In interactive mode this happens after every statement run by the interpreter.) Implied by `Py_DEBUG`.

Please refer to `Misc/SpecialBuilds.txt` in the Python source distribution for more detailed information.

STABLE APPLICATION BINARY INTERFACE

Traditionally, the C API of Python will change with every release. Most changes will be source-compatible, typically by only adding API, rather than changing existing API or removing API (although some interfaces do get removed after being deprecated first).

Unfortunately, the API compatibility does not extend to binary compatibility (the ABI). The reason is primarily the evolution of struct definitions, where addition of a new field, or changing the type of a field, might not break the API, but can break the ABI. As a consequence, extension modules need to be recompiled for every Python release (although an exception is possible on Unix when none of the affected interfaces are used). In addition, on Windows, extension modules link with a specific pythonXY.dll and need to be recompiled to link with a newer one.

Since Python 3.2, a subset of the API has been declared to guarantee a stable ABI. Extension modules wishing to use this API (called "limited API") need to define `Py_LIMITED_API`. A number of interpreter details then become hidden from the extension module; in return, a module is built that works on any 3.x version (x>=2) without recompilation.

In some cases, the stable ABI needs to be extended with new functions. Extension modules wishing to use these new APIs need to set `Py_LIMITED_API` to the `PY_VERSION_HEX` value (see *API and ABI Versioning*) of the minimum Python version they want to support (e.g. `0x03030000` for Python 3.3). Such modules will work on all subsequent Python releases, but fail to load (because of missing symbols) on the older releases.

As of Python 3.2, the set of functions available to the limited API is documented in PEP 384. In the C API documentation, API elements that are not part of the limited API are marked as "Not part of the limited API."

THE VERY HIGH LEVEL LAYER

The functions in this chapter will let you execute Python source code given in a file or a buffer, but they will not let you interact in a more detailed way with the interpreter.

Several of these functions accept a start symbol from the grammar as a parameter. The available start symbols are `Py_eval_input`, `Py_file_input`, and `Py_single_input`. These are described following the functions which accept them as parameters.

Note also that several of these functions take `FILE*` parameters. One particular issue which needs to be handled carefully is that the `FILE` structure for different C libraries can be different and incompatible. Under Windows (at least), it is possible for dynamically linked extensions to actually use different libraries, so care should be taken that `FILE*` parameters are only passed to these functions if it is certain that they were created by the same library that the Python runtime is using.

int **Py_Main**(int *argc*, wchar_t **argv*)

> The main program for the standard interpreter. This is made available for programs which embed Python. The *argc* and *argv* parameters should be prepared exactly as those which are passed to a C program's **main()** function (converted to wchar_t according to the user's locale). It is important to note that the argument list may be modified (but the contents of the strings pointed to by the argument list are not). The return value will be 0 if the interpreter exits normally (i.e., without an exception), 1 if the interpreter exits due to an exception, or 2 if the parameter list does not represent a valid Python command line.
>
> Note that if an otherwise unhandled **SystemExit** is raised, this function will not return 1, but exit the process, as long as **Py_InspectFlag** is not set.

int **PyRun_AnyFile**(FILE **fp*, const char **filename*)

> This is a simplified interface to *PyRun_AnyFileExFlags()* below, leaving *closeit* set to 0 and *flags* set to *NULL*.

int **PyRun_AnyFileFlags**(FILE **fp*, const char **filename*, *PyCompilerFlags* **flags*)

> This is a simplified interface to *PyRun_AnyFileExFlags()* below, leaving the *closeit* argument set to 0.

int **PyRun_AnyFileEx**(FILE **fp*, const char **filename*, int *closeit*)

> This is a simplified interface to *PyRun_AnyFileExFlags()* below, leaving the *flags* argument set to *NULL*.

int **PyRun_AnyFileExFlags**(FILE **fp*, const char **filename*, int *closeit*, *PyCompilerFlags* **flags*)

> If *fp* refers to a file associated with an interactive device (console or terminal input or Unix pseudo-terminal), return the value of *PyRun_InteractiveLoop()*, otherwise return the result of *PyRun_SimpleFile()*. *filename* is decoded from the filesystem encoding (**sys.getfilesystemencoding()**). If *filename* is *NULL*, this function uses "???" as the filename.

int **PyRun_SimpleString**(const char **command*)

> This is a simplified interface to *PyRun_SimpleStringFlags()* below, leaving the *PyCompilerFlags** argument set to NULL.

int **PyRun_SimpleStringFlags**(const char *command, *PyCompilerFlags* *flags*)

> Executes the Python source code from *command* in the `__main__` module according to the *flags* argument. If `__main__` does not already exist, it is created. Returns 0 on success or -1 if an exception was raised. If there was an error, there is no way to get the exception information. For the meaning of *flags*, see below.

> Note that if an otherwise unhandled `SystemExit` is raised, this function will not return -1, but exit the process, as long as `Py_InspectFlag` is not set.

int **PyRun_SimpleFile**(FILE *fp*, const char *filename*)

> This is a simplified interface to *PyRun_SimpleFileExFlags()* below, leaving *closeit* set to 0 and *flags* set to *NULL*.

int **PyRun_SimpleFileEx**(FILE *fp*, const char *filename*, int *closeit*)

> This is a simplified interface to *PyRun_SimpleFileExFlags()* below, leaving *flags* set to *NULL*.

int **PyRun_SimpleFileExFlags**(FILE *fp*, const char *filename*, int *closeit*, *PyCompilerFlags* *flags*)

> Similar to *PyRun_SimpleStringFlags()*, but the Python source code is read from *fp* instead of an in-memory string. *filename* should be the name of the file, it is decoded from the filesystem encoding (`sys.getfilesystemencoding()`). If *closeit* is true, the file is closed before PyRun_SimpleFileExFlags returns.

int **PyRun_InteractiveOne**(FILE *fp*, const char *filename*)

> This is a simplified interface to *PyRun_InteractiveOneFlags()* below, leaving *flags* set to *NULL*.

int **PyRun_InteractiveOneFlags**(FILE *fp*, const char *filename*, *PyCompilerFlags* *flags*)

> Read and execute a single statement from a file associated with an interactive device according to the *flags* argument. The user will be prompted using `sys.ps1` and `sys.ps2`. *filename* is decoded from the filesystem encoding (`sys.getfilesystemencoding()`).

> Returns 0 when the input was executed successfully, -1 if there was an exception, or an error code from the `errcode.h` include file distributed as part of Python if there was a parse error. (Note that `errcode.h` is not included by `Python.h`, so must be included specifically if needed.)

int **PyRun_InteractiveLoop**(FILE *fp*, const char *filename*)

> This is a simplified interface to *PyRun_InteractiveLoopFlags()* below, leaving *flags* set to *NULL*.

int **PyRun_InteractiveLoopFlags**(FILE *fp*, const char *filename*, *PyCompilerFlags* *flags*)

> Read and execute statements from a file associated with an interactive device until EOF is reached. The user will be prompted using `sys.ps1` and `sys.ps2`. *filename* is decoded from the filesystem encoding (`sys.getfilesystemencoding()`). Returns 0 at EOF or a negative number upon failure.

int (***PyOS_InputHook**)(void)

> Can be set to point to a function with the prototype `int func(void)`. The function will be called when Python's interpreter prompt is about to become idle and wait for user input from the terminal. The return value is ignored. Overriding this hook can be used to integrate the interpreter's prompt with other event loops, as done in the `Modules/_tkinter.c` in the Python source code.

char* (***PyOS_ReadlineFunctionPointer**)(FILE *, FILE *, const char *)

> Can be set to point to a function with the prototype `char *func(FILE *stdin, FILE *stdout, char *prompt)`, overriding the default function used to read a single line of input at the interpreter's prompt. The function is expected to output the string *prompt* if it's not *NULL*, and then read a line of input from the provided standard input file, returning the resulting string. For example, The `readline` module sets this hook to provide line-editing and tab-completion features.

> The result must be a string allocated by *PyMem_RawMalloc()* or *PyMem_RawRealloc()*, or *NULL* if an error occurred.

> Changed in version 3.4: The result must be allocated by *PyMem_RawMalloc()* or *PyMem_RawRealloc()*, instead of being allocated by *PyMem_Malloc()* or *PyMem_Realloc()*.

struct _node* **PyParser_SimpleParseString**(const char *str*, int *start*)
>   This is a simplified interface to *PyParser_SimpleParseStringFlagsFilename()* below, leaving *filename* set to *NULL* and *flags* set to 0.

struct _node* **PyParser_SimpleParseStringFlags**(const char *str*, int *start*, int *flags*)
>   This is a simplified interface to *PyParser_SimpleParseStringFlagsFilename()* below, leaving *filename* set to *NULL*.

struct _node* **PyParser_SimpleParseStringFlagsFilename**(const char *str*, const char *filename*, int *start*, int *flags*)
>   Parse Python source code from *str* using the start token *start* according to the *flags* argument. The result can be used to create a code object which can be evaluated efficiently. This is useful if a code fragment must be evaluated many times. *filename* is decoded from the filesystem encoding (sys.getfilesystemencoding()).

struct _node* **PyParser_SimpleParseFile**(FILE *fp*, const char *filename*, int *start*)
>   This is a simplified interface to *PyParser_SimpleParseFileFlags()* below, leaving *flags* set to 0.

struct _node* **PyParser_SimpleParseFileFlags**(FILE *fp*, const char *filename*, int *start*, int *flags*)
>   Similar to *PyParser_SimpleParseStringFlagsFilename()*, but the Python source code is read from *fp* instead of an in-memory string.

*PyObject** **PyRun_String**(const char *str*, int *start*, *PyObject* *globals*, *PyObject* *locals*)
>   *Return value: New reference.* This is a simplified interface to *PyRun_StringFlags()* below, leaving *flags* set to *NULL*.

*PyObject** **PyRun_StringFlags**(const char *str*, int *start*, *PyObject* *globals*, *PyObject* *locals*, *PyCompilerFlags* *flags*)
>   *Return value: New reference.* Execute Python source code from *str* in the context specified by the objects *globals* and *locals* with the compiler flags specified by *flags*. *globals* must be a dictionary; *locals* can be any object that implements the mapping protocol. The parameter *start* specifies the start token that should be used to parse the source code.
>
>   Returns the result of executing the code as a Python object, or *NULL* if an exception was raised.

*PyObject** **PyRun_File**(FILE *fp*, const char *filename*, int *start*, *PyObject* *globals*, *PyObject* *locals*)
>   *Return value: New reference.* This is a simplified interface to *PyRun_FileExFlags()* below, leaving *closeit* set to 0 and *flags* set to *NULL*.

*PyObject** **PyRun_FileEx**(FILE *fp*, const char *filename*, int *start*, *PyObject* *globals*, *PyObject* *locals*, int *closeit*)
>   *Return value: New reference.* This is a simplified interface to *PyRun_FileExFlags()* below, leaving *flags* set to *NULL*.

*PyObject** **PyRun_FileFlags**(FILE *fp*, const char *filename*, int *start*, *PyObject* *globals*, *PyObject* *locals*, *PyCompilerFlags* *flags*)
>   *Return value: New reference.* This is a simplified interface to *PyRun_FileExFlags()* below, leaving *closeit* set to 0.

*PyObject** **PyRun_FileExFlags**(FILE *fp*, const char *filename*, int *start*, *PyObject* *globals*, *PyObject* *locals*, int *closeit*, *PyCompilerFlags* *flags*)
>   *Return value: New reference.* Similar to *PyRun_StringFlags()*, but the Python source code is read from *fp* instead of an in-memory string. *filename* should be the name of the file, it is decoded from the filesystem encoding (sys.getfilesystemencoding()). If *closeit* is true, the file is closed before *PyRun_FileExFlags()* returns.

*PyObject** **Py_CompileString**(const char *str*, const char *filename*, int *start*)
>   *Return value: New reference.* This is a simplified interface to *Py_CompileStringFlags()* below, leaving *flags* set to *NULL*.

*PyObject** **Py_CompileStringFlags**(const char *str*, const char *filename*, int *start*, *PyCompilerFlags* *flags*)

Return value: New reference. This is a simplified interface to `Py_CompileStringExFlags()` below, with *optimize* set to −1.

*PyObject** **Py_CompileStringObject**(const char *str*, *PyObject* *filename*, int *start*, *PyCompiler-Flags* *flags*, int *optimize*)
    Parse and compile the Python source code in *str*, returning the resulting code object. The start token is given by *start*; this can be used to constrain the code which can be compiled and should be `Py_eval_input`, `Py_file_input`, or `Py_single_input`. The filename specified by *filename* is used to construct the code object and may appear in tracebacks or `SyntaxError` exception messages. This returns *NULL* if the code cannot be parsed or compiled.

    The integer *optimize* specifies the optimization level of the compiler; a value of −1 selects the optimization level of the interpreter as given by -O options. Explicit levels are 0 (no optimization; `__debug__` is true), 1 (asserts are removed, `__debug__` is false) or 2 (docstrings are removed too).

    New in version 3.4.

*PyObject** **Py_CompileStringExFlags**(const char *str*, const char *filename*, int *start*, *PyCompiler-Flags* *flags*, int *optimize*)
    Like `Py_CompileStringObject()`, but *filename* is a byte string decoded from the filesystem encoding (`os.fsdecode()`).

    New in version 3.2.

*PyObject** **PyEval_EvalCode**(*PyObject* *co*, *PyObject* *globals*, *PyObject* *locals*)
    Return value: New reference. This is a simplified interface to `PyEval_EvalCodeEx()`, with just the code object, and global and local variables. The other arguments are set to *NULL*.

*PyObject** **PyEval_EvalCodeEx**(*PyObject* *co*, *PyObject* *globals*, *PyObject* *locals*, *PyObject* **args*, int *argcount*, *PyObject* **kws*, int *kwcount*, *PyObject* **defs*, int *defcount*, *PyObject* *kwdefs*, *PyObject* *closure*)
    Evaluate a precompiled code object, given a particular environment for its evaluation. This environment consists of a dictionary of global variables, a mapping object of local variables, arrays of arguments, keywords and defaults, a dictionary of default values for *keyword-only* arguments and a closure tuple of cells.

PyFrameObject
    The C structure of the objects used to describe frame objects. The fields of this type are subject to change at any time.

*PyObject** **PyEval_EvalFrame**(*PyFrameObject* *f*)
    Evaluate an execution frame. This is a simplified interface to `PyEval_EvalFrameEx()`, for backward compatibility.

*PyObject** **PyEval_EvalFrameEx**(*PyFrameObject* *f*, int *throwflag*)
    This is the main, unvarnished function of Python interpretation. It is literally 2000 lines long. The code object associated with the execution frame *f* is executed, interpreting bytecode and executing calls as needed. The additional *throwflag* parameter can mostly be ignored - if true, then it causes an exception to immediately be thrown; this is used for the `throw()` methods of generator objects.

    Changed in version 3.4: This function now includes a debug assertion to help ensure that it does not silently discard an active exception.

int **PyEval_MergeCompilerFlags**(*PyCompilerFlags* *cf*)
    This function changes the flags of the current evaluation frame, and returns true on success, false on failure.

int **Py_eval_input**
    The start symbol from the Python grammar for isolated expressions; for use with `Py_CompileString()`.

int **Py_file_input**
    The start symbol from the Python grammar for sequences of statements as read from a file or other

source; for use with *Py_CompileString()*. This is the symbol to use when compiling arbitrarily long Python source code.

int **Py_single_input**

> The start symbol from the Python grammar for a single statement; for use with *Py_CompileString()*. This is the symbol used for the interactive interpreter loop.

struct **PyCompilerFlags**

> This is the structure used to hold compiler flags. In cases where code is only being compiled, it is passed as **int flags**, and in cases where code is being executed, it is passed as PyCompilerFlags *flags. In this case, from __future__ import can modify *flags*.

> Whenever PyCompilerFlags *flags is *NULL*, cf_flags is treated as equal to 0, and any modification due to from __future__ import is discarded.

```
struct PyCompilerFlags {
    int cf_flags;
}
```

int **CO_FUTURE_DIVISION**

> This bit can be set in *flags* to cause division operator / to be interpreted as "true division" according to PEP 238.

REFERENCE COUNTING

The macros in this section are used for managing reference counts of Python objects.

void **Py_INCREF**(*PyObject* *o*)

> Increment the reference count for object *o*. The object must not be *NULL*; if you aren't sure that it isn't *NULL*, use *Py_XINCREF()*.

void **Py_XINCREF**(*PyObject* *o*)

> Increment the reference count for object *o*. The object may be *NULL*, in which case the macro has no effect.

void **Py_DECREF**(*PyObject* *o*)

> Decrement the reference count for object *o*. The object must not be *NULL*; if you aren't sure that it isn't *NULL*, use *Py_XDECREF()*. If the reference count reaches zero, the object's type's deallocation function (which must not be *NULL*) is invoked.

> **Warning:** The deallocation function can cause arbitrary Python code to be invoked (e.g. when a class instance with a **__del__**() method is deallocated). While exceptions in such code are not propagated, the executed code has free access to all Python global variables. This means that any object that is reachable from a global variable should be in a consistent state before *Py_DECREF()* is invoked. For example, code to delete an object from a list should copy a reference to the deleted object in a temporary variable, update the list data structure, and then call *Py_DECREF()* for the temporary variable.

void **Py_XDECREF**(*PyObject* *o*)

> Decrement the reference count for object *o*. The object may be *NULL*, in which case the macro has no effect; otherwise the effect is the same as for *Py_DECREF()*, and the same warning applies.

void **Py_CLEAR**(*PyObject* *o*)

> Decrement the reference count for object *o*. The object may be *NULL*, in which case the macro has no effect; otherwise the effect is the same as for *Py_DECREF()*, except that the argument is also set to *NULL*. The warning for *Py_DECREF()* does not apply with respect to the object passed because the macro carefully uses a temporary variable and sets the argument to *NULL* before decrementing its reference count.

> It is a good idea to use this macro whenever decrementing the value of a variable that might be traversed during garbage collection.

The following functions are for runtime dynamic embedding of Python: **Py_IncRef(PyObject *o)**, **Py_DecRef(PyObject *o)**. They are simply exported function versions of *Py_XINCREF()* and *Py_XDECREF()*, respectively.

The following functions or macros are only for use within the interpreter core: **_Py_Dealloc()**, **_Py_ForgetReference()**, **_Py_NewReference()**, as well as the global variable **_Py_RefTotal**.

EXCEPTION HANDLING

The functions described in this chapter will let you handle and raise Python exceptions. It is important to understand some of the basics of Python exception handling. It works somewhat like the POSIX `errno` variable: there is a global indicator (per thread) of the last error that occurred. Most C API functions don't clear this on success, but will set it to indicate the cause of the error on failure. Most C API functions also return an error indicator, usually *NULL* if they are supposed to return a pointer, or `-1` if they return an integer (exception: the `PyArg_*()` functions return `1` for success and `0` for failure).

Concretely, the error indicator consists of three object pointers: the exception's type, the exception's value, and the traceback object. Any of those pointers can be NULL if non-set (although some combinations are forbidden, for example you can't have a non-NULL traceback if the exception type is NULL).

When a function must fail because some function it called failed, it generally doesn't set the error indicator; the function it called already set it. It is responsible for either handling the error and clearing the exception or returning after cleaning up any resources it holds (such as object references or memory allocations); it should *not* continue normally if it is not prepared to handle the error. If returning due to an error, it is important to indicate to the caller that an error has been set. If the error is not handled or carefully propagated, additional calls into the Python/C API may not behave as intended and may fail in mysterious ways.

Note: The error indicator is **not** the result of `sys.exc_info()`. The former corresponds to an exception that is not yet caught (and is therefore still propagating), while the latter returns an exception after it is caught (and has therefore stopped propagating).

5.1 Printing and clearing

void **PyErr_Clear**()
> Clear the error indicator. If the error indicator is not set, there is no effect.

void **PyErr_PrintEx**(int *set_sys_last_vars*)
> Print a standard traceback to `sys.stderr` and clear the error indicator. Call this function only when the error indicator is set. (Otherwise it will cause a fatal error!)
>
> If *set_sys_last_vars* is nonzero, the variables `sys.last_type`, `sys.last_value` and `sys.last_traceback` will be set to the type, value and traceback of the printed exception, respectively.

void **PyErr_Print**()
> Alias for `PyErr_PrintEx(1)`.

void **PyErr_WriteUnraisable**(*PyObject* *obj*)
> This utility function prints a warning message to `sys.stderr` when an exception has been set but it is impossible for the interpreter to actually raise the exception. It is used, for example, when an exception occurs in an `__del__`() method.

The function is called with a single argument *obj* that identifies the context in which the unraisable exception occurred. If possible, the repr of *obj* will be printed in the warning message.

5.2 Raising exceptions

These functions help you set the current thread's error indicator. For convenience, some of these functions will always return a NULL pointer for use in a **return** statement.

void **PyErr_SetString**(*PyObject *type*, const char **message*)
>   This is the most common way to set the error indicator. The first argument specifies the exception type; it is normally one of the standard exceptions, e.g. **PyExc_RuntimeError**. You need not increment its reference count. The second argument is an error message; it is decoded from '**utf-8**'.

void **PyErr_SetObject**(*PyObject *type*, *PyObject *value*)
>   This function is similar to *PyErr_SetString()* but lets you specify an arbitrary Python object for the "value" of the exception.

PyObject* **PyErr_Format**(*PyObject *exception*, const char **format*, ...)
>   *Return value: Always NULL.* This function sets the error indicator and returns *NULL*. *exception* should be a Python exception class. The *format* and subsequent parameters help format the error message; they have the same meaning and values as in *PyUnicode_FromFormat()*. *format* is an ASCII-encoded string.

PyObject* **PyErr_FormatV**(*PyObject *exception*, const char **format*, va_list *vargs*)
>   *Return value: Always NULL.* Same as *PyErr_Format()*, but taking a **va_list** argument rather than a variable number of arguments.

>   New in version 3.5.

void **PyErr_SetNone**(*PyObject *type*)
>   This is a shorthand for PyErr_SetObject(type, Py_None).

int **PyErr_BadArgument**()
>   This is a shorthand for PyErr_SetString(PyExc_TypeError, message), where *message* indicates that a built-in operation was invoked with an illegal argument. It is mostly for internal use.

PyObject* **PyErr_NoMemory**()
>   *Return value: Always NULL.* This is a shorthand for PyErr_SetNone(PyExc_MemoryError); it returns *NULL* so an object allocation function can write **return PyErr_NoMemory()**; when it runs out of memory.

PyObject* **PyErr_SetFromErrno**(*PyObject *type*)
>   *Return value: Always NULL.* This is a convenience function to raise an exception when a C library function has returned an error and set the C variable **errno**. It constructs a tuple object whose first item is the integer **errno** value and whose second item is the corresponding error message (gotten from **strerror()**), and then calls **PyErr_SetObject(type, object)**. On Unix, when the **errno** value is EINTR, indicating an interrupted system call, this calls *PyErr_CheckSignals()*, and if that set the error indicator, leaves it set to that. The function always returns *NULL*, so a wrapper function around a system call can write **return PyErr_SetFromErrno(type)**; when the system call returns an error.

PyObject* **PyErr_SetFromErrnoWithFilenameObject**(*PyObject *type*, *PyObject *filenameObject*)
>   Similar to *PyErr_SetFromErrno()*, with the additional behavior that if *filenameObject* is not *NULL*, it is passed to the constructor of *type* as a third parameter. In the case of **OSError** exception, this is used to define the **filename** attribute of the exception instance.

PyObject* **PyErr_SetFromErrnoWithFilenameObjects**(*PyObject *type*, *PyObject *filenameObject*, *PyObject *filenameObject2*)
>   Similar to *PyErr_SetFromErrnoWithFilenameObject()*, but takes a second filename object, for raising errors when a function that takes two filenames fails.

New in version 3.4.

PyObject* **PyErr_SetFromErrnoWithFilename**(*PyObject* *type, const char *filename)
> *Return value: Always NULL.* Similar to *PyErr_SetFromErrnoWithFilenameObject()*, but the filename is given as a C string. *filename* is decoded from the filesystem encoding (`os.fsdecode()`).

PyObject* **PyErr_SetFromWindowsErr**(int *ierr*)
> *Return value: Always NULL.* This is a convenience function to raise `WindowsError`. If called with *ierr* of 0, the error code returned by a call to `GetLastError()` is used instead. It calls the Win32 function `FormatMessage()` to retrieve the Windows description of error code given by *ierr* or `GetLastError()`, then it constructs a tuple object whose first item is the *ierr* value and whose second item is the corresponding error message (gotten from `FormatMessage()`), and then calls `PyErr_SetObject(PyExc_WindowsError, object)`. This function always returns *NULL*. Availability: Windows.

PyObject* **PyErr_SetExcFromWindowsErr**(*PyObject* *type, int *ierr*)
> *Return value: Always NULL.* Similar to *PyErr_SetFromWindowsErr()*, with an additional parameter specifying the exception type to be raised. Availability: Windows.

PyObject* **PyErr_SetFromWindowsErrWithFilename**(int *ierr*, const char *filename)
> *Return value: Always NULL.* Similar to `PyErr_SetFromWindowsErrWithFilenameObject()`, but the filename is given as a C string. *filename* is decoded from the filesystem encoding (`os.fsdecode()`). Availability: Windows.

PyObject* **PyErr_SetExcFromWindowsErrWithFilenameObject**(*PyObject* *type, int *ierr*, *PyObject* *filename)
> Similar to `PyErr_SetFromWindowsErrWithFilenameObject()`, with an additional parameter specifying the exception type to be raised. Availability: Windows.

PyObject* **PyErr_SetExcFromWindowsErrWithFilenameObjects**(*PyObject* *type, int *ierr*, *PyObject* *filename, *PyObject* *filename2)
> Similar to *PyErr_SetExcFromWindowsErrWithFilenameObject()*, but accepts a second filename object. Availability: Windows.

New in version 3.4.

PyObject* **PyErr_SetExcFromWindowsErrWithFilename**(*PyObject* *type, int *ierr*, const char *filename)
> *Return value: Always NULL.* Similar to *PyErr_SetFromWindowsErrWithFilename()*, with an additional parameter specifying the exception type to be raised. Availability: Windows.

PyObject* **PyErr_SetImportError**(*PyObject* *msg, *PyObject* *name, *PyObject* *path)
> This is a convenience function to raise `ImportError`. *msg* will be set as the exception's message string. *name* and *path*, both of which can be NULL, will be set as the `ImportError`'s respective `name` and `path` attributes.

New in version 3.3.

void **PyErr_SyntaxLocationObject**(*PyObject* *filename, int *lineno*, int *col_offset*)
> Set file, line, and offset information for the current exception. If the current exception is not a `SyntaxError`, then it sets additional attributes, which make the exception printing subsystem think the exception is a `SyntaxError`.

New in version 3.4.

void **PyErr_SyntaxLocationEx**(const char *filename, int *lineno*, int *col_offset*)
> Like *PyErr_SyntaxLocationObject()*, but *filename* is a byte string decoded from the filesystem encoding (`os.fsdecode()`).

New in version 3.2.

void **PyErr_SyntaxLocation**(const char *filename*, int *lineno*)
>   Like *PyErr_SyntaxLocationEx()*, but the col_offset parameter is omitted.

void **PyErr_BadInternalCall**()
>   This is a shorthand for **PyErr_SetString(PyExc_SystemError, message)**, where *message* indicates
>   that an internal operation (e.g. a Python/C API function) was invoked with an illegal argument. It is
>   mostly for internal use.

5.3 Issuing warnings

Use these functions to issue warnings from C code. They mirror similar functions exported by the Python
warnings module. They normally print a warning message to *sys.stderr*; however, it is also possible that the
user has specified that warnings are to be turned into errors, and in that case they will raise an exception.
It is also possible that the functions raise an exception because of a problem with the warning machinery.
The return value is 0 if no exception is raised, or -1 if an exception is raised. (It is not possible to determine
whether a warning message is actually printed, nor what the reason is for the exception; this is intentional.)
If an exception is raised, the caller should do its normal exception handling (for example, *Py_DECREF()*
owned references and return an error value).

int **PyErr_WarnEx**(*PyObject *category*, const char *message*, Py_ssize_t *stack_level*)
>   Issue a warning message. The *category* argument is a warning category (see below) or *NULL*; the
>   *message* argument is a UTF-8 encoded string. *stack_level* is a positive number giving a number of
>   stack frames; the warning will be issued from the currently executing line of code in that stack frame.
>   A *stack_level* of 1 is the function calling *PyErr_WarnEx()*, 2 is the function above that, and so forth.
>
>   Warning categories must be subclasses of **PyExc_Warning**; **PyExc_Warning** is a subclass of
>   **PyExc_Exception**; the default warning category is **PyExc_RuntimeWarning**. The standard Python
>   warning categories are available as global variables whose names are enumerated at *Standard Warning
>   Categories*.
>
>   For information about warning control, see the documentation for the **warnings** module and the -W
>   option in the command line documentation. There is no C API for warning control.

*PyObject** **PyErr_SetImportErrorSubclass**(*PyObject *msg*, *PyObject *name*, *PyObject *path*)
>   Much like *PyErr_SetImportError()* but this function allows for specifying a subclass of **ImportError**
>   to raise.
>
>   New in version 3.6.

int **PyErr_WarnExplicitObject**(*PyObject *category*, *PyObject *message*, *PyObject *filename*,
>   int *lineno*, *PyObject *module*, *PyObject *registry*)
>   Issue a warning message with explicit control over all warning attributes. This is a straightforward
>   wrapper around the Python function **warnings.warn_explicit()**, see there for more information.
>   The *module* and *registry* arguments may be set to *NULL* to get the default effect described there.
>
>   New in version 3.4.

int **PyErr_WarnExplicit**(*PyObject *category*, const char *message*, const char *filename*, int *lineno*,
>   const char *module*, *PyObject *registry*)
>   Similar to *PyErr_WarnExplicitObject()* except that *message* and *module* are UTF-8 encoded strings,
>   and *filename* is decoded from the filesystem encoding (**os.fsdecode()**).

int **PyErr_WarnFormat**(*PyObject *category*, Py_ssize_t *stack_level*, const char *format*, ...)
>   Function similar to *PyErr_WarnEx()*, but use *PyUnicode_FromFormat()* to format the warning mes-
>   sage. *format* is an ASCII-encoded string.
>
>   New in version 3.2.

int **PyErr_ResourceWarning**(*PyObject* *source*, Py_ssize_t *stack_level*, const char *format*, ...)
Function similar to *PyErr_WarnFormat()*, but *category* is **ResourceWarning** and pass *source* to
`warnings.WarningMessage()`.

New in version 3.6.

5.4 Querying the error indicator

*PyObject** **PyErr_Occurred**()
Return value: Borrowed reference. Test whether the error indicator is set. If set, return the exception
type (the first argument to the last call to one of the **PyErr_Set*()** functions or to *PyErr_Restore()*).
If not set, return *NULL*. You do not own a reference to the return value, so you do not need to
Py_DECREF() it.

Note: Do not compare the return value to a specific exception; use *PyErr_ExceptionMatches()*
instead, shown below. (The comparison could easily fail since the exception may be an instance
instead of a class, in the case of a class exception, or it may be a subclass of the expected exception.)

---

int **PyErr_ExceptionMatches**(*PyObject* *exc*)
Equivalent to **PyErr_GivenExceptionMatches(PyErr_Occurred(), exc)**. This should only be called
when an exception is actually set; a memory access violation will occur if no exception has been raised.

int **PyErr_GivenExceptionMatches**(*PyObject* *given*, *PyObject* *exc*)
Return true if the *given* exception matches the exception type in *exc*. If *exc* is a class object, this also
returns true when *given* is an instance of a subclass. If *exc* is a tuple, all exception types in the tuple
(and recursively in subtuples) are searched for a match.

void **PyErr_Fetch**(*PyObject* **ptype*, *PyObject* **pvalue*, *PyObject* **ptraceback*)
Retrieve the error indicator into three variables whose addresses are passed. If the error indicator is
not set, set all three variables to *NULL*. If it is set, it will be cleared and you own a reference to each
object retrieved. The value and traceback object may be *NULL* even when the type object is not.

Note: This function is normally only used by code that needs to catch exceptions or by code that
needs to save and restore the error indicator temporarily, e.g.:

```
{
    PyObject *type, *value, *traceback;
    PyErr_Fetch(&type, &value, &traceback);

    /* ... code that might produce other errors ... */

    PyErr_Restore(type, value, traceback);
}
```

---

void **PyErr_Restore**(*PyObject* *type*, *PyObject* *value*, *PyObject* *traceback*)
Set the error indicator from the three objects. If the error indicator is already set, it is cleared first. If
the objects are *NULL*, the error indicator is cleared. Do not pass a *NULL* type and non-*NULL* value
or traceback. The exception type should be a class. Do not pass an invalid exception type or value.
(Violating these rules will cause subtle problems later.) This call takes away a reference to each object:
you must own a reference to each object before the call and after the call you no longer own these
references. (If you don't understand this, don't use this function. I warned you.)

Note: This function is normally only used by code that needs to save and restore the error indicator temporarily. Use *PyErr_Fetch()* to save the current error indicator.

void **PyErr_NormalizeException**(*PyObject*****exc, *PyObject*****val, *PyObject*****tb)

Under certain circumstances, the values returned by *PyErr_Fetch()* below can be "unnormalized", meaning that ***exc** is a class object but ***val** is not an instance of the same class. This function can be used to instantiate the class in that case. If the values are already normalized, nothing happens. The delayed normalization is implemented to improve performance.

Note: This function *does not* implicitly set the **__traceback__** attribute on the exception value. If setting the traceback appropriately is desired, the following additional snippet is needed:

```
if (tb != NULL) {
  PyException_SetTraceback(val, tb);
}
```

void **PyErr_GetExcInfo**(*PyObject* ****ptype*, *PyObject* ****pvalue*, *PyObject* ****ptraceback*)

Retrieve the exception info, as known from **sys.exc_info()**. This refers to an exception that was *already caught*, not to an exception that was freshly raised. Returns new references for the three objects, any of which may be *NULL*. Does not modify the exception info state.

Note: This function is not normally used by code that wants to handle exceptions. Rather, it can be used when code needs to save and restore the exception state temporarily. Use *PyErr_SetExcInfo()* to restore or clear the exception state.

New in version **3.3**.

void **PyErr_SetExcInfo**(*PyObject* ***type*, *PyObject* ***value*, *PyObject* ***traceback*)

Set the exception info, as known from **sys.exc_info()**. This refers to an exception that was *already caught*, not to an exception that was freshly raised. This function steals the references of the arguments. To clear the exception state, pass *NULL* for all three arguments. For general rules about the three arguments, see *PyErr_Restore()*.

Note: This function is not normally used by code that wants to handle exceptions. Rather, it can be used when code needs to save and restore the exception state temporarily. Use *PyErr_GetExcInfo()* to read the exception state.

New in version **3.3**.

5.5 Signal Handling

int **PyErr_CheckSignals**()

This function interacts with Python's signal handling. It checks whether a signal has been sent to the processes and if so, invokes the corresponding signal handler. If the **signal** module is supported, this can invoke a signal handler written in Python. In all cases, the default effect for **SIGINT** is to raise the **KeyboardInterrupt** exception. If an exception is raised the error indicator is set and the function returns **-1**; otherwise the function returns **0**. The error indicator may or may not be cleared if it was previously set.

void **PyErr_SetInterrupt**()
> This function simulates the effect of a SIGINT signal arriving — the next time *PyErr_CheckSignals()* is called, KeyboardInterrupt will be raised. It may be called without holding the interpreter lock.

int **PySignal_SetWakeupFd**(int *fd*)
> This utility function specifies a file descriptor to which the signal number is written as a single byte whenever a signal is received. *fd* must be non-blocking. It returns the previous such file descriptor.
>
> The value -1 disables the feature; this is the initial state. This is equivalent to signal. set_wakeup_fd() in Python, but without any error checking. *fd* should be a valid file descriptor. The function should only be called from the main thread.
>
> Changed in version 3.5: On Windows, the function now also supports socket handles.

5.6 Exception Classes

*PyObject** **PyErr_NewException**(const char **name*, *PyObject* **base*, *PyObject* **dict*)
> *Return value: New reference.* This utility function creates and returns a new exception class. The *name* argument must be the name of the new exception, a C string of the form module.classname. The *base* and *dict* arguments are normally *NULL*. This creates a class object derived from Exception (accessible in C as PyExc_Exception).
>
> The __module__ attribute of the new class is set to the first part (up to the last dot) of the *name* argument, and the class name is set to the last part (after the last dot). The *base* argument can be used to specify alternate base classes; it can either be only one class or a tuple of classes. The *dict* argument can be used to specify a dictionary of class variables and methods.

*PyObject** **PyErr_NewExceptionWithDoc**(const char **name*, const char **doc*, *PyObject* **base*, *PyObject* **dict*)
> *Return value: New reference.* Same as *PyErr_NewException()*, except that the new exception class can easily be given a docstring: If *doc* is non-*NULL*, it will be used as the docstring for the exception class.
>
> New in version 3.2.

5.7 Exception Objects

*PyObject** **PyException_GetTraceback**(*PyObject* **ex*)
> *Return value: New reference.* Return the traceback associated with the exception as a new reference, as accessible from Python through __traceback__. If there is no traceback associated, this returns *NULL*.

int **PyException_SetTraceback**(*PyObject* **ex*, *PyObject* **tb*)
> Set the traceback associated with the exception to *tb*. Use Py_None to clear it.

*PyObject** **PyException_GetContext**(*PyObject* **ex*)
> Return the context (another exception instance during whose handling *ex* was raised) associated with the exception as a new reference, as accessible from Python through __context__. If there is no context associated, this returns *NULL*.

void **PyException_SetContext**(*PyObject* **ex*, *PyObject* **ctx*)
> Set the context associated with the exception to *ctx*. Use *NULL* to clear it. There is no type check to make sure that *ctx* is an exception instance. This steals a reference to *ctx*.

*PyObject** **PyException_GetCause**(*PyObject* **ex*)
> Return the cause (either an exception instance, or None, set by raise ... from ...) associated with the exception as a new reference, as accessible from Python through __cause__.

void **PyException_SetCause**(*PyObject* *ex, *PyObject* *cause)

> Set the cause associated with the exception to *cause*. Use *NULL* to clear it. There is no type check to make sure that *cause* is either an exception instance or None. This steals a reference to *cause*.
>
> **__suppress_context__** is implicitly set to True by this function.

5.8 Unicode Exception Objects

The following functions are used to create and modify Unicode exceptions from C.

PyObject* **PyUnicodeDecodeError_Create**(const char *encoding, const char *object, Py_ssize_t *length*, Py_ssize_t *start*, Py_ssize_t *end*, const char *reason)

> Create a UnicodeDecodeError object with the attributes *encoding*, *object*, *length*, *start*, *end* and *reason*. *encoding* and *reason* are UTF-8 encoded strings.

PyObject* **PyUnicodeEncodeError_Create**(const char *encoding, const *Py_UNICODE* *object, Py_ssize_t *length*, Py_ssize_t *start*, Py_ssize_t *end*, const char *reason)

> Create a UnicodeEncodeError object with the attributes *encoding*, *object*, *length*, *start*, *end* and *reason*. *encoding* and *reason* are UTF-8 encoded strings.

PyObject* **PyUnicodeTranslateError_Create**(const *Py_UNICODE* *object, Py_ssize_t *length*, Py_ssize_t *start*, Py_ssize_t *end*, const char *reason)

> Create a UnicodeTranslateError object with the attributes *object*, *length*, *start*, *end* and *reason*. *reason* is a UTF-8 encoded string.

PyObject* **PyUnicodeDecodeError_GetEncoding**(*PyObject* *exc)
PyObject* **PyUnicodeEncodeError_GetEncoding**(*PyObject* *exc)

> Return the *encoding* attribute of the given exception object.

PyObject* **PyUnicodeDecodeError_GetObject**(*PyObject* *exc)
PyObject* **PyUnicodeEncodeError_GetObject**(*PyObject* *exc)
PyObject* **PyUnicodeTranslateError_GetObject**(*PyObject* *exc)

> Return the *object* attribute of the given exception object.

int **PyUnicodeDecodeError_GetStart**(*PyObject* *exc, Py_ssize_t *start)
int **PyUnicodeEncodeError_GetStart**(*PyObject* *exc, Py_ssize_t *start)
int **PyUnicodeTranslateError_GetStart**(*PyObject* *exc, Py_ssize_t *start)

> Get the *start* attribute of the given exception object and place it into *start. *start* must not be *NULL*. Return 0 on success, -1 on failure.

int **PyUnicodeDecodeError_SetStart**(*PyObject* *exc, Py_ssize_t *start*)
int **PyUnicodeEncodeError_SetStart**(*PyObject* *exc, Py_ssize_t *start*)
int **PyUnicodeTranslateError_SetStart**(*PyObject* *exc, Py_ssize_t *start*)

> Set the *start* attribute of the given exception object to *start*. Return 0 on success, -1 on failure.

int **PyUnicodeDecodeError_GetEnd**(*PyObject* *exc, Py_ssize_t *end)
int **PyUnicodeEncodeError_GetEnd**(*PyObject* *exc, Py_ssize_t *end)
int **PyUnicodeTranslateError_GetEnd**(*PyObject* *exc, Py_ssize_t *end)

> Get the *end* attribute of the given exception object and place it into *end. *end* must not be *NULL*. Return 0 on success, -1 on failure.

int **PyUnicodeDecodeError_SetEnd**(*PyObject* *exc, Py_ssize_t *end*)
int **PyUnicodeEncodeError_SetEnd**(*PyObject* *exc, Py_ssize_t *end*)
int **PyUnicodeTranslateError_SetEnd**(*PyObject* *exc, Py_ssize_t *end*)

> Set the *end* attribute of the given exception object to *end*. Return 0 on success, -1 on failure.

PyObject* **PyUnicodeDecodeError_GetReason**(*PyObject* *exc)

PyObject* **PyUnicodeEncodeError_GetReason**(*PyObject *exc*)
PyObject* **PyUnicodeTranslateError_GetReason**(*PyObject *exc*)
>   Return the *reason* attribute of the given exception object.

int **PyUnicodeDecodeError_SetReason**(*PyObject *exc*, const char **reason*)
int **PyUnicodeEncodeError_SetReason**(*PyObject *exc*, const char **reason*)
int **PyUnicodeTranslateError_SetReason**(*PyObject *exc*, const char **reason*)
>   Set the *reason* attribute of the given exception object to *reason*. Return 0 on success, -1 on failure.

5.9 Recursion Control

These two functions provide a way to perform safe recursive calls at the C level, both in the core and in extension modules. They are needed if the recursive code does not necessarily invoke Python code (which tracks its recursion depth automatically).

int **Py_EnterRecursiveCall**(const char **where*)
>   Marks a point where a recursive C-level call is about to be performed.
>
>   If USE_STACKCHECK is defined, this function checks if the OS stack overflowed using *PyOS_CheckStack()*. In this is the case, it sets a MemoryError and returns a nonzero value.
>
>   The function then checks if the recursion limit is reached. If this is the case, a RecursionError is set and a nonzero value is returned. Otherwise, zero is returned.
>
>   *where* should be a string such as " in instance check" to be concatenated to the RecursionError message caused by the recursion depth limit.

void **Py_LeaveRecursiveCall**()
>   Ends a *Py_EnterRecursiveCall()*. Must be called once for each *successful* invocation of *Py_EnterRecursiveCall()*.

Properly implementing *tp_repr* for container types requires special recursion handling. In addition to protecting the stack, *tp_repr* also needs to track objects to prevent cycles. The following two functions facilitate this functionality. Effectively, these are the C equivalent to reprlib.recursive_repr().

int **Py_ReprEnter**(*PyObject *object*)
>   Called at the beginning of the *tp_repr* implementation to detect cycles.
>
>   If the object has already been processed, the function returns a positive integer. In that case the *tp_repr* implementation should return a string object indicating a cycle. As examples, dict objects return {...} and list objects return [...].
>
>   The function will return a negative integer if the recursion limit is reached. In that case the *tp_repr* implementation should typically return NULL.
>
>   Otherwise, the function returns zero and the *tp_repr* implementation can continue normally.

void **Py_ReprLeave**(*PyObject *object*)
>   Ends a *Py_ReprEnter()*. Must be called once for each invocation of *Py_ReprEnter()* that returns zero.

5.10 Standard Exceptions

All standard Python exceptions are available as global variables whose names are PyExc_ followed by the Python exception name. These have the type *PyObject**; they are all class objects. For completeness, here are all the variables:

C Name	Python Name	Notes
PyExc_BaseException	BaseException	(1)
PyExc_Exception	Exception	(1)
PyExc_ArithmeticError	ArithmeticError	(1)
PyExc_AssertionError	AssertionError	
PyExc_AttributeError	AttributeError	
PyExc_BlockingIOError	BlockingIOError	
PyExc_BrokenPipeError	BrokenPipeError	
PyExc_BufferError	BufferError	
PyExc_ChildProcessError	ChildProcessError	
PyExc_ConnectionAbortedError	ConnectionAbortedError	
PyExc_ConnectionError	ConnectionError	
PyExc_ConnectionRefusedError	ConnectionRefusedError	
PyExc_ConnectionResetError	ConnectionResetError	
PyExc_EOFError	EOFError	
PyExc_FileExistsError	FileExistsError	
PyExc_FileNotFoundError	FileNotFoundError	
PyExc_FloatingPointError	FloatingPointError	
PyExc_GeneratorExit	GeneratorExit	
PyExc_ImportError	ImportError	
PyExc_IndentationError	IndentationError	
PyExc_IndexError	IndexError	
PyExc_InterruptedError	InterruptedError	
PyExc_IsADirectoryError	IsADirectoryError	
PyExc_KeyError	KeyError	
PyExc_KeyboardInterrupt	KeyboardInterrupt	
PyExc_LookupError	LookupError	(1)
PyExc_MemoryError	MemoryError	
PyExc_ModuleNotFoundError	ModuleNotFoundError	
PyExc_NameError	NameError	
PyExc_NotADirectoryError	NotADirectoryError	
PyExc_NotImplementedError	NotImplementedError	
PyExc_OSError	OSError	(1)
PyExc_OverflowError	OverflowError	
PyExc_PermissionError	PermissionError	
PyExc_ProcessLookupError	ProcessLookupError	
PyExc_RecursionError	RecursionError	
PyExc_ReferenceError	ReferenceError	(2)
PyExc_RuntimeError	RuntimeError	
PyExc_StopAsyncIteration	StopAsyncIteration	
PyExc_StopIteration	StopIteration	
PyExc_SyntaxError	SyntaxError	
PyExc_SystemError	SystemError	
PyExc_SystemExit	SystemExit	
PyExc_TabError	TabError	
PyExc_TimeoutError	TimeoutError	
PyExc_TypeError	TypeError	
PyExc_UnboundLocalError	UnboundLocalError	
PyExc_UnicodeDecodeError	UnicodeDecodeError	
PyExc_UnicodeEncodeError	UnicodeEncodeError	
PyExc_UnicodeError	UnicodeError	

Continued on next page

Table 5.1 – continued from previous page

C Name	Python Name	Notes
PyExc_UnicodeTranslateError	UnicodeTranslateError	
PyExc_ValueError	ValueError	
PyExc_ZeroDivisionError	ZeroDivisionError	

New in version 3.3: PyExc_BlockingIOError, PyExc_BrokenPipeError, PyExc_ChildProcessError, PyExc_ConnectionError, PyExc_ConnectionAbortedError, PyExc_ConnectionRefusedError, PyExc_ConnectionResetError, PyExc_FileExistsError, PyExc_FileNotFoundError, PyExc_InterruptedError, PyExc_IsADirectoryError, PyExc_NotADirectoryError, PyExc_PermissionError, PyExc_ProcessLookupError and PyExc_TimeoutError were introduced following PEP 3151.

New in version 3.5: PyExc_StopAsyncIteration and PyExc_RecursionError.

New in version 3.6: PyExc_ModuleNotFoundError.

These are compatibility aliases to PyExc_OSError:

C Name	Notes
PyExc_EnvironmentError	
PyExc_IOError	
PyExc_WindowsError	(3)

Changed in version 3.3: These aliases used to be separate exception types.

Notes:

1. This is a base class for other standard exceptions.

2. This is the same as weakref.ReferenceError.

3. Only defined on Windows; protect code that uses this by testing that the preprocessor macro MS_WINDOWS is defined.

5.11 Standard Warning Categories

All standard Python warning categories are available as global variables whose names are PyExc_ followed by the Python exception name. These have the type *PyObject**; they are all class objects. For completeness, here are all the variables:

C Name	Python Name	Notes
PyExc_Warning	Warning	(1)
PyExc_BytesWarning	BytesWarning	
PyExc_DeprecationWarning	DeprecationWarning	
PyExc_FutureWarning	FutureWarning	
PyExc_ImportWarning	ImportWarning	
PyExc_PendingDeprecationWarning	PendingDeprecationWarning	
PyExc_ResourceWarning	ResourceWarning	
PyExc_RuntimeWarning	RuntimeWarning	
PyExc_SyntaxWarning	SyntaxWarning	
PyExc_UnicodeWarning	UnicodeWarning	
PyExc_UserWarning	UserWarning	

New in version 3.2: PyExc_ResourceWarning.

Notes:

1. This is a base class for other standard warning categories.

SIX

UTILITIES

The functions in this chapter perform various utility tasks, ranging from helping C code be more portable across platforms, using Python modules from C, and parsing function arguments and constructing Python values from C values.

6.1 Operating System Utilities

*PyObject*** **PyOS_FSPath**(*PyObject* *path*)

> *Return value: New reference.* Return the file system representation for *path*. If the object is a str or bytes object, then its reference count is incremented. If the object implements the os.PathLike interface, then __fspath__() is returned as long as it is a str or bytes object. Otherwise TypeError is raised and NULL is returned.

> New in version 3.6.

int **Py_FdIsInteractive**(FILE **fp*, const char **filename*)

> Return true (nonzero) if the standard I/O file *fp* with name *filename* is deemed interactive. This is the case for files for which isatty(fileno(fp)) is true. If the global flag Py_InteractiveFlag is true, this function also returns true if the *filename* pointer is *NULL* or if the name is equal to one of the strings '<stdin>' or '???'.

void **PyOS_AfterFork**()

> Function to update some internal state after a process fork; this should be called in the new process if the Python interpreter will continue to be used. If a new executable is loaded into the new process, this function does not need to be called.

int **PyOS_CheckStack**()

> Return true when the interpreter runs out of stack space. This is a reliable check, but is only available when USE_STACKCHECK is defined (currently on Windows using the Microsoft Visual C++ compiler). USE_STACKCHECK will be defined automatically; you should never change the definition in your own code.

PyOS_sighandler_t **PyOS_getsig**(int *i*)

> Return the current signal handler for signal *i*. This is a thin wrapper around either sigaction() or signal(). Do not call those functions directly! PyOS_sighandler_t is a typedef alias for void (*)(int).

PyOS_sighandler_t **PyOS_setsig**(int *i*, PyOS_sighandler_t *h*)

> Set the signal handler for signal *i* to be *h*; return the old signal handler. This is a thin wrapper around either sigaction() or signal(). Do not call those functions directly! PyOS_sighandler_t is a typedef alias for void (*)(int).

wchar_t* **Py_DecodeLocale**(const char* *arg*, size_t **size*)

> Decode a byte string from the locale encoding with the surrogateescape error handler: undecodable bytes are decoded as characters in range U+DC80..U+DCFF. If a byte sequence can be decoded as

a surrogate character, escape the bytes using the surrogateescape error handler instead of decoding them.

Encoding, highest priority to lowest priority:

- UTF-8 on macOS and Android;
- ASCII if the LC_CTYPE locale is "C", nl_langinfo(CODESET) returns the ASCII encoding (or an alias), and mbstowcs() and wcstombs() functions use the ISO-8859-1 encoding.
- the current locale encoding (LC_CTYPE locale).

Return a pointer to a newly allocated wide character string, use *PyMem_RawFree()* to free the memory. If size is not NULL, write the number of wide characters excluding the null character into ***size**.

Return NULL on decoding error or memory allocation error. If *size* is not NULL, ***size** is set to **(size_t)-1** on memory error or set to **(size_t)-2** on decoding error.

Decoding errors should never happen, unless there is a bug in the C library.

Use the *Py_EncodeLocale()* function to encode the character string back to a byte string.

See also:

The *PyUnicode_DecodeFSDefaultAndSize()* and *PyUnicode_DecodeLocaleAndSize()* functions.

New in version 3.5.

char* **Py_EncodeLocale**(const wchar_t *text*, size_t *error_pos*)

Encode a wide character string to the locale encoding with the surrogateescape error handler: surrogate characters in the range U+DC80..U+DCFF are converted to bytes 0x80..0xFF.

Encoding, highest priority to lowest priority:

- UTF-8 on macOS and Android;
- ASCII if the LC_CTYPE locale is "C", nl_langinfo(CODESET) returns the ASCII encoding (or an alias), and mbstowcs() and wcstombs() functions uses the ISO-8859-1 encoding.
- the current locale encoding.

Return a pointer to a newly allocated byte string, use *PyMem_Free()* to free the memory. Return NULL on encoding error or memory allocation error

If error_pos is not NULL, ***error_pos** is set to the index of the invalid character on encoding error, or set to **(size_t)-1** otherwise.

Use the *Py_DecodeLocale()* function to decode the bytes string back to a wide character string.

See also:

The *PyUnicode_EncodeFSDefault()* and *PyUnicode_EncodeLocale()* functions.

New in version 3.5.

6.2 System Functions

These are utility functions that make functionality from the **sys** module accessible to C code. They all work with the current interpreter thread's **sys** module's dict, which is contained in the internal thread state structure.

PyObject ****PySys_GetObject**(const char *name*)

Return value: Borrowed reference. Return the object *name* from the **sys** module or *NULL* if it does not exist, without setting an exception.

int **PySys_SetObject**(const char *name, *PyObject* *v*)
> Set *name* in the `sys` module to *v* unless *v* is *NULL*, in which case *name* is deleted from the sys module. Returns 0 on success, `-1` on error.

void **PySys_ResetWarnOptions**()
> Reset `sys.warnoptions` to an empty list.

void **PySys_AddWarnOption**(wchar_t *s*)
> Append *s* to `sys.warnoptions`.

void **PySys_AddWarnOptionUnicode**(*PyObject* *unicode*)
> Append *unicode* to `sys.warnoptions`.

void **PySys_SetPath**(wchar_t *path*)
> Set `sys.path` to a list object of paths found in *path* which should be a list of paths separated with the platform's search path delimiter (: on Unix, ; on Windows).

void **PySys_WriteStdout**(const char *format*, ...)
> Write the output string described by *format* to `sys.stdout`. No exceptions are raised, even if truncation occurs (see below).
>
> *format* should limit the total size of the formatted output string to 1000 bytes or less – after 1000 bytes, the output string is truncated. In particular, this means that no unrestricted "%s" formats should occur; these should be limited using "%.<N>s" where <N> is a decimal number calculated so that <N> plus the maximum size of other formatted text does not exceed 1000 bytes. Also watch out for "%f", which can print hundreds of digits for very large numbers.
>
> If a problem occurs, or `sys.stdout` is unset, the formatted message is written to the real (C level) *stdout*.

void **PySys_WriteStderr**(const char *format*, ...)
> As *PySys_WriteStdout()*, but write to `sys.stderr` or *stderr* instead.

void **PySys_FormatStdout**(const char *format*, ...)
> Function similar to PySys_WriteStdout() but format the message using *PyUnicode_FromFormatV()* and don't truncate the message to an arbitrary length.
>
> New in version 3.2.

void **PySys_FormatStderr**(const char *format*, ...)
> As *PySys_FormatStdout()*, but write to `sys.stderr` or *stderr* instead.
>
> New in version 3.2.

void **PySys_AddXOption**(const wchar_t *s*)
> Parse *s* as a set of `-X` options and add them to the current options mapping as returned by *PySys_GetXOptions()*.
>
> New in version 3.2.

PyObject ***PySys_GetXOptions**()
> *Return value: Borrowed reference.* Return the current dictionary of `-X` options, similarly to `sys._xoptions`. On error, *NULL* is returned and an exception is set.
>
> New in version 3.2.

6.3 Process Control

void **Py_FatalError**(const char *message*)
> Print a fatal error message and kill the process. No cleanup is performed. This function should only be invoked when a condition is detected that would make it dangerous to continue using the Python

interpreter; e.g., when the object administration appears to be corrupted. On Unix, the standard C library function **abort()** is called which will attempt to produce a **core** file.

void **Py_Exit**(int *status*)

Exit the current process. This calls *Py_FinalizeEx()* and then calls the standard C library function **exit(status)**. If *Py_FinalizeEx()* indicates an error, the exit status is set to 120.

Changed in version 3.6: Errors from finalization no longer ignored.

int **Py_AtExit**(void (*func*)())

Register a cleanup function to be called by *Py_FinalizeEx()*. The cleanup function will be called with no arguments and should return no value. At most 32 cleanup functions can be registered. When the registration is successful, *Py_AtExit()* returns 0; on failure, it returns -1. The cleanup function registered last is called first. Each cleanup function will be called at most once. Since Python's internal finalization will have completed before the cleanup function, no Python APIs should be called by *func*.

6.4 Importing Modules

*PyObject** **PyImport_ImportModule**(const char **name*)

Return value: New reference. This is a simplified interface to *PyImport_ImportModuleEx()* below, leaving the *globals* and *locals* arguments set to *NULL* and *level* set to 0. When the *name* argument contains a dot (when it specifies a submodule of a package), the *fromlist* argument is set to the list ['*'] so that the return value is the named module rather than the top-level package containing it as would otherwise be the case. (Unfortunately, this has an additional side effect when *name* in fact specifies a subpackage instead of a submodule: the submodules specified in the package's **__all__** variable are loaded.) Return a new reference to the imported module, or *NULL* with an exception set on failure. A failing import of a module doesn't leave the module in **sys.modules**.

This function always uses absolute imports.

*PyObject** **PyImport_ImportModuleNoBlock**(const char **name*)

This function is a deprecated alias of *PyImport_ImportModule()*.

Changed in version 3.3: This function used to fail immediately when the import lock was held by another thread. In Python 3.3 though, the locking scheme switched to per-module locks for most purposes, so this function's special behaviour isn't needed anymore.

*PyObject** **PyImport_ImportModuleEx**(const char **name*, *PyObject* **globals*, *PyObject* **locals*, *PyObject* **fromlist*)

Return value: New reference. Import a module. This is best described by referring to the built-in Python function **__import__()**.

The return value is a new reference to the imported module or top-level package, or *NULL* with an exception set on failure. Like for **__import__()**, the return value when a submodule of a package was requested is normally the top-level package, unless a non-empty *fromlist* was given.

Failing imports remove incomplete module objects, like with *PyImport_ImportModule()*.

*PyObject** **PyImport_ImportModuleLevelObject**(*PyObject* **name*, *PyObject* **globals*, *PyObject* **locals*, *PyObject* **fromlist*, int *level*)

Import a module. This is best described by referring to the built-in Python function **__import__()**, as the standard **__import__()** function calls this function directly.

The return value is a new reference to the imported module or top-level package, or *NULL* with an exception set on failure. Like for **__import__()**, the return value when a submodule of a package was requested is normally the top-level package, unless a non-empty *fromlist* was given.

New in version 3.3.

PyObject* **PyImport_ImportModuleLevel**(const char **name*, *PyObject *globals*, *PyObject *locals*, *Py-Object *fromlist*, int *level*)

> *Return value: New reference.* Similar to *PyImport_ImportModuleLevelObject()*, but the name is a UTF-8 encoded string instead of a Unicode object.

> Changed in version 3.3: Negative values for *level* are no longer accepted.

PyObject* **PyImport_Import**(*PyObject *name*)

> *Return value: New reference.* This is a higher-level interface that calls the current "import hook function" (with an explicit *level* of 0, meaning absolute import). It invokes the __import__() function from the __builtins__ of the current globals. This means that the import is done using whatever import hooks are installed in the current environment.

> This function always uses absolute imports.

PyObject* **PyImport_ReloadModule**(*PyObject *m*)

> *Return value: New reference.* Reload a module. Return a new reference to the reloaded module, or *NULL* with an exception set on failure (the module still exists in this case).

PyObject* **PyImport_AddModuleObject**(*PyObject *name*)

> Return the module object corresponding to a module name. The *name* argument may be of the form package.module. First check the modules dictionary if there's one there, and if not, create a new one and insert it in the modules dictionary. Return *NULL* with an exception set on failure.

> ---
> **Note:** This function does not load or import the module; if the module wasn't already loaded, you will get an empty module object. Use *PyImport_ImportModule()* or one of its variants to import a module. Package structures implied by a dotted name for *name* are not created if not already present.
> ---

> New in version 3.3.

PyObject* **PyImport_AddModule**(const char **name*)

> *Return value: Borrowed reference.* Similar to *PyImport_AddModuleObject()*, but the name is a UTF-8 encoded string instead of a Unicode object.

PyObject* **PyImport_ExecCodeModule**(const char **name*, *PyObject *co*)

> *Return value: New reference.* Given a module name (possibly of the form package.module) and a code object read from a Python bytecode file or obtained from the built-in function compile(), load the module. Return a new reference to the module object, or *NULL* with an exception set if an error occurred. *name* is removed from sys.modules in error cases, even if *name* was already in sys.modules on entry to *PyImport_ExecCodeModule()*. Leaving incompletely initialized modules in sys.modules is dangerous, as imports of such modules have no way to know that the module object is an unknown (and probably damaged with respect to the module author's intents) state.

> The module's __spec__ and __loader__ will be set, if not set already, with the appropriate values. The spec's loader will be set to the module's __loader__ (if set) and to an instance of SourceFileLoader otherwise.

> The module's __file__ attribute will be set to the code object's co_filename. If applicable, __cached__ will also be set.

> This function will reload the module if it was already imported. See *PyImport_ReloadModule()* for the intended way to reload a module.

> If *name* points to a dotted name of the form package.module, any package structures not already created will still not be created.

> See also *PyImport_ExecCodeModuleEx()* and *PyImport_ExecCodeModuleWithPathnames()*.

PyObject* **PyImport_ExecCodeModuleEx**(const char **name*, *PyObject *co*, const char **pathname*)

> *Return value: New reference.* Like *PyImport_ExecCodeModule()*, but the __file__ attribute of the module object is set to *pathname* if it is non-NULL.

See also *PyImport_ExecCodeModuleWithPathnames()*.

PyObject* **PyImport_ExecCodeModuleObject**(*PyObject *name*, *PyObject *co*, *PyObject *pathname*, *PyObject *cpathname*)

Like *PyImport_ExecCodeModuleEx()*, but the `__cached__` attribute of the module object is set to *cpathname* if it is non-NULL. Of the three functions, this is the preferred one to use.

New in version 3.3.

PyObject* **PyImport_ExecCodeModuleWithPathnames**(const char **name*, *PyObject *co*, const char **pathname*, const char **cpathname*)

Like *PyImport_ExecCodeModuleObject()*, but *name*, *pathname* and *cpathname* are UTF-8 encoded strings. Attempts are also made to figure out what the value for *pathname* should be from *cpathname* if the former is set to NULL.

New in version 3.2.

Changed in version 3.3: Uses `imp.source_from_cache()` in calculating the source path if only the bytecode path is provided.

long **PyImport_GetMagicNumber**()

Return the magic number for Python bytecode files (a.k.a. `.pyc` file). The magic number should be present in the first four bytes of the bytecode file, in little-endian byte order. Returns -1 on error.

Changed in version 3.3: Return value of -1 upon failure.

const char * **PyImport_GetMagicTag**()

Return the magic tag string for PEP 3147 format Python bytecode file names. Keep in mind that the value at `sys.implementation.cache_tag` is authoritative and should be used instead of this function.

New in version 3.2.

PyObject* **PyImport_GetModuleDict**()

Return value: Borrowed reference. Return the dictionary used for the module administration (a.k.a. `sys.modules`). Note that this is a per-interpreter variable.

PyObject* **PyImport_GetImporter**(*PyObject *path*)

Return a finder object for a `sys.path/pkg.__path__` item *path*, possibly by fetching it from the `sys.path_importer_cache` dict. If it wasn't yet cached, traverse `sys.path_hooks` until a hook is found that can handle the path item. Return None if no hook could; this tells our caller that the *path based finder* could not find a finder for this path item. Cache the result in `sys.path_importer_cache`. Return a new reference to the finder object.

void **_PyImport_Init**()

Initialize the import mechanism. For internal use only.

void **PyImport_Cleanup**()

Empty the module table. For internal use only.

void **_PyImport_Fini**()

Finalize the import mechanism. For internal use only.

PyObject* **_PyImport_FindExtension**(char *, char *)

For internal use only.

int **PyImport_ImportFrozenModuleObject**(*PyObject *name*)

Load a frozen module named *name*. Return 1 for success, 0 if the module is not found, and -1 with an exception set if the initialization failed. To access the imported module on a successful load, use *PyImport_ImportModule()*. (Note the misnomer — this function would reload the module if it was already imported.)

New in version 3.3.

Changed in version 3.4: The `__file__` attribute is no longer set on the module.

int **PyImport_ImportFrozenModule**(const char *name*)

> Similar to *PyImport_ImportFrozenModuleObject()*, but the name is a UTF-8 encoded string instead of a Unicode object.

struct **_frozen**

> This is the structure type definition for frozen module descriptors, as generated by the **freeze** utility (see **Tools/freeze/** in the Python source distribution). Its definition, found in **Include/import.h**, is:

```
struct _frozen {
    char *name;
    unsigned char *code;
    int size;
};
```

const struct *_frozen** **PyImport_FrozenModules**

> This pointer is initialized to point to an array of **struct _frozen** records, terminated by one whose members are all *NULL* or zero. When a frozen module is imported, it is searched in this table. Third-party code could play tricks with this to provide a dynamically created collection of frozen modules.

int **PyImport_AppendInittab**(const char *name*, PyObject* (*initfunc*)(void))

> Add a single module to the existing table of built-in modules. This is a convenience wrapper around *PyImport_ExtendInittab()*, returning -1 if the table could not be extended. The new module can be imported by the name *name*, and uses the function *initfunc* as the initialization function called on the first attempted import. This should be called before *Py_Initialize()*.

struct **_inittab**

> Structure describing a single entry in the list of built-in modules. Each of these structures gives the name and initialization function for a module built into the interpreter. The name is an ASCII encoded string. Programs which embed Python may use an array of these structures in conjunction with *PyImport_ExtendInittab()* to provide additional built-in modules. The structure is defined in **Include/import.h** as:

```
struct _inittab {
    char *name;                 /* ASCII encoded string */
    PyObject* (*initfunc)(void);
};
```

int **PyImport_ExtendInittab**(struct *_inittab* *newtab*)

> Add a collection of modules to the table of built-in modules. The *newtab* array must end with a sentinel entry which contains *NULL* for the **name** field; failure to provide the sentinel value can result in a memory fault. Returns 0 on success or -1 if insufficient memory could be allocated to extend the internal table. In the event of failure, no modules are added to the internal table. This should be called before *Py_Initialize()*.

6.5 Data marshalling support

These routines allow C code to work with serialized objects using the same data format as the **marshal** module. There are functions to write data into the serialization format, and additional functions that can be used to read the data back. Files used to store marshalled data must be opened in binary mode.

Numeric values are stored with the least significant byte first.

The module supports two versions of the data format: version 0 is the historical version, version 1 shares interned strings in the file, and upon unmarshalling. Version 2 uses a binary format for floating point numbers. *Py_MARSHAL_VERSION* indicates the current file format (currently 2).

void **PyMarshal_WriteLongToFile**(long *value*, FILE **file*, int *version*)
> Marshal a **long** integer, *value*, to *file*. This will only write the least-significant 32 bits of *value*; regardless of the size of the native **long** type. *version* indicates the file format.

void **PyMarshal_WriteObjectToFile**(*PyObject* *value*, FILE **file*, int *version*)
> Marshal a Python object, *value*, to *file*. *version* indicates the file format.

PyObject* **PyMarshal_WriteObjectToString**(*PyObject* *value*, int *version*)
> *Return value: New reference.* Return a bytes object containing the marshalled representation of *value*. *version* indicates the file format.

The following functions allow marshalled values to be read back in.

XXX What about error detection? It appears that reading past the end of the file will always result in a negative numeric value (where that's relevant), but it's not clear that negative values won't be handled properly when there's no error. What's the right way to tell? Should only non-negative values be written using these routines?

long **PyMarshal_ReadLongFromFile**(FILE **file*)
> Return a C **long** from the data stream in a **FILE*** opened for reading. Only a 32-bit value can be read in using this function, regardless of the native size of **long**.

> On error, raise an exception and return **-1**.

int **PyMarshal_ReadShortFromFile**(FILE **file*)
> Return a C **short** from the data stream in a **FILE*** opened for reading. Only a 16-bit value can be read in using this function, regardless of the native size of **short**.

> On error, raise an exception and return **-1**.

PyObject* **PyMarshal_ReadObjectFromFile**(FILE **file*)
> *Return value: New reference.* Return a Python object from the data stream in a **FILE*** opened for reading.

> On error, sets the appropriate exception (**EOFError** or **TypeError**) and returns *NULL*.

PyObject* **PyMarshal_ReadLastObjectFromFile**(FILE **file*)
> *Return value: New reference.* Return a Python object from the data stream in a **FILE*** opened for reading. Unlike *PyMarshal_ReadObjectFromFile()*, this function assumes that no further objects will be read from the file, allowing it to aggressively load file data into memory so that the de-serialization can operate from data in memory rather than reading a byte at a time from the file. Only use these variant if you are certain that you won't be reading anything else from the file.

> On error, sets the appropriate exception (**EOFError** or **TypeError**) and returns *NULL*.

PyObject* **PyMarshal_ReadObjectFromString**(const char **data*, Py_ssize_t *len*)
> *Return value: New reference.* Return a Python object from the data stream in a byte buffer containing *len* bytes pointed to by *data*.

> On error, sets the appropriate exception (**EOFError** or **TypeError**) and returns *NULL*.

6.6 Parsing arguments and building values

These functions are useful when creating your own extensions functions and methods. Additional information and examples are available in extending-index.

The first three of these functions described, *PyArg_ParseTuple()*, *PyArg_ParseTupleAndKeywords()*, and *PyArg_Parse()*, all use *format strings* which are used to tell the function about the expected arguments. The format strings use the same syntax for each of these functions.

6.6.1 Parsing arguments

A format string consists of zero or more "format units." A format unit describes one Python object; it is usually a single character or a parenthesized sequence of format units. With a few exceptions, a format unit that is not a parenthesized sequence normally corresponds to a single address argument to these functions. In the following description, the quoted form is the format unit; the entry in (round) parentheses is the Python object type that matches the format unit; and the entry in [square] brackets is the type of the C variable(s) whose address should be passed.

Strings and buffers

These formats allow accessing an object as a contiguous chunk of memory. You don't have to provide raw storage for the returned unicode or bytes area.

In general, when a format sets a pointer to a buffer, the buffer is managed by the corresponding Python object, and the buffer shares the lifetime of this object. You won't have to release any memory yourself. The only exceptions are es, es#, et and et#.

However, when a *Py_buffer* structure gets filled, the underlying buffer is locked so that the caller can subsequently use the buffer even inside a *Py_BEGIN_ALLOW_THREADS* block without the risk of mutable data being resized or destroyed. As a result, **you have to call** *PyBuffer_Release()* after you have finished processing the data (or in any early abort case).

Unless otherwise stated, buffers are not NUL-terminated.

Some formats require a read-only *bytes-like object*, and set a pointer instead of a buffer structure. They work by checking that the object's *PyBufferProcs.bf_releasebuffer* field is *NULL*, which disallows mutable objects such as bytearray.

Note: For all # variants of formats (s#, y#, etc.), the type of the length argument (int or Py_ssize_t) is controlled by defining the macro PY_SSIZE_T_CLEAN before including Python.h. If the macro was defined, length is a Py_ssize_t rather than an int. This behavior will change in a future Python version to only support Py_ssize_t and drop int support. It is best to always define PY_SSIZE_T_CLEAN.

---

s (str) [**const char ***] Convert a Unicode object to a C pointer to a character string. A pointer to an existing string is stored in the character pointer variable whose address you pass. The C string is NUL-terminated. The Python string must not contain embedded null code points; if it does, a **ValueError** exception is raised. Unicode objects are converted to C strings using 'utf-8' encoding. If this conversion fails, a **UnicodeError** is raised.

Note: This format does not accept *bytes-like objects*. If you want to accept filesystem paths and convert them to C character strings, it is preferable to use the O& format with *PyUnicode_FSConverter()* as *converter*.

Changed in version 3.5: Previously, **TypeError** was raised when embedded null code points were encountered in the Python string.

s* (str or *bytes-like object*) [**Py_buffer**] This format accepts Unicode objects as well as bytes-like objects. It fills a *Py_buffer* structure provided by the caller. In this case the resulting C string may contain embedded NUL bytes. Unicode objects are converted to C strings using 'utf-8' encoding.

s# (str, read-only *bytes-like object*) [**const char *, int or Py_ssize_t**] Like **s***, except that it doesn't accept mutable objects. The result is stored into two C variables, the first one a pointer to a C string, the second one its length. The string may contain embedded null bytes. Unicode objects are converted to C strings using 'utf-8' encoding.

---

z (str or None) [**const char ***] Like **s**, but the Python object may also be **None**, in which case the C pointer is set to *NULL*.

z* (str, *bytes-like object* or None) [**Py_buffer**] Like **s***, but the Python object may also be **None**, in which case the **buf** member of the *Py_buffer* structure is set to *NULL*.

z# (str, read-only *bytes-like object* or None) [**const char ***, int] Like **s#**, but the Python object may also be **None**, in which case the C pointer is set to *NULL*.

y (read-only *bytes-like object*) [**const char ***] This format converts a bytes-like object to a C pointer to a character string; it does not accept Unicode objects. The bytes buffer must not contain embedded null bytes; if it does, a **ValueError** exception is raised.

Changed in version 3.5: Previously, **TypeError** was raised when embedded null bytes were encountered in the bytes buffer.

y* (*bytes-like object*) [**Py_buffer**] This variant on **s*** doesn't accept Unicode objects, only bytes-like objects. **This is the recommended way to accept binary data.**

y# (read-only *bytes-like object*) [**const char ***, int] This variant on **s#** doesn't accept Unicode objects, only bytes-like objects.

S (bytes) [**PyBytesObject ***] Requires that the Python object is a **bytes** object, without attempting any conversion. Raises **TypeError** if the object is not a bytes object. The C variable may also be declared as *PyObject**.

Y (bytearray) [**PyByteArrayObject ***] Requires that the Python object is a **bytearray** object, without attempting any conversion. Raises **TypeError** if the object is not a **bytearray** object. The C variable may also be declared as *PyObject**.

u (str) [**Py_UNICODE ***] Convert a Python Unicode object to a C pointer to a NUL-terminated buffer of Unicode characters. You must pass the address of a *Py_UNICODE* pointer variable, which will be filled with the pointer to an existing Unicode buffer. Please note that the width of a *Py_UNICODE* character depends on compilation options (it is either 16 or 32 bits). The Python string must not contain embedded null code points; if it does, a **ValueError** exception is raised.

Changed in version 3.5: Previously, **TypeError** was raised when embedded null code points were encountered in the Python string.

u# (str) [**Py_UNICODE ***, int] This variant on **u** stores into two C variables, the first one a pointer to a Unicode data buffer, the second one its length. This variant allows null code points.

Z (str or None) [**Py_UNICODE ***] Like **u**, but the Python object may also be **None**, in which case the *Py_UNICODE* pointer is set to *NULL*.

Z# (str or None) [**Py_UNICODE ***, int] Like **u#**, but the Python object may also be **None**, in which case the *Py_UNICODE* pointer is set to *NULL*.

U (str) [**PyObject ***] Requires that the Python object is a Unicode object, without attempting any conversion. Raises **TypeError** if the object is not a Unicode object. The C variable may also be declared as *PyObject**.

w* (read-write *bytes-like object*) [**Py_buffer**] This format accepts any object which implements the read-write buffer interface. It fills a *Py_buffer* structure provided by the caller. The buffer may contain embedded null bytes. The caller have to call *PyBuffer_Release()* when it is done with the buffer.

es (str) [**const char *encoding, char **buffer**] This variant on **s** is used for encoding Unicode into a character buffer. It only works for encoded data without embedded NUL bytes.

This format requires two arguments. The first is only used as input, and must be a **const char*** which points to the name of an encoding as a NUL-terminated string, or *NULL*, in which case 'utf-8' encoding is used. An exception is raised if the named encoding is not known to Python. The second argument must be a **char****; the value of the pointer it references will be set to a buffer with the contents of the argument text. The text will be encoded in the encoding specified by the first argument.

PyArg_ParseTuple() will allocate a buffer of the needed size, copy the encoded data into this buffer and adjust **buffer* to reference the newly allocated storage. The caller is responsible for calling *PyMem_Free()* to free the allocated buffer after use.

et (str, bytes or bytearray) [const char *encoding, char **buffer] Same as **es** except that byte string objects are passed through without recoding them. Instead, the implementation assumes that the byte string object uses the encoding passed in as parameter.

es# (str) [const char *encoding, char **buffer, int *buffer_length] This variant on **s#** is used for encoding Unicode into a character buffer. Unlike the **es** format, this variant allows input data which contains NUL characters.

It requires three arguments. The first is only used as input, and must be a **const char*** which points to the name of an encoding as a NUL-terminated string, or *NULL*, in which case 'utf-8' encoding is used. An exception is raised if the named encoding is not known to Python. The second argument must be a **char****; the value of the pointer it references will be set to a buffer with the contents of the argument text. The text will be encoded in the encoding specified by the first argument. The third argument must be a pointer to an integer; the referenced integer will be set to the number of bytes in the output buffer.

There are two modes of operation:

If **buffer* points a *NULL* pointer, the function will allocate a buffer of the needed size, copy the encoded data into this buffer and set **buffer* to reference the newly allocated storage. The caller is responsible for calling *PyMem_Free()* to free the allocated buffer after usage.

If **buffer* points to a non-*NULL* pointer (an already allocated buffer), *PyArg_ParseTuple()* will use this location as the buffer and interpret the initial value of **buffer_length* as the buffer size. It will then copy the encoded data into the buffer and NUL-terminate it. If the buffer is not large enough, a **ValueError** will be set.

In both cases, **buffer_length* is set to the length of the encoded data without the trailing NUL byte.

et# (str, bytes or bytearray) [const char *encoding, char **buffer, int *buffer_length] Same as **es#** except that byte string objects are passed through without recoding them. Instead, the implementation assumes that the byte string object uses the encoding passed in as parameter.

Numbers

b (int) [unsigned char] Convert a nonnegative Python integer to an unsigned tiny int, stored in a C **unsigned char**.

B (int) [unsigned char] Convert a Python integer to a tiny int without overflow checking, stored in a C **unsigned char**.

h (int) [short int] Convert a Python integer to a C **short int**.

H (int) [unsigned short int] Convert a Python integer to a C **unsigned short int**, without overflow checking.

i (int) [int] Convert a Python integer to a plain C **int**.

I (int) [unsigned int] Convert a Python integer to a C **unsigned int**, without overflow checking.

l (int) [long int] Convert a Python integer to a C **long int**.

k (int) [unsigned long] Convert a Python integer to a C **unsigned long** without overflow checking.

L (int) [long long] Convert a Python integer to a C **long long**.

K (int) [**unsigned long long**] Convert a Python integer to a C `unsigned long long` without overflow checking.

n (int) [**Py_ssize_t**] Convert a Python integer to a C `Py_ssize_t`.

c (**bytes or bytearray of length 1**) [**char**] Convert a Python byte, represented as a `bytes` or `bytearray` object of length 1, to a C `char`.

Changed in version 3.3: Allow `bytearray` objects.

C (**str of length 1**) [**int**] Convert a Python character, represented as a `str` object of length 1, to a C `int`.

f (float) [**float**] Convert a Python floating point number to a C `float`.

d (float) [**double**] Convert a Python floating point number to a C `double`.

D (complex) [**Py_complex**] Convert a Python complex number to a C `Py_complex` structure.

Other objects

O (**object**) [**PyObject ***] Store a Python object (without any conversion) in a C object pointer. The C program thus receives the actual object that was passed. The object's reference count is not increased. The pointer stored is not *NULL*.

O! (**object**) [*typeobject*, **PyObject ***] Store a Python object in a C object pointer. This is similar to O, but takes two C arguments: the first is the address of a Python type object, the second is the address of the C variable (of type `PyObject*`) into which the object pointer is stored. If the Python object does not have the required type, `TypeError` is raised.

O& (**object**) [*converter, anything*] Convert a Python object to a C variable through a *converter* function. This takes two arguments: the first is a function, the second is the address of a C variable (of arbitrary type), converted to `void *`. The *converter* function in turn is called as follows:

```
status = converter(object, address);
```

where *object* is the Python object to be converted and *address* is the `void*` argument that was passed to the `PyArg_Parse*()` function. The returned *status* should be 1 for a successful conversion and 0 if the conversion has failed. When the conversion fails, the *converter* function should raise an exception and leave the content of *address* unmodified.

If the *converter* returns `Py_CLEANUP_SUPPORTED`, it may get called a second time if the argument parsing eventually fails, giving the converter a chance to release any memory that it had already allocated. In this second call, the *object* parameter will be NULL; *address* will have the same value as in the original call.

Changed in version 3.1: `Py_CLEANUP_SUPPORTED` was added.

p (bool) [**int**] Tests the value passed in for truth (a boolean **p**redicate) and converts the result to its equivalent C true/false integer value. Sets the int to 1 if the expression was true and 0 if it was false. This accepts any valid Python value. See truth for more information about how Python tests values for truth.

New in version 3.3.

(**items**) (**tuple**) [*matching-items*] The object must be a Python sequence whose length is the number of format units in *items*. The C arguments must correspond to the individual format units in *items*. Format units for sequences may be nested.

It is possible to pass "long" integers (integers whose value exceeds the platform's `LONG_MAX`) however no proper range checking is done — the most significant bits are silently truncated when the receiving field is too small to receive the value (actually, the semantics are inherited from downcasts in C — your mileage may vary).

A few other characters have a meaning in a format string. These may not occur inside nested parentheses. They are:

| Indicates that the remaining arguments in the Python argument list are optional. The C variables corresponding to optional arguments should be initialized to their default value — when an optional argument is not specified, *PyArg_ParseTuple()* does not touch the contents of the corresponding C variable(s).

$ *PyArg_ParseTupleAndKeywords()* only: Indicates that the remaining arguments in the Python argument list are keyword-only. Currently, all keyword-only arguments must also be optional arguments, so | must always be specified before $ in the format string.

New in version 3.3.

: The list of format units ends here; the string after the colon is used as the function name in error messages (the "associated value" of the exception that *PyArg_ParseTuple()* raises).

; The list of format units ends here; the string after the semicolon is used as the error message *instead* of the default error message. : and ; mutually exclude each other.

Note that any Python object references which are provided to the caller are *borrowed* references; do not decrement their reference count!

Additional arguments passed to these functions must be addresses of variables whose type is determined by the format string; these are used to store values from the input tuple. There are a few cases, as described in the list of format units above, where these parameters are used as input values; they should match what is specified for the corresponding format unit in that case.

For the conversion to succeed, the *arg* object must match the format and the format must be exhausted. On success, the *PyArg_Parse*()* functions return true, otherwise they return false and raise an appropriate exception. When the *PyArg_Parse*()* functions fail due to conversion failure in one of the format units, the variables at the addresses corresponding to that and the following format units are left untouched.

API Functions

int **PyArg_ParseTuple**(*PyObject* *args, const char *format, ...)
> Parse the parameters of a function that takes only positional parameters into local variables. Returns true on success; on failure, it returns false and raises the appropriate exception.

int **PyArg_VaParse**(*PyObject* *args, const char *format, va_list *vargs*)
> Identical to *PyArg_ParseTuple()*, except that it accepts a va_list rather than a variable number of arguments.

int **PyArg_ParseTupleAndKeywords**(*PyObject* *args, *PyObject* *kw, const char *format, char *keywords[], ...)
> Parse the parameters of a function that takes both positional and keyword parameters into local variables. The *keywords* argument is a *NULL*-terminated array of keyword parameter names. Empty names denote *positional-only parameters*. Returns true on success; on failure, it returns false and raises the appropriate exception.
>
> Changed in version 3.6: Added support for *positional-only parameters*.

int **PyArg_VaParseTupleAndKeywords**(*PyObject* *args, *PyObject* *kw, const char *format, char *keywords[], va_list *vargs*)
> Identical to *PyArg_ParseTupleAndKeywords()*, except that it accepts a va_list rather than a variable number of arguments.

int **PyArg_ValidateKeywordArguments**(*PyObject* *)
> Ensure that the keys in the keywords argument dictionary are strings. This is only needed if *PyArg_ParseTupleAndKeywords()* is not used, since the latter already does this check.
>
> New in version 3.2.

int **PyArg_Parse**(*PyObject* *args*, const char *format*, ...)

> Function used to deconstruct the argument lists of "old-style" functions — these are functions which use the `METH_OLDARGS` parameter parsing method, which has been removed in Python 3. This is not recommended for use in parameter parsing in new code, and most code in the standard interpreter has been modified to no longer use this for that purpose. It does remain a convenient way to decompose other tuples, however, and may continue to be used for that purpose.

int **PyArg_UnpackTuple**(*PyObject* *args*, const char *name*, Py_ssize_t *min*, Py_ssize_t *max*, ...)

> A simpler form of parameter retrieval which does not use a format string to specify the types of the arguments. Functions which use this method to retrieve their parameters should be declared as *METH_VARARGS* in function or method tables. The tuple containing the actual parameters should be passed as *args*; it must actually be a tuple. The length of the tuple must be at least *min* and no more than *max*; *min* and *max* may be equal. Additional arguments must be passed to the function, each of which should be a pointer to a *PyObject** variable; these will be filled in with the values from *args*; they will contain borrowed references. The variables which correspond to optional parameters not given by *args* will not be filled in; these should be initialized by the caller. This function returns true on success and false if *args* is not a tuple or contains the wrong number of elements; an exception will be set if there was a failure.
>
> This is an example of the use of this function, taken from the sources for the **_weakref** helper module for weak references:

```
static PyObject *
weakref_ref(PyObject *self, PyObject *args)
{
    PyObject *object;
    PyObject *callback = NULL;
    PyObject *result = NULL;

    if (PyArg_UnpackTuple(args, "ref", 1, 2, &object, &callback)) {
        result = PyWeakref_NewRef(object, callback);
    }
    return result;
}
```

> The call to *PyArg_UnpackTuple()* in this example is entirely equivalent to this call to *PyArg_ParseTuple()*:

```
PyArg_ParseTuple(args, "O|O:ref", &object, &callback)
```

6.6.2 Building values

PyObject* **Py_BuildValue**(const char *format*, ...)

> *Return value: New reference.* Create a new value based on a format string similar to those accepted by the *PyArg_Parse*()* family of functions and a sequence of values. Returns the value or *NULL* in the case of an error; an exception will be raised if *NULL* is returned.
>
> *Py_BuildValue()* does not always build a tuple. It builds a tuple only if its format string contains two or more format units. If the format string is empty, it returns **None**; if it contains exactly one format unit, it returns whatever object is described by that format unit. To force it to return a tuple of size 0 or one, parenthesize the format string.
>
> When memory buffers are passed as parameters to supply data to build objects, as for the **s** and **s#** formats, the required data is copied. Buffers provided by the caller are never referenced by the objects created by *Py_BuildValue()*. In other words, if your code invokes **malloc()** and passes the allocated memory to *Py_BuildValue()*, your code is responsible for calling **free()** for that memory once *Py_BuildValue()* returns.

In the following description, the quoted form is the format unit; the entry in (round) parentheses is the Python object type that the format unit will return; and the entry in [square] brackets is the type of the C value(s) to be passed.

The characters space, tab, colon and comma are ignored in format strings (but not within format units such as **s#**). This can be used to make long format strings a tad more readable.

s (**str or None**) [**char ***] Convert a null-terminated C string to a Python **str** object using `'utf-8'` encoding. If the C string pointer is *NULL*, **None** is used.

s# (**str or None**) [**char *, int**] Convert a C string and its length to a Python **str** object using `'utf-8'` encoding. If the C string pointer is *NULL*, the length is ignored and **None** is returned.

y (**bytes**) [**char ***] This converts a C string to a Python **bytes** object. If the C string pointer is *NULL*, **None** is returned.

y# (**bytes**) [**char *, int**] This converts a C string and its lengths to a Python object. If the C string pointer is *NULL*, **None** is returned.

z (**str or None**) [**char ***] Same as **s**.

z# (**str or None**) [**char *, int**] Same as **s#**.

u (**str**) [**Py_UNICODE ***] Convert a null-terminated buffer of Unicode (UCS-2 or UCS-4) data to a Python Unicode object. If the Unicode buffer pointer is *NULL*, **None** is returned.

u# (**str**) [**Py_UNICODE *, int**] Convert a Unicode (UCS-2 or UCS-4) data buffer and its length to a Python Unicode object. If the Unicode buffer pointer is *NULL*, the length is ignored and **None** is returned.

U (**str or None**) [**char ***] Same as **s**.

U# (**str or None**) [**char *, int**] Same as **s#**.

i (**int**) [**int**] Convert a plain C **int** to a Python integer object.

b (**int**) [**char**] Convert a plain C **char** to a Python integer object.

h (**int**) [**short int**] Convert a plain C **short int** to a Python integer object.

l (**int**) [**long int**] Convert a C **long int** to a Python integer object.

B (**int**) [**unsigned char**] Convert a C **unsigned char** to a Python integer object.

H (**int**) [**unsigned short int**] Convert a C **unsigned short int** to a Python integer object.

I (**int**) [**unsigned int**] Convert a C **unsigned int** to a Python integer object.

k (**int**) [**unsigned long**] Convert a C **unsigned long** to a Python integer object.

L (**int**) [**long long**] Convert a C **long long** to a Python integer object.

K (**int**) [**unsigned long long**] Convert a C **unsigned long long** to a Python integer object.

n (**int**) [**Py_ssize_t**] Convert a C **Py_ssize_t** to a Python integer.

c (**bytes of length 1**) [**char**] Convert a C **int** representing a byte to a Python **bytes** object of length 1.

C (**str of length 1**) [**int**] Convert a C **int** representing a character to Python **str** object of length 1.

d (**float**) [**double**] Convert a C **double** to a Python floating point number.

f (**float**) [**float**] Convert a C **float** to a Python floating point number.

D (**complex**) [**Py_complex ***] Convert a C *Py_complex* structure to a Python complex number.

O (object) [**PyObject ***] Pass a Python object untouched (except for its reference count, which is incremented by one). If the object passed in is a *NULL* pointer, it is assumed that this was caused because the call producing the argument found an error and set an exception. Therefore, *Py_BuildValue()* will return *NULL* but won't raise an exception. If no exception has been raised yet, SystemError is set.

S (object) [**PyObject ***] Same as O.

N (object) [**PyObject ***] Same as O, except it doesn't increment the reference count on the object. Useful when the object is created by a call to an object constructor in the argument list.

O& (object) [*converter, anything*] Convert *anything* to a Python object through a *converter* function. The function is called with *anything* (which should be compatible with void *) as its argument and should return a "new" Python object, or *NULL* if an error occurred.

(items) (tuple) [*matching-items*] Convert a sequence of C values to a Python tuple with the same number of items.

[items] (list) [*matching-items*] Convert a sequence of C values to a Python list with the same number of items.

{items} (dict) [*matching-items*] Convert a sequence of C values to a Python dictionary. Each pair of consecutive C values adds one item to the dictionary, serving as key and value, respectively.

If there is an error in the format string, the SystemError exception is set and *NULL* returned.

PyObject* **Py_VaBuildValue**(const char **format*, va_list *vargs*)
Identical to *Py_BuildValue()*, except that it accepts a va_list rather than a variable number of arguments.

6.7 String conversion and formatting

Functions for number conversion and formatted string output.

int **PyOS_snprintf**(char **str*, size_t *size*, const char **format*, ...)
Output not more than *size* bytes to *str* according to the format string *format* and the extra arguments. See the Unix man page *snprintf(2)*.

int **PyOS_vsnprintf**(char **str*, size_t *size*, const char **format*, va_list *va*)
Output not more than *size* bytes to *str* according to the format string *format* and the variable argument list *va*. Unix man page *vsnprintf(2)*.

PyOS_snprintf() and *PyOS_vsnprintf()* wrap the Standard C library functions snprintf() and vsnprintf(). Their purpose is to guarantee consistent behavior in corner cases, which the Standard C functions do not.

The wrappers ensure that *str***[*size*-1] is always '\0' upon return. They never write more than *size* bytes (including the trailing '\0') into str. Both functions require that str != NULL, size > 0 and format != NULL.

If the platform doesn't have vsnprintf() and the buffer size needed to avoid truncation exceeds *size* by more than 512 bytes, Python aborts with a *Py_FatalError*.

The return value (*rv*) for these functions should be interpreted as follows:

- When 0 <= rv < size, the output conversion was successful and *rv* characters were written to *str* (excluding the trailing '\0' byte at *str***[*rv*]).

- When rv >= size, the output conversion was truncated and a buffer with rv + 1 bytes would have been needed to succeed. *str***[*size*-1] is '\0' in this case.

- When `rv` < 0, "something bad happened." *str**[**size*-1] is '\0' in this case too, but the rest of *str* is undefined. The exact cause of the error depends on the underlying platform.

The following functions provide locale-independent string to number conversions.

double **PyOS_string_to_double**(const char **s*, char ***endptr*, *PyObject *overflow_exception*)

Convert a string **s** to a **double**, raising a Python exception on failure. The set of accepted strings corresponds to the set of strings accepted by Python's **float()** constructor, except that **s** must not have leading or trailing whitespace. The conversion is independent of the current locale.

If **endptr** is NULL, convert the whole string. Raise ValueError and return -1.0 if the string is not a valid representation of a floating-point number.

If endptr is not NULL, convert as much of the string as possible and set ***endptr** to point to the first unconverted character. If no initial segment of the string is the valid representation of a floating-point number, set ***endptr** to point to the beginning of the string, raise ValueError, and return -1.0.

If **s** represents a value that is too large to store in a float (for example, "1e500" is such a string on many platforms) then if **overflow_exception** is NULL return Py_HUGE_VAL (with an appropriate sign) and don't set any exception. Otherwise, **overflow_exception** must point to a Python exception object; raise that exception and return -1.0. In both cases, set ***endptr** to point to the first character after the converted value.

If any other error occurs during the conversion (for example an out-of-memory error), set the appropriate Python exception and return -1.0.

New in version 3.1.

char* **PyOS_double_to_string**(double *val*, char *format_code*, int *precision*, int *flags*, int **ptype*)

Convert a **double** *val* to a string using supplied *format_code*, *precision*, and *flags*.

format_code must be one of 'e', 'E', 'f', 'F', 'g', 'G' or 'r'. For 'r', the supplied *precision* must be 0 and is ignored. The 'r' format code specifies the standard **repr()** format.

flags can be zero or more of the values *Py_DTSF_SIGN*, *Py_DTSF_ADD_DOT_0*, or *Py_DTSF_ALT*, or-ed together:

- *Py_DTSF_SIGN* means to always precede the returned string with a sign character, even if *val* is non-negative.

- *Py_DTSF_ADD_DOT_0* means to ensure that the returned string will not look like an integer.

- *Py_DTSF_ALT* means to apply "alternate" formatting rules. See the documentation for the *PyOS_snprintf()* '#' specifier for details.

If *ptype* is non-NULL, then the value it points to will be set to one of *Py_DTST_FINITE*, *Py_DTST_INFINITE*, or *Py_DTST_NAN*, signifying that *val* is a finite number, an infinite number, or not a number, respectively.

The return value is a pointer to *buffer* with the converted string or *NULL* if the conversion failed. The caller is responsible for freeing the returned string by calling *PyMem_Free()*.

New in version 3.1.

int **PyOS_stricmp**(const char **s1*, const char **s2*)

Case insensitive comparison of strings. The function works almost identically to **strcmp()** except that it ignores the case.

int **PyOS_strnicmp**(const char **s1*, const char **s2*, Py_ssize_t *size*)

Case insensitive comparison of strings. The function works almost identically to **strncmp()** except that it ignores the case.

6.8 Reflection

*PyObject** **PyEval_GetBuiltins()**
> *Return value: Borrowed reference.* Return a dictionary of the builtins in the current execution frame, or the interpreter of the thread state if no frame is currently executing.

*PyObject** **PyEval_GetLocals()**
> *Return value: Borrowed reference.* Return a dictionary of the local variables in the current execution frame, or *NULL* if no frame is currently executing.

*PyObject** **PyEval_GetGlobals()**
> *Return value: Borrowed reference.* Return a dictionary of the global variables in the current execution frame, or *NULL* if no frame is currently executing.

*PyFrameObject** **PyEval_GetFrame()**
> *Return value: Borrowed reference.* Return the current thread state's frame, which is *NULL* if no frame is currently executing.

int **PyFrame_GetLineNumber**(*PyFrameObject *frame*)
> Return the line number that *frame* is currently executing.

const char* **PyEval_GetFuncName**(*PyObject *func*)
> Return the name of *func* if it is a function, class or instance object, else the name of *func*s type.

const char* **PyEval_GetFuncDesc**(*PyObject *func*)
> Return a description string, depending on the type of *func*. Return values include "()" for functions and methods, " constructor", " instance", and " object". Concatenated with the result of *PyEval_GetFuncName()*, the result will be a description of *func*.

6.9 Codec registry and support functions

int **PyCodec_Register**(*PyObject *search_function*)
> Register a new codec search function.
>
> As side effect, this tries to load the **encodings** package, if not yet done, to make sure that it is always first in the list of search functions.

int **PyCodec_KnownEncoding**(const char *encoding*)
> Return 1 or 0 depending on whether there is a registered codec for the given *encoding*.

*PyObject** **PyCodec_Encode**(*PyObject *object*, const char *encoding*, const char *errors*)
> Generic codec based encoding API.
>
> *object* is passed through the encoder function found for the given *encoding* using the error handling method defined by *errors*. *errors* may be *NULL* to use the default method defined for the codec. Raises a **LookupError** if no encoder can be found.

*PyObject** **PyCodec_Decode**(*PyObject *object*, const char *encoding*, const char *errors*)
> Generic codec based decoding API.
>
> *object* is passed through the decoder function found for the given *encoding* using the error handling method defined by *errors*. *errors* may be *NULL* to use the default method defined for the codec. Raises a **LookupError** if no encoder can be found.

6.9.1 Codec lookup API

In the following functions, the *encoding* string is looked up converted to all lower-case characters, which makes encodings looked up through this mechanism effectively case-insensitive. If no codec is found, a

`KeyError` is set and *NULL* returned.

PyObject* **PyCodec_Encoder**(const char *encoding)
> Get an encoder function for the given *encoding*.

PyObject* **PyCodec_Decoder**(const char *encoding)
> Get a decoder function for the given *encoding*.

PyObject* **PyCodec_IncrementalEncoder**(const char *encoding, const char *errors)
> Get an `IncrementalEncoder` object for the given *encoding*.

PyObject* **PyCodec_IncrementalDecoder**(const char *encoding, const char *errors)
> Get an `IncrementalDecoder` object for the given *encoding*.

PyObject* **PyCodec_StreamReader**(const char *encoding, *PyObject* *stream, const char *errors)
> Get a `StreamReader` factory function for the given *encoding*.

PyObject* **PyCodec_StreamWriter**(const char *encoding, *PyObject* *stream, const char *errors)
> Get a `StreamWriter` factory function for the given *encoding*.

6.9.2 Registry API for Unicode encoding error handlers

int **PyCodec_RegisterError**(const char *name, *PyObject* *error)
> Register the error handling callback function *error* under the given *name*. This callback function will be called by a codec when it encounters unencodable characters/undecodable bytes and *name* is specified as the error parameter in the call to the encode/decode function.
>
> The callback gets a single argument, an instance of `UnicodeEncodeError`, `UnicodeDecodeError` or `UnicodeTranslateError` that holds information about the problematic sequence of characters or bytes and their offset in the original string (see *Unicode Exception Objects* for functions to extract this information). The callback must either raise the given exception, or return a two-item tuple containing the replacement for the problematic sequence, and an integer giving the offset in the original string at which encoding/decoding should be resumed.
>
> Return 0 on success, -1 on error.

PyObject* **PyCodec_LookupError**(const char *name)
> Lookup the error handling callback function registered under *name*. As a special case *NULL* can be passed, in which case the error handling callback for "strict" will be returned.

PyObject* **PyCodec_StrictErrors**(*PyObject* *exc)
> Raise *exc* as an exception.

PyObject* **PyCodec_IgnoreErrors**(*PyObject* *exc)
> Ignore the unicode error, skipping the faulty input.

PyObject* **PyCodec_ReplaceErrors**(*PyObject* *exc)
> Replace the unicode encode error with ? or U+FFFD.

PyObject* **PyCodec_XMLCharRefReplaceErrors**(*PyObject* *exc)
> Replace the unicode encode error with XML character references.

PyObject* **PyCodec_BackslashReplaceErrors**(*PyObject* *exc)
> Replace the unicode encode error with backslash escapes (\x, \u and \U).

PyObject* **PyCodec_NameReplaceErrors**(*PyObject* *exc)
> Replace the unicode encode error with \N{...} escapes.
>
> New in version 3.5.

SEVEN

ABSTRACT OBJECTS LAYER

The functions in this chapter interact with Python objects regardless of their type, or with wide classes of object types (e.g. all numerical types, or all sequence types). When used on object types for which they do not apply, they will raise a Python exception.

It is not possible to use these functions on objects that are not properly initialized, such as a list object that has been created by *PyList_New()*, but whose items have not been set to some non-NULL value yet.

7.1 Object Protocol

*PyObject** **Py_NotImplemented**
> The NotImplemented singleton, used to signal that an operation is not implemented for the given type combination.

Py_RETURN_NOTIMPLEMENTED
> Properly handle returning *Py_NotImplemented* from within a C function (that is, increment the reference count of NotImplemented and return it).

int **PyObject_Print**(*PyObject* *o*, FILE *fp*, int *flags*)
> Print an object *o*, on file *fp*. Returns −1 on error. The flags argument is used to enable certain printing options. The only option currently supported is Py_PRINT_RAW; if given, the str() of the object is written instead of the repr().

int **PyObject_HasAttr**(*PyObject* *o*, *PyObject* *attr_name*)
> Returns 1 if *o* has the attribute *attr_name*, and 0 otherwise. This is equivalent to the Python expression hasattr(o, attr_name). This function always succeeds.

int **PyObject_HasAttrString**(*PyObject* *o*, const char *attr_name*)
> Returns 1 if *o* has the attribute *attr_name*, and 0 otherwise. This is equivalent to the Python expression hasattr(o, attr_name). This function always succeeds.

*PyObject** **PyObject_GetAttr**(*PyObject* *o*, *PyObject* *attr_name*)
> *Return value: New reference.* Retrieve an attribute named *attr_name* from object *o*. Returns the attribute value on success, or *NULL* on failure. This is the equivalent of the Python expression o.attr_name.

*PyObject** **PyObject_GetAttrString**(*PyObject* *o*, const char *attr_name*)
> *Return value: New reference.* Retrieve an attribute named *attr_name* from object *o*. Returns the attribute value on success, or *NULL* on failure. This is the equivalent of the Python expression o.attr_name.

*PyObject** **PyObject_GenericGetAttr**(*PyObject* *o*, *PyObject* *name*)
> Generic attribute getter function that is meant to be put into a type object's tp_getattro slot. It looks for a descriptor in the dictionary of classes in the object's MRO as well as an attribute in the object's __dict__ (if present). As outlined in descriptors, data descriptors take preference over instance attributes, while non-data descriptors don't. Otherwise, an AttributeError is raised.

int **PyObject_SetAttr**(*PyObject* *o, *PyObject* *attr_name, *PyObject* *v)

> Set the value of the attribute named *attr_name*, for object *o*, to the value *v*. Raise an exception and return -1 on failure; return 0 on success. This is the equivalent of the Python statement o.attr_name = v.

> If *v* is *NULL*, the attribute is deleted, however this feature is deprecated in favour of using *PyObject_DelAttr()*.

int **PyObject_SetAttrString**(*PyObject* *o, const char *attr_name, *PyObject* *v)

> Set the value of the attribute named *attr_name*, for object *o*, to the value *v*. Raise an exception and return -1 on failure; return 0 on success. This is the equivalent of the Python statement o.attr_name = v.

> If *v* is *NULL*, the attribute is deleted, however this feature is deprecated in favour of using *PyObject_DelAttrString()*.

int **PyObject_GenericSetAttr**(*PyObject* *o, *PyObject* *name, *PyObject* *value)

> Generic attribute setter and deleter function that is meant to be put into a type object's *tp_setattro* slot. It looks for a data descriptor in the dictionary of classes in the object's MRO, and if found it takes preference over setting or deleting the attribute in the instance dictionary. Otherwise, the attribute is set or deleted in the object's __dict__ (if present). On success, 0 is returned, otherwise an **AttributeError** is raised and -1 is returned.

int **PyObject_DelAttr**(*PyObject* *o, *PyObject* *attr_name)

> Delete attribute named *attr_name*, for object *o*. Returns -1 on failure. This is the equivalent of the Python statement del o.attr_name.

int **PyObject_DelAttrString**(*PyObject* *o, const char *attr_name)

> Delete attribute named *attr_name*, for object *o*. Returns -1 on failure. This is the equivalent of the Python statement del o.attr_name.

PyObject* **PyObject_GenericGetDict**(*PyObject* *o, void *context)

> A generic implementation for the getter of a __dict__ descriptor. It creates the dictionary if necessary.

> New in version 3.3.

int **PyObject_GenericSetDict**(*PyObject* *o, void *context)

> A generic implementation for the setter of a __dict__ descriptor. This implementation does not allow the dictionary to be deleted.

> New in version 3.3.

PyObject* **PyObject_RichCompare**(*PyObject* *o1, *PyObject* *o2, int *opid*)

> *Return value: New reference.* Compare the values of *o1* and *o2* using the operation specified by *opid*, which must be one of Py_LT, Py_LE, Py_EQ, Py_NE, Py_GT, or Py_GE, corresponding to <, <=, ==, !=, >, or >= respectively. This is the equivalent of the Python expression o1 op o2, where op is the operator corresponding to *opid*. Returns the value of the comparison on success, or *NULL* on failure.

int **PyObject_RichCompareBool**(*PyObject* *o1, *PyObject* *o2, int *opid*)

> Compare the values of *o1* and *o2* using the operation specified by *opid*, which must be one of Py_LT, Py_LE, Py_EQ, Py_NE, Py_GT, or Py_GE, corresponding to <, <=, ==, !=, >, or >= respectively. Returns -1 on error, 0 if the result is false, 1 otherwise. This is the equivalent of the Python expression o1 op o2, where op is the operator corresponding to *opid*.

Note: If *o1* and *o2* are the same object, *PyObject_RichCompareBool()* will always return 1 for Py_EQ and 0 for Py_NE.

PyObject* **PyObject_Repr**(*PyObject* *o)

> *Return value: New reference.* Compute a string representation of object *o*. Returns the string rep-

resentation on success, *NULL* on failure. This is the equivalent of the Python expression `repr(o)`. Called by the `repr()` built-in function.

Changed in version 3.4: This function now includes a debug assertion to help ensure that it does not silently discard an active exception.

PyObject* **PyObject_ASCII**(*PyObject* *o)

As *PyObject_Repr()*, compute a string representation of object *o*, but escape the non-ASCII characters in the string returned by *PyObject_Repr()* with \x, \u or \U escapes. This generates a string similar to that returned by *PyObject_Repr()* in Python 2. Called by the `ascii()` built-in function.

PyObject* **PyObject_Str**(*PyObject* *o)

Return value: New reference. Compute a string representation of object *o*. Returns the string representation on success, *NULL* on failure. This is the equivalent of the Python expression `str(o)`. Called by the `str()` built-in function and, therefore, by the `print()` function.

Changed in version 3.4: This function now includes a debug assertion to help ensure that it does not silently discard an active exception.

PyObject* **PyObject_Bytes**(*PyObject* *o)

Compute a bytes representation of object *o*. *NULL* is returned on failure and a bytes object on success. This is equivalent to the Python expression `bytes(o)`, when *o* is not an integer. Unlike `bytes(o)`, a TypeError is raised when *o* is an integer instead of a zero-initialized bytes object.

int **PyObject_IsSubclass**(*PyObject* *derived, *PyObject* *cls)

Return 1 if the class *derived* is identical to or derived from the class *cls*, otherwise return 0. In case of an error, return -1.

If *cls* is a tuple, the check will be done against every entry in *cls*. The result will be 1 when at least one of the checks returns 1, otherwise it will be 0.

If *cls* has a `__subclasscheck__()` method, it will be called to determine the subclass status as described in PEP 3119. Otherwise, *derived* is a subclass of *cls* if it is a direct or indirect subclass, i.e. contained in `cls.__mro__`.

Normally only class objects, i.e. instances of `type` or a derived class, are considered classes. However, objects can override this by having a `__bases__` attribute (which must be a tuple of base classes).

int **PyObject_IsInstance**(*PyObject* *inst, *PyObject* *cls)

Return 1 if *inst* is an instance of the class *cls* or a subclass of *cls*, or 0 if not. On error, returns -1 and sets an exception.

If *cls* is a tuple, the check will be done against every entry in *cls*. The result will be 1 when at least one of the checks returns 1, otherwise it will be 0.

If *cls* has a `__instancecheck__()` method, it will be called to determine the subclass status as described in PEP 3119. Otherwise, *inst* is an instance of *cls* if its class is a subclass of *cls*.

An instance *inst* can override what is considered its class by having a `__class__` attribute.

An object *cls* can override if it is considered a class, and what its base classes are, by having a `__bases__` attribute (which must be a tuple of base classes).

int **PyCallable_Check**(*PyObject* *o)

Determine if the object *o* is callable. Return 1 if the object is callable and 0 otherwise. This function always succeeds.

PyObject* **PyObject_Call**(*PyObject* *callable_object, *PyObject* *args, *PyObject* *kw)

Return value: New reference. Call a callable Python object *callable_object*, with arguments given by the tuple *args*, and named arguments given by the dictionary *kw*. If no named arguments are needed, *kw* may be *NULL*. *args* must not be *NULL*, use an empty tuple if no arguments are needed. Returns the result of the call on success, or *NULL* on failure. This is the equivalent of the Python expression `callable_object(*args, **kw)`.

*PyObject** **PyObject_CallObject**(*PyObject* *callable_object*, *PyObject* *args*)

> *Return value: New reference.* Call a callable Python object *callable_object*, with arguments given by the tuple *args*. If no arguments are needed, then *args* may be *NULL*. Returns the result of the call on success, or *NULL* on failure. This is the equivalent of the Python expression `callable_object(*args)`.

*PyObject** **PyObject_CallFunction**(*PyObject* *callable*, const char *format*, ...)

> *Return value: New reference.* Call a callable Python object *callable*, with a variable number of C arguments. The C arguments are described using a *Py_BuildValue()* style format string. The format may be *NULL*, indicating that no arguments are provided. Returns the result of the call on success, or *NULL* on failure. This is the equivalent of the Python expression `callable(*args)`. Note that if you only pass *PyObject* * args, *PyObject_CallFunctionObjArgs()* is a faster alternative.

> Changed in version 3.4: The type of *format* was changed from `char *`.

*PyObject** **PyObject_CallMethod**(*PyObject* *o*, const char *method*, const char *format*, ...)

> *Return value: New reference.* Call the method named *method* of object *o* with a variable number of C arguments. The C arguments are described by a *Py_BuildValue()* format string that should produce a tuple. The format may be *NULL*, indicating that no arguments are provided. Returns the result of the call on success, or *NULL* on failure. This is the equivalent of the Python expression `o.method(args)`. Note that if you only pass *PyObject* * args, *PyObject_CallMethodObjArgs()* is a faster alternative.

> Changed in version 3.4: The types of *method* and *format* were changed from `char *`.

*PyObject** **PyObject_CallFunctionObjArgs**(*PyObject* *callable*, ..., NULL)

> *Return value: New reference.* Call a callable Python object *callable*, with a variable number of *PyObject** arguments. The arguments are provided as a variable number of parameters followed by *NULL*. Returns the result of the call on success, or *NULL* on failure.

*PyObject** **PyObject_CallMethodObjArgs**(*PyObject* *o*, *PyObject* *name*, ..., NULL)

> *Return value: New reference.* Calls a method of the object *o*, where the name of the method is given as a Python string object in *name*. It is called with a variable number of *PyObject** arguments. The arguments are provided as a variable number of parameters followed by *NULL*. Returns the result of the call on success, or *NULL* on failure.

Py_hash_t **PyObject_Hash**(*PyObject* *o*)

> Compute and return the hash value of an object *o*. On failure, return -1. This is the equivalent of the Python expression `hash(o)`.

> Changed in version 3.2: The return type is now Py_hash_t. This is a signed integer the same size as Py_ssize_t.

Py_hash_t **PyObject_HashNotImplemented**(*PyObject* *o*)

> Set a **TypeError** indicating that `type(o)` is not hashable and return -1. This function receives special treatment when stored in a **tp_hash** slot, allowing a type to explicitly indicate to the interpreter that it is not hashable.

int **PyObject_IsTrue**(*PyObject* *o*)

> Returns 1 if the object *o* is considered to be true, and 0 otherwise. This is equivalent to the Python expression `not not o`. On failure, return -1.

int **PyObject_Not**(*PyObject* *o*)

> Returns 0 if the object *o* is considered to be true, and 1 otherwise. This is equivalent to the Python expression `not o`. On failure, return -1.

*PyObject** **PyObject_Type**(*PyObject* *o*)

> *Return value: New reference.* When *o* is non-*NULL*, returns a type object corresponding to the object type of object *o*. On failure, raises **SystemError** and returns *NULL*. This is equivalent to the Python expression `type(o)`. This function increments the reference count of the return value. There's really no reason to use this function instead of the common expression `o->ob_type`, which returns a pointer of type *PyTypeObject**, except when the incremented reference count is needed.

int **PyObject_TypeCheck**(*PyObject* *o, *PyTypeObject* *type)
> Return true if the object *o* is of type *type* or a subtype of *type*. Both parameters must be non-*NULL*.

Py_ssize_t **PyObject_Length**(*PyObject* *o)
Py_ssize_t **PyObject_Size**(*PyObject* *o)
> Return the length of object *o*. If the object *o* provides either the sequence and mapping protocols, the sequence length is returned. On error, -1 is returned. This is the equivalent to the Python expression len(o).

Py_ssize_t **PyObject_LengthHint**(*PyObject* *o, Py_ssize_t *default*)
> Return an estimated length for the object *o*. First try to return its actual length, then an estimate using __length_hint__(), and finally return the default value. On error return -1. This is the equivalent to the Python expression operator.length_hint(o, default).

> New in version 3.4.

PyObject* **PyObject_GetItem**(*PyObject* *o, *PyObject* *key)
> *Return value: New reference.* Return element of *o* corresponding to the object *key* or *NULL* on failure. This is the equivalent of the Python expression o[key].

int **PyObject_SetItem**(*PyObject* *o, *PyObject* *key, *PyObject* *v)
> Map the object *key* to the value *v*. Raise an exception and return -1 on failure; return 0 on success. This is the equivalent of the Python statement o[key] = v.

int **PyObject_DelItem**(*PyObject* *o, *PyObject* *key)
> Delete the mapping for *key* from *o*. Returns -1 on failure. This is the equivalent of the Python statement del o[key].

PyObject* **PyObject_Dir**(*PyObject* *o)
> *Return value: New reference.* This is equivalent to the Python expression dir(o), returning a (possibly empty) list of strings appropriate for the object argument, or *NULL* if there was an error. If the argument is *NULL*, this is like the Python dir(), returning the names of the current locals; in this case, if no execution frame is active then *NULL* is returned but *PyErr_Occurred()* will return false.

PyObject* **PyObject_GetIter**(*PyObject* *o)
> *Return value: New reference.* This is equivalent to the Python expression iter(o). It returns a new iterator for the object argument, or the object itself if the object is already an iterator. Raises **TypeError** and returns *NULL* if the object cannot be iterated.

7.2 Number Protocol

int **PyNumber_Check**(*PyObject* *o)
> Returns 1 if the object *o* provides numeric protocols, and false otherwise. This function always succeeds.

PyObject* **PyNumber_Add**(*PyObject* *o1, *PyObject* *o2)
> *Return value: New reference.* Returns the result of adding *o1* and *o2*, or *NULL* on failure. This is the equivalent of the Python expression o1 + o2.

PyObject* **PyNumber_Subtract**(*PyObject* *o1, *PyObject* *o2)
> *Return value: New reference.* Returns the result of subtracting *o2* from *o1*, or *NULL* on failure. This is the equivalent of the Python expression o1 - o2.

PyObject* **PyNumber_Multiply**(*PyObject* *o1, *PyObject* *o2)
> *Return value: New reference.* Returns the result of multiplying *o1* and *o2*, or *NULL* on failure. This is the equivalent of the Python expression o1 * o2.

PyObject* **PyNumber_MatrixMultiply**(*PyObject* *o1, *PyObject* *o2)
> Returns the result of matrix multiplication on *o1* and *o2*, or *NULL* on failure. This is the equivalent of the Python expression o1 @ o2.

New in version 3.5.

PyObject* **PyNumber_FloorDivide**(*PyObject *o1*, *PyObject *o2*)

> *Return value: New reference.* Return the floor of *o1* divided by *o2*, or *NULL* on failure. This is equivalent to the "classic" division of integers.

PyObject* **PyNumber_TrueDivide**(*PyObject *o1*, *PyObject *o2*)

> *Return value: New reference.* Return a reasonable approximation for the mathematical value of *o1* divided by *o2*, or *NULL* on failure. The return value is "approximate" because binary floating point numbers are approximate; it is not possible to represent all real numbers in base two. This function can return a floating point value when passed two integers.

PyObject* **PyNumber_Remainder**(*PyObject *o1*, *PyObject *o2*)

> *Return value: New reference.* Returns the remainder of dividing *o1* by *o2*, or *NULL* on failure. This is the equivalent of the Python expression o1 % o2.

PyObject* **PyNumber_Divmod**(*PyObject *o1*, *PyObject *o2*)

> *Return value: New reference.* See the built-in function divmod(). Returns *NULL* on failure. This is the equivalent of the Python expression divmod(o1, o2).

PyObject* **PyNumber_Power**(*PyObject *o1*, *PyObject *o2*, *PyObject *o3*)

> *Return value: New reference.* See the built-in function pow(). Returns *NULL* on failure. This is the equivalent of the Python expression pow(o1, o2, o3), where *o3* is optional. If *o3* is to be ignored, pass *Py_None* in its place (passing *NULL* for *o3* would cause an illegal memory access).

PyObject* **PyNumber_Negative**(*PyObject *o*)

> *Return value: New reference.* Returns the negation of *o* on success, or *NULL* on failure. This is the equivalent of the Python expression -o.

PyObject* **PyNumber_Positive**(*PyObject *o*)

> *Return value: New reference.* Returns *o* on success, or *NULL* on failure. This is the equivalent of the Python expression +o.

PyObject* **PyNumber_Absolute**(*PyObject *o*)

> *Return value: New reference.* Returns the absolute value of *o*, or *NULL* on failure. This is the equivalent of the Python expression abs(o).

PyObject* **PyNumber_Invert**(*PyObject *o*)

> *Return value: New reference.* Returns the bitwise negation of *o* on success, or *NULL* on failure. This is the equivalent of the Python expression ~o.

PyObject* **PyNumber_Lshift**(*PyObject *o1*, *PyObject *o2*)

> *Return value: New reference.* Returns the result of left shifting *o1* by *o2* on success, or *NULL* on failure. This is the equivalent of the Python expression o1 << o2.

PyObject* **PyNumber_Rshift**(*PyObject *o1*, *PyObject *o2*)

> *Return value: New reference.* Returns the result of right shifting *o1* by *o2* on success, or *NULL* on failure. This is the equivalent of the Python expression o1 >> o2.

PyObject* **PyNumber_And**(*PyObject *o1*, *PyObject *o2*)

> *Return value: New reference.* Returns the "bitwise and" of *o1* and *o2* on success and *NULL* on failure. This is the equivalent of the Python expression o1 & o2.

PyObject* **PyNumber_Xor**(*PyObject *o1*, *PyObject *o2*)

> *Return value: New reference.* Returns the "bitwise exclusive or" of *o1* by *o2* on success, or *NULL* on failure. This is the equivalent of the Python expression o1 ^ o2.

PyObject* **PyNumber_Or**(*PyObject *o1*, *PyObject *o2*)

> *Return value: New reference.* Returns the "bitwise or" of *o1* and *o2* on success, or *NULL* on failure. This is the equivalent of the Python expression o1 | o2.

PyObject* **PyNumber_InPlaceAdd**(*PyObject *o1*, *PyObject *o2*)

> *Return value: New reference.* Returns the result of adding *o1* and *o2*, or *NULL* on failure. The

operation is done *in-place* when *o1* supports it. This is the equivalent of the Python statement o1 +=
o2.

*PyObject** **PyNumber_InPlaceSubtract**(*PyObject* **o1*, *PyObject* **o2*)
    Return value: New reference. Returns the result of subtracting *o2* from *o1*, or *NULL* on failure. The
    operation is done *in-place* when *o1* supports it. This is the equivalent of the Python statement o1 -=
    o2.

*PyObject** **PyNumber_InPlaceMultiply**(*PyObject* **o1*, *PyObject* **o2*)
    Return value: New reference. Returns the result of multiplying *o1* and *o2*, or *NULL* on failure. The
    operation is done *in-place* when *o1* supports it. This is the equivalent of the Python statement o1 *=
    o2.

*PyObject** **PyNumber_InPlaceMatrixMultiply**(*PyObject* **o1*, *PyObject* **o2*)
    Returns the result of matrix multiplication on *o1* and *o2*, or *NULL* on failure. The operation is done
    in-place when *o1* supports it. This is the equivalent of the Python statement o1 @= o2.

    New in version 3.5.

*PyObject** **PyNumber_InPlaceFloorDivide**(*PyObject* **o1*, *PyObject* **o2*)
    Return value: New reference. Returns the mathematical floor of dividing *o1* by *o2*, or *NULL* on failure.
    The operation is done *in-place* when *o1* supports it. This is the equivalent of the Python statement o1
    //= o2.

*PyObject** **PyNumber_InPlaceTrueDivide**(*PyObject* **o1*, *PyObject* **o2*)
    Return value: New reference. Return a reasonable approximation for the mathematical value of *o1*
    divided by *o2*, or *NULL* on failure. The return value is "approximate" because binary floating point
    numbers are approximate; it is not possible to represent all real numbers in base two. This function
    can return a floating point value when passed two integers. The operation is done *in-place* when *o1*
    supports it.

*PyObject** **PyNumber_InPlaceRemainder**(*PyObject* **o1*, *PyObject* **o2*)
    Return value: New reference. Returns the remainder of dividing *o1* by *o2*, or *NULL* on failure. The
    operation is done *in-place* when *o1* supports it. This is the equivalent of the Python statement o1 %=
    o2.

*PyObject** **PyNumber_InPlacePower**(*PyObject* **o1*, *PyObject* **o2*, *PyObject* **o3*)
    Return value: New reference. See the built-in function pow(). Returns *NULL* on failure. The operation
    is done *in-place* when *o1* supports it. This is the equivalent of the Python statement o1 **= o2 when
    o3 is *Py_None*, or an in-place variant of pow(o1, o2, o3) otherwise. If *o3* is to be ignored, pass
    Py_None in its place (passing *NULL* for *o3* would cause an illegal memory access).

*PyObject** **PyNumber_InPlaceLshift**(*PyObject* **o1*, *PyObject* **o2*)
    Return value: New reference. Returns the result of left shifting *o1* by *o2* on success, or *NULL* on
    failure. The operation is done *in-place* when *o1* supports it. This is the equivalent of the Python
    statement o1 <<= o2.

*PyObject** **PyNumber_InPlaceRshift**(*PyObject* **o1*, *PyObject* **o2*)
    Return value: New reference. Returns the result of right shifting *o1* by *o2* on success, or *NULL* on
    failure. The operation is done *in-place* when *o1* supports it. This is the equivalent of the Python
    statement o1 >>= o2.

*PyObject** **PyNumber_InPlaceAnd**(*PyObject* **o1*, *PyObject* **o2*)
    Return value: New reference. Returns the "bitwise and" of *o1* and *o2* on success and *NULL* on failure.
    The operation is done *in-place* when *o1* supports it. This is the equivalent of the Python statement o1
    &= o2.

*PyObject** **PyNumber_InPlaceXor**(*PyObject* **o1*, *PyObject* **o2*)
    Return value: New reference. Returns the "bitwise exclusive or" of *o1* by *o2* on success, or *NULL*
    on failure. The operation is done *in-place* when *o1* supports it. This is the equivalent of the Python
    statement o1 ^= o2.

*PyObject** **PyNumber_InPlaceOr**(*PyObject* *o1*, *PyObject* *o2*)

> *Return value: New reference.* Returns the "bitwise or" of *o1* and *o2* on success, or *NULL* on failure. The operation is done *in-place* when *o1* supports it. This is the equivalent of the Python statement o1 |= o2.

*PyObject** **PyNumber_Long**(*PyObject* *o*)

> *Return value: New reference.* Returns the *o* converted to an integer object on success, or *NULL* on failure. This is the equivalent of the Python expression int(o).

*PyObject** **PyNumber_Float**(*PyObject* *o*)

> *Return value: New reference.* Returns the *o* converted to a float object on success, or *NULL* on failure. This is the equivalent of the Python expression float(o).

*PyObject** **PyNumber_Index**(*PyObject* *o*)

> Returns the *o* converted to a Python int on success or *NULL* with a **TypeError** exception raised on failure.

*PyObject** **PyNumber_ToBase**(*PyObject* *n*, int *base*)

> Returns the integer *n* converted to base *base* as a string. The *base* argument must be one of 2, 8, 10, or 16. For base 2, 8, or 16, the returned string is prefixed with a base marker of '0b', '0o', or '0x', respectively. If *n* is not a Python int, it is converted with *PyNumber_Index()* first.

Py_ssize_t **PyNumber_AsSsize_t**(*PyObject* *o*, *PyObject* *exc*)

> Returns *o* converted to a Py_ssize_t value if *o* can be interpreted as an integer. If the call fails, an exception is raised and −1 is returned.
>
> If *o* can be converted to a Python int but the attempt to convert to a Py_ssize_t value would raise an **OverflowError**, then the *exc* argument is the type of exception that will be raised (usually **IndexError** or **OverflowError**). If *exc* is *NULL*, then the exception is cleared and the value is clipped to *PY_SSIZE_T_MIN* for a negative integer or *PY_SSIZE_T_MAX* for a positive integer.

int **PyIndex_Check**(*PyObject* *o*)

> Returns 1 if *o* is an index integer (has the nb_index slot of the tp_as_number structure filled in), and 0 otherwise.

7.3 Sequence Protocol

int **PySequence_Check**(*PyObject* *o*)

> Return 1 if the object provides sequence protocol, and 0 otherwise. This function always succeeds.

Py_ssize_t **PySequence_Size**(*PyObject* *o*)
Py_ssize_t **PySequence_Length**(*PyObject* *o*)

> Returns the number of objects in sequence *o* on success, and −1 on failure. For objects that do not provide sequence protocol, this is equivalent to the Python expression len(o).

*PyObject** **PySequence_Concat**(*PyObject* *o1*, *PyObject* *o2*)

> *Return value: New reference.* Return the concatenation of *o1* and *o2* on success, and *NULL* on failure. This is the equivalent of the Python expression o1 + o2.

*PyObject** **PySequence_Repeat**(*PyObject* *o*, Py_ssize_t *count*)

> *Return value: New reference.* Return the result of repeating sequence object *o* count times, or *NULL* on failure. This is the equivalent of the Python expression o * count.

*PyObject** **PySequence_InPlaceConcat**(*PyObject* *o1*, *PyObject* *o2*)

> *Return value: New reference.* Return the concatenation of *o1* and *o2* on success, and *NULL* on failure. The operation is done *in-place* when *o1* supports it. This is the equivalent of the Python expression o1 += o2.

*PyObject** **PySequence_InPlaceRepeat**(*PyObject* *o*, Py_ssize_t *count*)

> *Return value: New reference.* Return the result of repeating sequence object *o count* times, or *NULL* on failure. The operation is done *in-place* when *o* supports it. This is the equivalent of the Python expression o *= count.

*PyObject** **PySequence_GetItem**(*PyObject* *o*, Py_ssize_t *i*)

> *Return value: New reference.* Return the *i*th element of *o*, or *NULL* on failure. This is the equivalent of the Python expression o[i].

*PyObject** **PySequence_GetSlice**(*PyObject* *o*, Py_ssize_t *i1*, Py_ssize_t *i2*)

> *Return value: New reference.* Return the slice of sequence object *o* between *i1* and *i2*, or *NULL* on failure. This is the equivalent of the Python expression o[i1:i2].

int **PySequence_SetItem**(*PyObject* *o*, Py_ssize_t *i*, *PyObject* *v*)

> Assign object *v* to the *i*th element of *o*. Raise an exception and return -1 on failure; return 0 on success. This is the equivalent of the Python statement o[i] = v. This function *does not* steal a reference to *v*.

> If *v* is *NULL*, the element is deleted, however this feature is deprecated in favour of using *PySequence_DelItem()*.

int **PySequence_DelItem**(*PyObject* *o*, Py_ssize_t *i*)

> Delete the *i*th element of object *o*. Returns -1 on failure. This is the equivalent of the Python statement del o[i].

int **PySequence_SetSlice**(*PyObject* *o*, Py_ssize_t *i1*, Py_ssize_t *i2*, *PyObject* *v*)

> Assign the sequence object *v* to the slice in sequence object *o* from *i1* to *i2*. This is the equivalent of the Python statement o[i1:i2] = v.

int **PySequence_DelSlice**(*PyObject* *o*, Py_ssize_t *i1*, Py_ssize_t *i2*)

> Delete the slice in sequence object *o* from *i1* to *i2*. Returns -1 on failure. This is the equivalent of the Python statement del o[i1:i2].

Py_ssize_t **PySequence_Count**(*PyObject* *o*, *PyObject* *value*)

> Return the number of occurrences of *value* in *o*, that is, return the number of keys for which o[key] == value. On failure, return -1. This is equivalent to the Python expression o.count(value).

int **PySequence_Contains**(*PyObject* *o*, *PyObject* *value*)

> Determine if *o* contains *value*. If an item in *o* is equal to *value*, return 1, otherwise return 0. On error, return -1. This is equivalent to the Python expression value in o.

Py_ssize_t **PySequence_Index**(*PyObject* *o*, *PyObject* *value*)

> Return the first index *i* for which o[i] == value. On error, return -1. This is equivalent to the Python expression o.index(value).

*PyObject** **PySequence_List**(*PyObject* *o*)

> *Return value: New reference.* Return a list object with the same contents as the sequence or iterable *o*, or *NULL* on failure. The returned list is guaranteed to be new. This is equivalent to the Python expression list(o).

*PyObject** **PySequence_Tuple**(*PyObject* *o*)

> *Return value: New reference.* Return a tuple object with the same contents as the arbitrary sequence *o* or *NULL* on failure. If *o* is a tuple, a new reference will be returned, otherwise a tuple will be constructed with the appropriate contents. This is equivalent to the Python expression tuple(o).

*PyObject** **PySequence_Fast**(*PyObject* *o*, const char *m*)

> *Return value: New reference.* Return the sequence *o* as a list, unless it is already a tuple or list, in which case *o* is returned. Use *PySequence_Fast_GET_ITEM()* to access the members of the result. Returns *NULL* on failure. If the object is not a sequence, raises **TypeError** with *m* as the message text.

PyObject* **PySequence_Fast_GET_ITEM**(*PyObject *o*, Py_ssize_t *i*)
> *Return value: Borrowed reference.* Return the *i*th element of *o*, assuming that *o* was returned by *PySequence_Fast()*, *o* is not *NULL*, and that *i* is within bounds.

PyObject** **PySequence_Fast_ITEMS**(*PyObject *o*)
> Return the underlying array of PyObject pointers. Assumes that *o* was returned by *PySequence_Fast()* and *o* is not *NULL*.
>
> Note, if a list gets resized, the reallocation may relocate the items array. So, only use the underlying array pointer in contexts where the sequence cannot change.

PyObject* **PySequence_ITEM**(*PyObject *o*, Py_ssize_t *i*)
> *Return value: New reference.* Return the *i*th element of *o* or *NULL* on failure. Macro form of *PySequence_GetItem()* but without checking that *PySequence_Check()* on *o* is true and without adjustment for negative indices.

Py_ssize_t **PySequence_Fast_GET_SIZE**(*PyObject *o*)
> Returns the length of *o*, assuming that *o* was returned by *PySequence_Fast()* and that *o* is not *NULL*. The size can also be gotten by calling *PySequence_Size()* on *o*, but *PySequence_Fast_GET_SIZE()* is faster because it can assume *o* is a list or tuple.

7.4 Mapping Protocol

int **PyMapping_Check**(*PyObject *o*)
> Return 1 if the object provides mapping protocol, and 0 otherwise. This function always succeeds.

Py_ssize_t **PyMapping_Size**(*PyObject *o*)
Py_ssize_t **PyMapping_Length**(*PyObject *o*)
> Returns the number of keys in object *o* on success, and -1 on failure. For objects that do not provide mapping protocol, this is equivalent to the Python expression `len(o)`.

int **PyMapping_DelItemString**(*PyObject *o*, const char **key*)
> Remove the mapping for object *key* from the object *o*. Return -1 on failure. This is equivalent to the Python statement `del o[key]`.

int **PyMapping_DelItem**(*PyObject *o*, *PyObject *key*)
> Remove the mapping for object *key* from the object *o*. Return -1 on failure. This is equivalent to the Python statement `del o[key]`.

int **PyMapping_HasKeyString**(*PyObject *o*, const char **key*)
> On success, return 1 if the mapping object has the key *key* and 0 otherwise. This is equivalent to the Python expression `key in o`. This function always succeeds.

int **PyMapping_HasKey**(*PyObject *o*, *PyObject *key*)
> Return 1 if the mapping object has the key *key* and 0 otherwise. This is equivalent to the Python expression `key in o`. This function always succeeds.

PyObject* **PyMapping_Keys**(*PyObject *o*)
> *Return value: New reference.* On success, return a list or tuple of the keys in object *o*. On failure, return *NULL*.

PyObject* **PyMapping_Values**(*PyObject *o*)
> *Return value: New reference.* On success, return a list or tuple of the values in object *o*. On failure, return *NULL*.

PyObject* **PyMapping_Items**(*PyObject *o*)
> *Return value: New reference.* On success, return a list or tuple of the items in object *o*, where each item is a tuple containing a key-value pair. On failure, return *NULL*.

PyObject* **PyMapping_GetItemString**(*PyObject* *o*, const char **key*)

> *Return value: New reference.* Return element of *o* corresponding to the object *key* or *NULL* on failure. This is the equivalent of the Python expression o[key].

int **PyMapping_SetItemString**(*PyObject* *o*, const char **key*, *PyObject* **v*)

> Map the object *key* to the value *v* in object *o*. Returns -1 on failure. This is the equivalent of the Python statement o[key] = v.

7.5 Iterator Protocol

There are two functions specifically for working with iterators.

int **PyIter_Check**(*PyObject* **o*)

> Return true if the object *o* supports the iterator protocol.

PyObject* **PyIter_Next**(*PyObject* **o*)

> *Return value: New reference.* Return the next value from the iteration *o*. The object must be an iterator (it is up to the caller to check this). If there are no remaining values, returns *NULL* with no exception set. If an error occurs while retrieving the item, returns *NULL* and passes along the exception.

To write a loop which iterates over an iterator, the C code should look something like this:

```
PyObject *iterator = PyObject_GetIter(obj);
PyObject *item;

if (iterator == NULL) {
    /* propagate error */
}

while (item = PyIter_Next(iterator)) {
    /* do something with item */
    ...
    /* release reference when done */
    Py_DECREF(item);
}

Py_DECREF(iterator);

if (PyErr_Occurred()) {
    /* propagate error */
}
else {
    /* continue doing useful work */
}
```

7.6 Buffer Protocol

Certain objects available in Python wrap access to an underlying memory array or *buffer*. Such objects include the built-in bytes and bytearray, and some extension types like array.array. Third-party libraries may define their own types for special purposes, such as image processing or numeric analysis.

While each of these types have their own semantics, they share the common characteristic of being backed by a possibly large memory buffer. It is then desirable, in some situations, to access that buffer directly and without intermediate copying.

Python provides such a facility at the C level in the form of the *buffer protocol*. This protocol has two sides:

- on the producer side, a type can export a "buffer interface" which allows objects of that type to expose information about their underlying buffer. This interface is described in the section *Buffer Object Structures*;

- on the consumer side, several means are available to obtain a pointer to the raw underlying data of an object (for example a method parameter).

Simple objects such as `bytes` and `bytearray` expose their underlying buffer in byte-oriented form. Other forms are possible; for example, the elements exposed by an `array.array` can be multi-byte values.

An example consumer of the buffer interface is the `write()` method of file objects: any object that can export a series of bytes through the buffer interface can be written to a file. While `write()` only needs read-only access to the internal contents of the object passed to it, other methods such as `readinto()` need write access to the contents of their argument. The buffer interface allows objects to selectively allow or reject exporting of read-write and read-only buffers.

There are two ways for a consumer of the buffer interface to acquire a buffer over a target object:

- call *PyObject_GetBuffer()* with the right parameters;

- call *PyArg_ParseTuple()* (or one of its siblings) with one of the `y*`, `w*` or `s*` *format codes*.

In both cases, *PyBuffer_Release()* must be called when the buffer isn't needed anymore. Failure to do so could lead to various issues such as resource leaks.

7.6.1 Buffer structure

Buffer structures (or simply "buffers") are useful as a way to expose the binary data from another object to the Python programmer. They can also be used as a zero-copy slicing mechanism. Using their ability to reference a block of memory, it is possible to expose any data to the Python programmer quite easily. The memory could be a large, constant array in a C extension, it could be a raw block of memory for manipulation before passing to an operating system library, or it could be used to pass around structured data in its native, in-memory format.

Contrary to most data types exposed by the Python interpreter, buffers are not *PyObject* pointers but rather simple C structures. This allows them to be created and copied very simply. When a generic wrapper around a buffer is needed, a *memoryview* object can be created.

For short instructions how to write an exporting object, see *Buffer Object Structures*. For obtaining a buffer, see *PyObject_GetBuffer()*.

Py_buffer

> void *`buf`
>> A pointer to the start of the logical structure described by the buffer fields. This can be any location within the underlying physical memory block of the exporter. For example, with negative *strides* the value may point to the end of the memory block.
>>
>> For *contiguous* arrays, the value points to the beginning of the memory block.

> void *`obj`
>> A new reference to the exporting object. The reference is owned by the consumer and automatically decremented and set to *NULL* by *PyBuffer_Release()*. The field is the equivalent of the return value of any standard C-API function.
>>
>> As a special case, for *temporary* buffers that are wrapped by *PyMemoryView_FromBuffer()* or *PyBuffer_FillInfo()* this field is *NULL*. In general, exporting objects MUST NOT use this scheme.

Py_ssize_t **len**

> product(shape) * itemsize. For contiguous arrays, this is the length of the underlying memory block. For non-contiguous arrays, it is the length that the logical structure would have if it were copied to a contiguous representation.
>
> Accessing ((char *)buf)[0] up to ((char *)buf)[len-1] is only valid if the buffer has been obtained by a request that guarantees contiguity. In most cases such a request will be *PyBUF_SIMPLE* or *PyBUF_WRITABLE*.

int **readonly**

> An indicator of whether the buffer is read-only. This field is controlled by the *PyBUF_WRITABLE* flag.

Py_ssize_t **itemsize**

> Item size in bytes of a single element. Same as the value of **struct.calcsize()** called on non-NULL *format* values.
>
> Important exception: If a consumer requests a buffer without the *PyBUF_FORMAT* flag, *format* will be set to *NULL*, but *itemsize* still has the value for the original format.
>
> If *shape* is present, the equality product(shape) * itemsize == len still holds and the consumer can use *itemsize* to navigate the buffer.
>
> If *shape* is *NULL* as a result of a *PyBUF_SIMPLE* or a *PyBUF_WRITABLE* request, the consumer must disregard *itemsize* and assume itemsize == 1.

const char ***format**

> A *NUL* terminated string in **struct** module style syntax describing the contents of a single item. If this is *NULL*, "B" (unsigned bytes) is assumed.
>
> This field is controlled by the *PyBUF_FORMAT* flag.

int **ndim**

> The number of dimensions the memory represents as an n-dimensional array. If it is 0, *buf* points to a single item representing a scalar. In this case, *shape*, *strides* and *suboffsets* MUST be *NULL*.
>
> The macro **PyBUF_MAX_NDIM** limits the maximum number of dimensions to 64. Exporters MUST respect this limit, consumers of multi-dimensional buffers SHOULD be able to handle up to **PyBUF_MAX_NDIM** dimensions.

Py_ssize_t ***shape**

> An array of **Py_ssize_t** of length *ndim* indicating the shape of the memory as an n-dimensional array. Note that shape[0] * ... * shape[ndim-1] * itemsize MUST be equal to *len*.
>
> Shape values are restricted to shape[n] >= 0. The case shape[n] == 0 requires special attention. See *complex arrays* for further information.
>
> The shape array is read-only for the consumer.

Py_ssize_t ***strides**

> An array of **Py_ssize_t** of length *ndim* giving the number of bytes to skip to get to a new element in each dimension.
>
> Stride values can be any integer. For regular arrays, strides are usually positive, but a consumer MUST be able to handle the case strides[n] <= 0. See *complex arrays* for further information.
>
> The strides array is read-only for the consumer.

Py_ssize_t ***suboffsets**

> An array of **Py_ssize_t** of length *ndim*. If suboffsets[n] >= 0, the values stored along the nth dimension are pointers and the suboffset value dictates how many bytes to add to each pointer after de-referencing. A suboffset value that is negative indicates that no de-referencing should occur (striding in a contiguous memory block).

If all suboffsets are negative (i.e. no de-referencing is needed, then this field must be NULL (the default value).

This type of array representation is used by the Python Imaging Library (PIL). See *complex arrays* for further information how to access elements of such an array.

The suboffsets array is read-only for the consumer.

void *`internal`
> This is for use internally by the exporting object. For example, this might be re-cast as an integer by the exporter and used to store flags about whether or not the shape, strides, and suboffsets arrays must be freed when the buffer is released. The consumer MUST NOT alter this value.

7.6.2 Buffer request types

Buffers are usually obtained by sending a buffer request to an exporting object via `PyObject_GetBuffer()`. Since the complexity of the logical structure of the memory can vary drastically, the consumer uses the *flags* argument to specify the exact buffer type it can handle.

All `Py_buffer` fields are unambiguously defined by the request type.

request-independent fields

The following fields are not influenced by *flags* and must always be filled in with the correct values: `obj`, `buf`, `len`, `itemsize`, `ndim`.

readonly, format

> **PyBUF_WRITABLE**
> > Controls the *readonly* field. If set, the exporter MUST provide a writable buffer or else report failure. Otherwise, the exporter MAY provide either a read-only or writable buffer, but the choice MUST be consistent for all consumers.
>
> **PyBUF_FORMAT**
> > Controls the *format* field. If set, this field MUST be filled in correctly. Otherwise, this field MUST be *NULL*.

PyBUF_WRITABLE can be |'d to any of the flags in the next section. Since *PyBUF_SIMPLE* is defined as 0, *PyBUF_WRITABLE* can be used as a stand-alone flag to request a simple writable buffer.

PyBUF_FORMAT can be |'d to any of the flags except *PyBUF_SIMPLE*. The latter already implies format B (unsigned bytes).

shape, strides, suboffsets

The flags that control the logical structure of the memory are listed in decreasing order of complexity. Note that each flag contains all bits of the flags below it.

Request	shape	strides	suboffsets
PyBUF_INDIRECT	yes	yes	if needed
PyBUF_STRIDES	yes	yes	NULL
PyBUF_ND	yes	NULL	NULL
PyBUF_SIMPLE	NULL	NULL	NULL

contiguity requests

C or Fortran *contiguity* can be explicitly requested, with and without stride information. Without stride information, the buffer must be C-contiguous.

Request	shape	strides	suboffsets	contig
PyBUF_C_CONTIGUOUS	yes	yes	NULL	C
PyBUF_F_CONTIGUOUS	yes	yes	NULL	F
PyBUF_ANY_CONTIGUOUS	yes	yes	NULL	C or F
PyBUF_ND	yes	NULL	NULL	C

compound requests

All possible requests are fully defined by some combination of the flags in the previous section. For convenience, the buffer protocol provides frequently used combinations as single flags.

In the following table U stands for undefined contiguity. The consumer would have to call *PyBuffer_IsContiguous()* to determine contiguity.

Request	shape	strides	suboffsets	contig	readonly	format
`PyBUF_FULL`	yes	yes	if needed	U	0	yes
`PyBUF_FULL_RO`	yes	yes	if needed	U	1 or 0	yes
`PyBUF_RECORDS`	yes	yes	NULL	U	0	yes
`PyBUF_RECORDS_RO`	yes	yes	NULL	U	1 or 0	yes
`PyBUF_STRIDED`	yes	yes	NULL	U	0	NULL
`PyBUF_STRIDED_RO`	yes	yes	NULL	U	1 or 0	NULL
`PyBUF_CONTIG`	yes	NULL	NULL	C	0	NULL
`PyBUF_CONTIG_RO`	yes	NULL	NULL	C	1 or 0	NULL

7.6.3 Complex arrays

NumPy-style: shape and strides

The logical structure of NumPy-style arrays is defined by *itemsize*, *ndim*, *shape* and *strides*.

If `ndim == 0`, the memory location pointed to by *buf* is interpreted as a scalar of size *itemsize*. In that case, both *shape* and *strides* are *NULL*.

If *strides* is *NULL*, the array is interpreted as a standard n-dimensional C-array. Otherwise, the consumer must access an n-dimensional array as follows:

```
ptr = (char *)buf + indices[0] * strides[0] + ... + indices[n-1] * strides[n-1]
item = *((typeof(item) *)ptr);
```

As noted above, *buf* can point to any location within the actual memory block. An exporter can check the validity of a buffer with this function:

```
def verify_structure(memlen, itemsize, ndim, shape, strides, offset):
    """Verify that the parameters represent a valid array within
    the bounds of the allocated memory:
        char *mem: start of the physical memory block
        memlen: length of the physical memory block
        offset: (char *)buf - mem
    """
    if offset % itemsize:
        return False
    if offset < 0 or offset+itemsize > memlen:
        return False
    if any(v % itemsize for v in strides):
        return False

    if ndim <= 0:
```

Chapter 7. Abstract Objects Layer

```
        return ndim == 0 and not shape and not strides
    if 0 in shape:
        return True

    imin = sum(strides[j]*(shape[j]-1) for j in range(ndim)
            if strides[j] <= 0)
    imax = sum(strides[j]*(shape[j]-1) for j in range(ndim)
            if strides[j] > 0)

    return 0 <= offset+imin and offset+imax+itemsize <= memlen
```

PIL-style: shape, strides and suboffsets

In addition to the regular items, PIL-style arrays can contain pointers that must be followed in order to get to the next element in a dimension. For example, the regular three-dimensional C-array char v[2][2][3] can also be viewed as an array of 2 pointers to 2 two-dimensional arrays: char (*v[2])[2][3]. In suboffsets representation, those two pointers can be embedded at the start of *buf*, pointing to two char x[2][3] arrays that can be located anywhere in memory.

Here is a function that returns a pointer to the element in an N-D array pointed to by an N-dimensional index when there are both non-NULL strides and suboffsets:

```
void *get_item_pointer(int ndim, void *buf, Py_ssize_t *strides,
                    Py_ssize_t *suboffsets, Py_ssize_t *indices) {
    char *pointer = (char*)buf;
    int i;
    for (i = 0; i < ndim; i++) {
        pointer += strides[i] * indices[i];
        if (suboffsets[i] >=0 ) {
            pointer = *((char**)pointer) + suboffsets[i];
        }
    }
    return (void*)pointer;
}
```

7.6.4 Buffer-related functions

int **PyObject_CheckBuffer**(*PyObject *obj*)

Return 1 if *obj* supports the buffer interface otherwise 0. When 1 is returned, it doesn't guarantee that *PyObject_GetBuffer()* will succeed.

int **PyObject_GetBuffer**(*PyObject *exporter*, *Py_buffer *view*, int *flags*)

Send a request to *exporter* to fill in *view* as specified by *flags*. If the exporter cannot provide a buffer of the exact type, it MUST raise PyExc_BufferError, set view->obj to *NULL* and return -1.

On success, fill in *view*, set view->obj to a new reference to *exporter* and return 0. In the case of chained buffer providers that redirect requests to a single object, view->obj MAY refer to this object instead of *exporter* (See *Buffer Object Structures*).

Successful calls to *PyObject_GetBuffer()* must be paired with calls to *PyBuffer_Release()*, similar to malloc() and free(). Thus, after the consumer is done with the buffer, *PyBuffer_Release()* must be called exactly once.

void **PyBuffer_Release**(*Py_buffer *view*)

Release the buffer *view* and decrement the reference count for view->obj. This function MUST be called when the buffer is no longer being used, otherwise reference leaks may occur.

It is an error to call this function on a buffer that was not obtained via *PyObject_GetBuffer()*.

Py_ssize_t **PyBuffer_SizeFromFormat**(const char *)
> Return the implied *itemsize* from *format*. This function is not yet implemented.

int **PyBuffer_IsContiguous**(*Py_buffer* *view*, char *order*)
> Return 1 if the memory defined by the *view* is C-style (*order* is `'C'`) or Fortran-style (*order* is `'F'`) *contiguous* or either one (*order* is `'A'`). Return 0 otherwise.

void **PyBuffer_FillContiguousStrides**(int *ndims*, Py_ssize_t *shape*, Py_ssize_t *strides*, int *itemsize*, char *order*)
> Fill the *strides* array with byte-strides of a *contiguous* (C-style if *order* is `'C'` or Fortran-style if *order* is `'F'`) array of the given shape with the given number of bytes per element.

int **PyBuffer_FillInfo**(*Py_buffer* *view*, *PyObject* *exporter*, void *buf*, Py_ssize_t *len*, int *readonly*, int *flags*)
> Handle buffer requests for an exporter that wants to expose *buf* of size *len* with writability set according to *readonly*. *buf* is interpreted as a sequence of unsigned bytes.
>
> The *flags* argument indicates the request type. This function always fills in *view* as specified by flags, unless *buf* has been designated as read-only and *PyBUF_WRITABLE* is set in *flags*.
>
> On success, set `view->obj` to a new reference to *exporter* and return 0. Otherwise, raise `PyExc_BufferError`, set `view->obj` to *NULL* and return `-1`;
>
> If this function is used as part of a *getbufferproc*, *exporter* MUST be set to the exporting object and *flags* must be passed unmodified. Otherwise, *exporter* MUST be NULL.

7.7 Old Buffer Protocol

Deprecated since version 3.0.

These functions were part of the "old buffer protocol" API in Python 2. In Python 3, this protocol doesn't exist anymore but the functions are still exposed to ease porting 2.x code. They act as a compatibility wrapper around the *new buffer protocol*, but they don't give you control over the lifetime of the resources acquired when a buffer is exported.

Therefore, it is recommended that you call *PyObject_GetBuffer()* (or the **y*** or **w*** *format codes* with the *PyArg_ParseTuple()* family of functions) to get a buffer view over an object, and *PyBuffer_Release()* when the buffer view can be released.

int **PyObject_AsCharBuffer**(*PyObject* *obj*, const char **buffer*, Py_ssize_t *buffer_len*)
> Returns a pointer to a read-only memory location usable as character-based input. The *obj* argument must support the single-segment character buffer interface. On success, returns 0, sets *buffer* to the memory location and *buffer_len* to the buffer length. Returns `-1` and sets a `TypeError` on error.

int **PyObject_AsReadBuffer**(*PyObject* *obj*, const void **buffer*, Py_ssize_t *buffer_len*)
> Returns a pointer to a read-only memory location containing arbitrary data. The *obj* argument must support the single-segment readable buffer interface. On success, returns 0, sets *buffer* to the memory location and *buffer_len* to the buffer length. Returns `-1` and sets a `TypeError` on error.

int **PyObject_CheckReadBuffer**(*PyObject* *o*)
> Returns 1 if *o* supports the single-segment readable buffer interface. Otherwise returns 0.

int **PyObject_AsWriteBuffer**(*PyObject* *obj*, void **buffer*, Py_ssize_t *buffer_len*)
> Returns a pointer to a writable memory location. The *obj* argument must support the single-segment, character buffer interface. On success, returns 0, sets *buffer* to the memory location and *buffer_len* to the buffer length. Returns `-1` and sets a `TypeError` on error.

CONCRETE OBJECTS LAYER

The functions in this chapter are specific to certain Python object types. Passing them an object of the wrong type is not a good idea; if you receive an object from a Python program and you are not sure that it has the right type, you must perform a type check first; for example, to check that an object is a dictionary, use *PyDict_Check()*. The chapter is structured like the "family tree" of Python object types.

> **Warning:** While the functions described in this chapter carefully check the type of the objects which are passed in, many of them do not check for *NULL* being passed instead of a valid object. Allowing *NULL* to be passed in can cause memory access violations and immediate termination of the interpreter.

8.1 Fundamental Objects

This section describes Python type objects and the singleton object `None`.

8.1.1 Type Objects

`PyTypeObject`
> The C structure of the objects used to describe built-in types.

*PyObject** **PyType_Type**
> This is the type object for type objects; it is the same object as `type` in the Python layer.

int **PyType_Check**(*PyObject* *o*)
> Return true if the object *o* is a type object, including instances of types derived from the standard type object. Return false in all other cases.

int **PyType_CheckExact**(*PyObject* *o*)
> Return true if the object *o* is a type object, but not a subtype of the standard type object. Return false in all other cases.

unsigned int **PyType_ClearCache**()
> Clear the internal lookup cache. Return the current version tag.

long **PyType_GetFlags**(*PyTypeObject** *type*)
> Return the *tp_flags* member of *type*. This function is primarily meant for use with *Py_LIMITED_API*; the individual flag bits are guaranteed to be stable across Python releases, but access to *tp_flags* itself is not part of the limited API.
>
> New in version 3.2.

void **PyType_Modified**(*PyTypeObject* *type*)
> Invalidate the internal lookup cache for the type and all of its subtypes. This function must be called after any manual modification of the attributes or base classes of the type.

int **PyType_HasFeature**(*PyTypeObject* *o*, int *feature*)
>   Return true if the type object *o* sets the feature *feature*. Type features are denoted by single bit flags.

int **PyType_IS_GC**(*PyTypeObject* *o*)
>   Return true if the type object includes support for the cycle detector; this tests the type flag
>   *Py_TPFLAGS_HAVE_GC*.

int **PyType_IsSubtype**(*PyTypeObject* *a*, *PyTypeObject* *b*)
>   Return true if *a* is a subtype of *b*.

>   This function only checks for actual subtypes, which means that **__subclasscheck__**() is not called
>   on *b*. Call *PyObject_IsSubclass()* to do the same check that **issubclass**() would do.

*PyObject** **PyType_GenericAlloc**(*PyTypeObject* *type*, Py_ssize_t *nitems*)
>   *Return value: New reference.* Generic handler for the *tp_alloc* slot of a type object. Use Python's
>   default memory allocation mechanism to allocate a new instance and initialize all its contents to *NULL*.

*PyObject** **PyType_GenericNew**(*PyTypeObject* *type*, *PyObject* *args*, *PyObject* *kwds*)
>   *Return value: New reference.* Generic handler for the *tp_new* slot of a type object. Create a new
>   instance using the type's *tp_alloc* slot.

int **PyType_Ready**(*PyTypeObject* *type*)
>   Finalize a type object. This should be called on all type objects to finish their initialization. This
>   function is responsible for adding inherited slots from a type's base class. Return 0 on success, or
>   return -1 and sets an exception on error.

*PyObject** **PyType_FromSpec**(PyType_Spec *spec*)
>   Creates and returns a heap type object from the *spec* passed to the function.

*PyObject** **PyType_FromSpecWithBases**(PyType_Spec *spec*, *PyObject* *bases*)
>   Creates and returns a heap type object from the *spec*. In addition to that, the created heap type
>   contains all types contained by the *bases* tuple as base types. This allows the caller to reference other
>   heap types as base types.

>   New in version 3.3.

void* **PyType_GetSlot**(*PyTypeObject* *type*, int *slot*)
>   Return the function pointer stored in the given slot. If the result is *NULL*, this indicates that either
>   the slot is *NULL*, or that the function was called with invalid parameters. Callers will typically cast
>   the result pointer into the appropriate function type.

>   New in version 3.4.

8.1.2 The None Object

Note that the *PyTypeObject* for None is not directly exposed in the Python/C API. Since None is a singleton,
testing for object identity (using == in C) is sufficient. There is no **PyNone_Check**() function for the same
reason.

*PyObject** **Py_None**
>   The Python None object, denoting lack of value. This object has no methods. It needs to be treated
>   just like any other object with respect to reference counts.

Py_RETURN_NONE
>   Properly handle returning *Py_None* from within a C function (that is, increment the reference count
>   of None and return it.)

8.2 Numeric Objects

8.2.1 Integer Objects

All integers are implemented as "long" integer objects of arbitrary size.

On error, most `PyLong_As*` APIs return `(return type)-1` which cannot be distinguished from a number. Use *PyErr_Occurred()* to disambiguate.

PyLongObject
> This subtype of *PyObject* represents a Python integer object.

PyTypeObject **PyLong_Type**
> This instance of *PyTypeObject* represents the Python integer type. This is the same object as `int` in the Python layer.

int **PyLong_Check**(*PyObject* **p*)
> Return true if its argument is a *PyLongObject* or a subtype of *PyLongObject*.

int **PyLong_CheckExact**(*PyObject* **p*)
> Return true if its argument is a *PyLongObject*, but not a subtype of *PyLongObject*.

PyObject* **PyLong_FromLong**(long *v*)
> *Return value: New reference.* Return a new *PyLongObject* object from *v*, or *NULL* on failure.
>
> The current implementation keeps an array of integer objects for all integers between −5 and 256, when you create an int in that range you actually just get back a reference to the existing object. So it should be possible to change the value of 1. I suspect the behaviour of Python in this case is undefined. :-)

PyObject* **PyLong_FromUnsignedLong**(unsigned long *v*)
> *Return value: New reference.* Return a new *PyLongObject* object from a C `unsigned long`, or *NULL* on failure.

PyObject* **PyLong_FromSsize_t**(Py_ssize_t *v*)
> Return a new *PyLongObject* object from a C `Py_ssize_t`, or *NULL* on failure.

PyObject* **PyLong_FromSize_t**(size_t *v*)
> Return a new *PyLongObject* object from a C `size_t`, or *NULL* on failure.

PyObject* **PyLong_FromLongLong**(long long *v*)
> *Return value: New reference.* Return a new *PyLongObject* object from a C `long long`, or *NULL* on failure.

PyObject* **PyLong_FromUnsignedLongLong**(unsigned long long *v*)
> *Return value: New reference.* Return a new *PyLongObject* object from a C `unsigned long long`, or *NULL* on failure.

PyObject* **PyLong_FromDouble**(double *v*)
> *Return value: New reference.* Return a new *PyLongObject* object from the integer part of *v*, or *NULL* on failure.

PyObject* **PyLong_FromString**(const char **str*, char ***pend*, int *base*)
> *Return value: New reference.* Return a new *PyLongObject* based on the string value in *str*, which is interpreted according to the radix in *base*. If *pend* is non-*NULL*, **pend* will point to the first character in *str* which follows the representation of the number. If *base* is 0, *str* is interpreted using the integers definition; in this case, leading zeros in a non-zero decimal number raises a `ValueError`. If *base* is not 0, it must be between 2 and 36, inclusive. Leading spaces and single underscores after a base specifier and between digits are ignored. If there are no digits, `ValueError` will be raised.

PyObject* **PyLong_FromUnicode**(*Py_UNICODE* **u*, Py_ssize_t *length*, int *base*)
> *Return value: New reference.* Convert a sequence of Unicode digits to a Python integer value. The

Unicode string is first encoded to a byte string using `PyUnicode_EncodeDecimal()` and then converted using *PyLong_FromString()*.

Deprecated since version 3.3, will be removed in version 4.0: Part of the old-style *Py_UNICODE* API; please migrate to using *PyLong_FromUnicodeObject()*.

*PyObject** **PyLong_FromUnicodeObject**(*PyObject* *u*, int *base*)
Convert a sequence of Unicode digits in the string *u* to a Python integer value. The Unicode string is first encoded to a byte string using `PyUnicode_EncodeDecimal()` and then converted using *PyLong_FromString()*.

New in version 3.3.

*PyObject** **PyLong_FromVoidPtr**(void *p*)
Return value: New reference. Create a Python integer from the pointer *p*. The pointer value can be retrieved from the resulting value using *PyLong_AsVoidPtr()*.

long **PyLong_AsLong**(*PyObject* *obj*)
Return a C `long` representation of *obj*. If *obj* is not an instance of *PyLongObject*, first call its `__int__()` method (if present) to convert it to a *PyLongObject*.

Raise `OverflowError` if the value of *obj* is out of range for a `long`.

Returns -1 on error. Use *PyErr_Occurred()* to disambiguate.

long **PyLong_AsLongAndOverflow**(*PyObject* *obj*, int *overflow*)
Return a C `long` representation of *obj*. If *obj* is not an instance of *PyLongObject*, first call its `__int__()` method (if present) to convert it to a *PyLongObject*.

If the value of *obj* is greater than `LONG_MAX` or less than `LONG_MIN`, set *overflow* to 1 or -1, respectively, and return -1; otherwise, set *overflow* to 0. If any other exception occurs set *overflow* to 0 and return -1 as usual.

Returns -1 on error. Use *PyErr_Occurred()* to disambiguate.

long long **PyLong_AsLongLong**(*PyObject* *obj*)
Return a C `long long` representation of *obj*. If *obj* is not an instance of *PyLongObject*, first call its `__int__()` method (if present) to convert it to a *PyLongObject*.

Raise `OverflowError` if the value of *obj* is out of range for a `long`.

Returns -1 on error. Use *PyErr_Occurred()* to disambiguate.

long long **PyLong_AsLongLongAndOverflow**(*PyObject* *obj*, int *overflow*)
Return a C `long long` representation of *obj*. If *obj* is not an instance of *PyLongObject*, first call its `__int__()` method (if present) to convert it to a *PyLongObject*.

If the value of *obj* is greater than `PY_LLONG_MAX` or less than `PY_LLONG_MIN`, set *overflow* to 1 or -1, respectively, and return -1; otherwise, set *overflow* to 0. If any other exception occurs set *overflow* to 0 and return -1 as usual.

Returns -1 on error. Use *PyErr_Occurred()* to disambiguate.

New in version 3.2.

Py_ssize_t **PyLong_AsSsize_t**(*PyObject* *pylong*)
Return a C `Py_ssize_t` representation of *pylong*. *pylong* must be an instance of *PyLongObject*.

Raise `OverflowError` if the value of *pylong* is out of range for a `Py_ssize_t`.

Returns -1 on error. Use *PyErr_Occurred()* to disambiguate.

unsigned long **PyLong_AsUnsignedLong**(*PyObject* *pylong*)
Return a C `unsigned long` representation of *pylong*. *pylong* must be an instance of *PyLongObject*.

Raise `OverflowError` if the value of *pylong* is out of range for a `unsigned long`.

Returns (unsigned long)-1 on error. Use *PyErr_Occurred()* to disambiguate.

size_t **PyLong_AsSize_t**(*PyObject *pylong*)

Return a C size_t representation of *pylong*. *pylong* must be an instance of *PyLongObject*.

Raise OverflowError if the value of *pylong* is out of range for a size_t.

Returns (size_t)-1 on error. Use *PyErr_Occurred()* to disambiguate.

unsigned long long **PyLong_AsUnsignedLongLong**(*PyObject *pylong*)

Return a C unsigned long long representation of *pylong*. *pylong* must be an instance of *PyLongObject*.

Raise OverflowError if the value of *pylong* is out of range for an unsigned long long.

Returns (unsigned long long)-1 on error. Use *PyErr_Occurred()* to disambiguate.

Changed in version 3.1: A negative *pylong* now raises OverflowError, not TypeError.

unsigned long **PyLong_AsUnsignedLongMask**(*PyObject *obj*)

Return a C unsigned long representation of *obj*. If *obj* is not an instance of *PyLongObject*, first call its __int__() method (if present) to convert it to a *PyLongObject*.

If the value of *obj* is out of range for an unsigned long, return the reduction of that value modulo ULONG_MAX + 1.

Returns -1 on error. Use *PyErr_Occurred()* to disambiguate.

unsigned long long **PyLong_AsUnsignedLongLongMask**(*PyObject *obj*)

Return a C unsigned long long representation of *obj*. If *obj* is not an instance of *PyLongObject*, first call its __int__() method (if present) to convert it to a *PyLongObject*.

If the value of *obj* is out of range for an unsigned long long, return the reduction of that value modulo PY_ULLONG_MAX + 1.

Returns -1 on error. Use *PyErr_Occurred()* to disambiguate.

double **PyLong_AsDouble**(*PyObject *pylong*)

Return a C double representation of *pylong*. *pylong* must be an instance of *PyLongObject*.

Raise OverflowError if the value of *pylong* is out of range for a double.

Returns -1.0 on error. Use *PyErr_Occurred()* to disambiguate.

void* **PyLong_AsVoidPtr**(*PyObject *pylong*)

Convert a Python integer *pylong* to a C void pointer. If *pylong* cannot be converted, an OverflowError will be raised. This is only assured to produce a usable void pointer for values created with *PyLong_FromVoidPtr()*.

Returns NULL on error. Use *PyErr_Occurred()* to disambiguate.

8.2.2 Boolean Objects

Booleans in Python are implemented as a subclass of integers. There are only two booleans, Py_False and Py_True. As such, the normal creation and deletion functions don't apply to booleans. The following macros are available, however.

int **PyBool_Check**(*PyObject *o*)

Return true if *o* is of type PyBool_Type.

PyObject* **Py_False**

The Python False object. This object has no methods. It needs to be treated just like any other object with respect to reference counts.

PyObject **Py_True**
> The Python True object. This object has no methods. It needs to be treated just like any other object with respect to reference counts.

Py_RETURN_FALSE
> Return Py_False from a function, properly incrementing its reference count.

Py_RETURN_TRUE
> Return Py_True from a function, properly incrementing its reference count.

PyObject **PyBool_FromLong**(long *v*)
> *Return value: New reference.* Return a new reference to Py_True or Py_False depending on the truth value of *v*.

8.2.3 Floating Point Objects

PyFloatObject
> This subtype of *PyObject* represents a Python floating point object.

PyTypeObject **PyFloat_Type**
> This instance of *PyTypeObject* represents the Python floating point type. This is the same object as float in the Python layer.

int **PyFloat_Check**(*PyObject* **p*)
> Return true if its argument is a *PyFloatObject* or a subtype of *PyFloatObject*.

int **PyFloat_CheckExact**(*PyObject* **p*)
> Return true if its argument is a *PyFloatObject*, but not a subtype of *PyFloatObject*.

PyObject **PyFloat_FromString**(*PyObject* **str*)
> *Return value: New reference.* Create a *PyFloatObject* object based on the string value in *str*, or *NULL* on failure.

PyObject **PyFloat_FromDouble**(double *v*)
> *Return value: New reference.* Create a *PyFloatObject* object from *v*, or *NULL* on failure.

double **PyFloat_AsDouble**(*PyObject* **pyfloat*)
> Return a C double representation of the contents of *pyfloat*. If *pyfloat* is not a Python floating point object but has a __float__() method, this method will first be called to convert *pyfloat* into a float. This method returns -1.0 upon failure, so one should call *PyErr_Occurred()* to check for errors.

double **PyFloat_AS_DOUBLE**(*PyObject* **pyfloat*)
> Return a C double representation of the contents of *pyfloat*, but without error checking.

PyObject **PyFloat_GetInfo**(void)
> Return a structseq instance which contains information about the precision, minimum and maximum values of a float. It's a thin wrapper around the header file float.h.

double **PyFloat_GetMax**()
> Return the maximum representable finite float *DBL_MAX* as C double.

double **PyFloat_GetMin**()
> Return the minimum normalized positive float *DBL_MIN* as C double.

int **PyFloat_ClearFreeList**()
> Clear the float free list. Return the number of items that could not be freed.

8.2.4 Complex Number Objects

Python's complex number objects are implemented as two distinct types when viewed from the C API: one is the Python object exposed to Python programs, and the other is a C structure which represents the actual complex number value. The API provides functions for working with both.

Complex Numbers as C Structures

Note that the functions which accept these structures as parameters and return them as results do so *by value* rather than dereferencing them through pointers. This is consistent throughout the API.

Py_complex
> The C structure which corresponds to the value portion of a Python complex number object. Most of the functions for dealing with complex number objects use structures of this type as input or output values, as appropriate. It is defined as:

```
typedef struct {
   double real;
   double imag;
} Py_complex;
```

Py_complex **_Py_c_sum**(*Py_complex left*, *Py_complex right*)
> Return the sum of two complex numbers, using the C *Py_complex* representation.

Py_complex **_Py_c_diff**(*Py_complex left*, *Py_complex right*)
> Return the difference between two complex numbers, using the C *Py_complex* representation.

Py_complex **_Py_c_neg**(*Py_complex complex*)
> Return the negation of the complex number *complex*, using the C *Py_complex* representation.

Py_complex **_Py_c_prod**(*Py_complex left*, *Py_complex right*)
> Return the product of two complex numbers, using the C *Py_complex* representation.

Py_complex **_Py_c_quot**(*Py_complex dividend*, *Py_complex divisor*)
> Return the quotient of two complex numbers, using the C *Py_complex* representation.

> If *divisor* is null, this method returns zero and sets **errno** to EDOM.

Py_complex **_Py_c_pow**(*Py_complex num*, *Py_complex exp*)
> Return the exponentiation of *num* by *exp*, using the C *Py_complex* representation.

> If *num* is null and *exp* is not a positive real number, this method returns zero and sets **errno** to EDOM.

Complex Numbers as Python Objects

PyComplexObject
> This subtype of *PyObject* represents a Python complex number object.

PyTypeObject **PyComplex_Type**
> This instance of *PyTypeObject* represents the Python complex number type. It is the same object as **complex** in the Python layer.

int **PyComplex_Check**(*PyObject *p*)
> Return true if its argument is a *PyComplexObject* or a subtype of *PyComplexObject*.

int **PyComplex_CheckExact**(*PyObject *p*)
> Return true if its argument is a *PyComplexObject*, but not a subtype of *PyComplexObject*.

*PyObject** **PyComplex_FromCComplex**(*Py_complex v*)
> *Return value: New reference.* Create a new Python complex number object from a C *Py_complex* value.

*PyObject** **PyComplex_FromDoubles**(double *real*, double *imag*)
> *Return value: New reference.* Return a new *PyComplexObject* object from *real* and *imag*.

double **PyComplex_RealAsDouble**(*PyObject* *op)

> Return the real part of *op* as a C double.

double **PyComplex_ImagAsDouble**(*PyObject* *op)

> Return the imaginary part of *op* as a C double.

Py_complex **PyComplex_AsCComplex**(*PyObject* *op)

> Return the *Py_complex* value of the complex number *op*.

> If *op* is not a Python complex number object but has a __complex__() method, this method will first be called to convert *op* to a Python complex number object. Upon failure, this method returns -1.0 as a real value.

8.3 Sequence Objects

Generic operations on sequence objects were discussed in the previous chapter; this section deals with the specific kinds of sequence objects that are intrinsic to the Python language.

8.3.1 Bytes Objects

These functions raise **TypeError** when expecting a bytes parameter and are called with a non-bytes parameter.

PyBytesObject

> This subtype of *PyObject* represents a Python bytes object.

PyTypeObject **PyBytes_Type**

> This instance of *PyTypeObject* represents the Python bytes type; it is the same object as **bytes** in the Python layer.

int **PyBytes_Check**(*PyObject* *o)

> Return true if the object *o* is a bytes object or an instance of a subtype of the bytes type.

int **PyBytes_CheckExact**(*PyObject* *o)

> Return true if the object *o* is a bytes object, but not an instance of a subtype of the bytes type.

PyObject* **PyBytes_FromString**(const char *v)

> Return a new bytes object with a copy of the string *v* as value on success, and *NULL* on failure. The parameter *v* must not be *NULL*; it will not be checked.

PyObject* **PyBytes_FromStringAndSize**(const char *v, Py_ssize_t *len*)

> Return a new bytes object with a copy of the string *v* as value and length *len* on success, and *NULL* on failure. If *v* is *NULL*, the contents of the bytes object are uninitialized.

PyObject* **PyBytes_FromFormat**(const char *format, ...)

> Take a C **printf**()-style *format* string and a variable number of arguments, calculate the size of the resulting Python bytes object and return a bytes object with the values formatted into it. The variable arguments must be C types and must correspond exactly to the format characters in the *format* string. The following format characters are allowed:

Format Characters	Type	Comment
%%	*n/a*	The literal % character.
%c	int	A single byte, represented as a C int.
%d	int	Exactly equivalent to `printf("%d")`.
%u	unsigned int	Exactly equivalent to `printf("%u")`.
%ld	long	Exactly equivalent to `printf("%ld")`.
%lu	unsigned long	Exactly equivalent to `printf("%lu")`.
%zd	Py_ssize_t	Exactly equivalent to `printf("%zd")`.
%zu	size_t	Exactly equivalent to `printf("%zu")`.
%i	int	Exactly equivalent to `printf("%i")`.
%x	int	Exactly equivalent to `printf("%x")`.
%s	char*	A null-terminated C character array.
%p	void*	The hex representation of a C pointer. Mostly equivalent to `printf("%p")` except that it is guaranteed to start with the literal 0x regardless of what the platform's `printf` yields.

An unrecognized format character causes all the rest of the format string to be copied as-is to the result object, and any extra arguments discarded.

PyObject* **PyBytes_FromFormatV**(const char **format*, va_list *vargs*)
> Identical to *PyBytes_FromFormat()* except that it takes exactly two arguments.

PyObject* **PyBytes_FromObject**(*PyObject *o*)
> Return the bytes representation of object *o* that implements the buffer protocol.

Py_ssize_t **PyBytes_Size**(*PyObject *o*)
> Return the length of the bytes in bytes object *o*.

Py_ssize_t **PyBytes_GET_SIZE**(*PyObject *o*)
> Macro form of *PyBytes_Size()* but without error checking.

char* **PyBytes_AsString**(*PyObject *o*)
> Return a pointer to the contents of *o*. The pointer refers to the internal buffer of *o*, which consists of `len(o) + 1` bytes. The last byte in the buffer is always null, regardless of whether there are any other null bytes. The data must not be modified in any way, unless the object was just created using `PyBytes_FromStringAndSize(NULL, size)`. It must not be deallocated. If *o* is not a bytes object at all, *PyBytes_AsString()* returns *NULL* and raises **TypeError**.

char* **PyBytes_AS_STRING**(*PyObject *string*)
> Macro form of *PyBytes_AsString()* but without error checking.

int **PyBytes_AsStringAndSize**(*PyObject *obj*, char ***buffer*, Py_ssize_t **length*)
> Return the null-terminated contents of the object *obj* through the output variables *buffer* and *length*.

> If *length* is *NULL*, the bytes object may not contain embedded null bytes; if it does, the function returns -1 and a **ValueError** is raised.

> The buffer refers to an internal buffer of *obj*, which includes an additional null byte at the end (not counted in *length*). The data must not be modified in any way, unless the object was just created using `PyBytes_FromStringAndSize(NULL, size)`. It must not be deallocated. If *obj* is not a bytes object at all, *PyBytes_AsStringAndSize()* returns -1 and raises **TypeError**.

> Changed in version 3.5: Previously, **TypeError** was raised when embedded null bytes were encountered in the bytes object.

void **PyBytes_Concat**(*PyObject **bytes*, *PyObject *newpart*)
> Create a new bytes object in **bytes* containing the contents of *newpart* appended to *bytes*; the caller will own the new reference. The reference to the old value of *bytes* will be stolen. If the new object

cannot be created, the old reference to *bytes* will still be discarded and the value of *bytes will be set to *NULL*; the appropriate exception will be set.

void **PyBytes_ConcatAndDel**(*PyObject* **bytes, *PyObject* *newpart)

Create a new bytes object in *bytes containing the contents of *newpart* appended to *bytes*. This version decrements the reference count of *newpart*.

int **_PyBytes_Resize**(*PyObject* **bytes, Py_ssize_t *newsize*)

A way to resize a bytes object even though it is "immutable". Only use this to build up a brand new bytes object; don't use this if the bytes may already be known in other parts of the code. It is an error to call this function if the refcount on the input bytes object is not one. Pass the address of an existing bytes object as an lvalue (it may be written into), and the new size desired. On success, *bytes holds the resized bytes object and 0 is returned; the address in *bytes may differ from its input value. If the reallocation fails, the original bytes object at *bytes is deallocated, *bytes is set to *NULL*, MemoryError is set, and -1 is returned.

8.3.2 Byte Array Objects

PyByteArrayObject

This subtype of *PyObject* represents a Python bytearray object.

PyTypeObject **PyByteArray_Type**

This instance of *PyTypeObject* represents the Python bytearray type; it is the same object as bytearray in the Python layer.

Type check macros

int **PyByteArray_Check**(*PyObject* *o)

Return true if the object *o* is a bytearray object or an instance of a subtype of the bytearray type.

int **PyByteArray_CheckExact**(*PyObject* *o)

Return true if the object *o* is a bytearray object, but not an instance of a subtype of the bytearray type.

Direct API functions

PyObject* **PyByteArray_FromObject**(*PyObject* *o)

Return a new bytearray object from any object, *o*, that implements the *buffer protocol*.

PyObject* **PyByteArray_FromStringAndSize**(const char *string, Py_ssize_t *len*)

Create a new bytearray object from *string* and its length, *len*. On failure, *NULL* is returned.

PyObject* **PyByteArray_Concat**(*PyObject* *a, *PyObject* *b)

Concat bytearrays *a* and *b* and return a new bytearray with the result.

Py_ssize_t **PyByteArray_Size**(*PyObject* *bytearray)

Return the size of *bytearray* after checking for a *NULL* pointer.

char* **PyByteArray_AsString**(*PyObject* *bytearray)

Return the contents of *bytearray* as a char array after checking for a *NULL* pointer. The returned array always has an extra null byte appended.

int **PyByteArray_Resize**(*PyObject* *bytearray, Py_ssize_t *len*)

Resize the internal buffer of *bytearray* to *len*.

Macros

These macros trade safety for speed and they don't check pointers.

char* **PyByteArray_AS_STRING**(*PyObject *bytearray*)
> Macro version of *PyByteArray_AsString()*.

Py_ssize_t **PyByteArray_GET_SIZE**(*PyObject *bytearray*)
> Macro version of *PyByteArray_Size()*.

8.3.3 Unicode Objects and Codecs

Unicode Objects

Since the implementation of PEP 393 in Python 3.3, Unicode objects internally use a variety of representations, in order to allow handling the complete range of Unicode characters while staying memory efficient. There are special cases for strings where all code points are below 128, 256, or 65536; otherwise, code points must be below 1114112 (which is the full Unicode range).

Py_UNICODE* and UTF-8 representations are created on demand and cached in the Unicode object. The *Py_UNICODE** representation is deprecated and inefficient; it should be avoided in performance- or memory-sensitive situations.

Due to the transition between the old APIs and the new APIs, unicode objects can internally be in two states depending on how they were created:

- "canonical" unicode objects are all objects created by a non-deprecated unicode API. They use the most efficient representation allowed by the implementation.

- "legacy" unicode objects have been created through one of the deprecated APIs (typically *PyUnicode_FromUnicode()*) and only bear the *Py_UNICODE** representation; you will have to call *PyUnicode_READY()* on them before calling any other API.

Unicode Type

These are the basic Unicode object types used for the Unicode implementation in Python:

Py_UCS4
Py_UCS2
Py_UCS1
> These types are typedefs for unsigned integer types wide enough to contain characters of 32 bits, 16 bits and 8 bits, respectively. When dealing with single Unicode characters, use *Py_UCS4*.
>
> New in version 3.3.

Py_UNICODE
> This is a typedef of **wchar_t**, which is a 16-bit type or 32-bit type depending on the platform.
>
> Changed in version 3.3: In previous versions, this was a 16-bit type or a 32-bit type depending on whether you selected a "narrow" or "wide" Unicode version of Python at build time.

PyASCIIObject
PyCompactUnicodeObject
PyUnicodeObject
> These subtypes of *PyObject* represent a Python Unicode object. In almost all cases, they shouldn't be used directly, since all API functions that deal with Unicode objects take and return *PyObject* pointers.
>
> New in version 3.3.

PyTypeObject **PyUnicode_Type**

> This instance of *PyTypeObject* represents the Python Unicode type. It is exposed to Python code as `str`.

The following APIs are really C macros and can be used to do fast checks and to access internal read-only data of Unicode objects:

int **PyUnicode_Check**(*PyObject* *o)

> Return true if the object *o* is a Unicode object or an instance of a Unicode subtype.

int **PyUnicode_CheckExact**(*PyObject* *o)

> Return true if the object *o* is a Unicode object, but not an instance of a subtype.

int **PyUnicode_READY**(*PyObject* *o)

> Ensure the string object *o* is in the "canonical" representation. This is required before using any of the access macros described below.

> Returns 0 on success and −1 with an exception set on failure, which in particular happens if memory allocation fails.

> New in version 3.3.

Py_ssize_t **PyUnicode_GET_LENGTH**(*PyObject* *o)

> Return the length of the Unicode string, in code points. *o* has to be a Unicode object in the "canonical" representation (not checked).

> New in version 3.3.

Py_UCS1* **PyUnicode_1BYTE_DATA**(*PyObject* *o)
Py_UCS2* **PyUnicode_2BYTE_DATA**(*PyObject* *o)
Py_UCS4* **PyUnicode_4BYTE_DATA**(*PyObject* *o)

> Return a pointer to the canonical representation cast to UCS1, UCS2 or UCS4 integer types for direct character access. No checks are performed if the canonical representation has the correct character size; use *PyUnicode_KIND()* to select the right macro. Make sure *PyUnicode_READY()* has been called before accessing this.

> New in version 3.3.

PyUnicode_WCHAR_KIND
PyUnicode_1BYTE_KIND
PyUnicode_2BYTE_KIND
PyUnicode_4BYTE_KIND

> Return values of the *PyUnicode_KIND()* macro.

> New in version 3.3.

int **PyUnicode_KIND**(*PyObject* *o)

> Return one of the PyUnicode kind constants (see above) that indicate how many bytes per character this Unicode object uses to store its data. *o* has to be a Unicode object in the "canonical" representation (not checked).

> New in version 3.3.

void* **PyUnicode_DATA**(*PyObject* *o)

> Return a void pointer to the raw unicode buffer. *o* has to be a Unicode object in the "canonical" representation (not checked).

> New in version 3.3.

void **PyUnicode_WRITE**(int *kind*, void *data, Py_ssize_t *index*, *Py_UCS4 value*)

> Write into a canonical representation *data* (as obtained with *PyUnicode_DATA()*). This macro does not do any sanity checks and is intended for usage in loops. The caller should cache the *kind* value and *data* pointer as obtained from other macro calls. *index* is the index in the string (starts at 0) and *value* is the new code point value which should be written to that location.

New in version 3.3.

Py_UCS4 **PyUnicode_READ**(int *kind*, void **data*, Py_ssize_t *index*)
Read a code point from a canonical representation *data* (as obtained with *PyUnicode_DATA()*). No checks or ready calls are performed.

New in version 3.3.

Py_UCS4 **PyUnicode_READ_CHAR**(*PyObject* **o*, Py_ssize_t *index*)
Read a character from a Unicode object *o*, which must be in the "canonical" representation. This is less efficient than *PyUnicode_READ()* if you do multiple consecutive reads.

New in version 3.3.

PyUnicode_MAX_CHAR_VALUE(*PyObject* **o*)
Return the maximum code point that is suitable for creating another string based on *o*, which must be in the "canonical" representation. This is always an approximation but more efficient than iterating over the string.

New in version 3.3.

int **PyUnicode_ClearFreeList**()
Clear the free list. Return the total number of freed items.

Py_ssize_t **PyUnicode_GET_SIZE**(*PyObject* **o*)
Return the size of the deprecated *Py_UNICODE* representation, in code units (this includes surrogate pairs as 2 units). *o* has to be a Unicode object (not checked).

Deprecated since version 3.3, will be removed in version 4.0: Part of the old-style Unicode API, please migrate to using *PyUnicode_GET_LENGTH()*.

Py_ssize_t **PyUnicode_GET_DATA_SIZE**(*PyObject* **o*)
Return the size of the deprecated *Py_UNICODE* representation in bytes. *o* has to be a Unicode object (not checked).

Deprecated since version 3.3, will be removed in version 4.0: Part of the old-style Unicode API, please migrate to using *PyUnicode_GET_LENGTH()*.

Py_UNICODE* **PyUnicode_AS_UNICODE**(*PyObject* **o*)
const char* **PyUnicode_AS_DATA**(*PyObject* **o*)
Return a pointer to a *Py_UNICODE* representation of the object. The returned buffer is always terminated with an extra null code point. It may also contain embedded null code points, which would cause the string to be truncated when used in most C functions. The AS_DATA form casts the pointer to const char *. The *o* argument has to be a Unicode object (not checked).

Changed in version 3.3: This macro is now inefficient – because in many cases the *Py_UNICODE* representation does not exist and needs to be created – and can fail (return *NULL* with an exception set). Try to port the code to use the new **PyUnicode_nBYTE_DATA()** macros or use *PyUnicode_WRITE()* or *PyUnicode_READ()*.

Deprecated since version 3.3, will be removed in version 4.0: Part of the old-style Unicode API, please migrate to using the **PyUnicode_nBYTE_DATA()** family of macros.

Unicode Character Properties

Unicode provides many different character properties. The most often needed ones are available through these macros which are mapped to C functions depending on the Python configuration.

int **Py_UNICODE_ISSPACE**(*Py_UNICODE* *ch*)
Return 1 or 0 depending on whether *ch* is a whitespace character.

int **Py_UNICODE_ISLOWER**(*Py_UNICODE ch*)

> Return 1 or 0 depending on whether *ch* is a lowercase character.

int **Py_UNICODE_ISUPPER**(*Py_UNICODE ch*)

> Return 1 or 0 depending on whether *ch* is an uppercase character.

int **Py_UNICODE_ISTITLE**(*Py_UNICODE ch*)

> Return 1 or 0 depending on whether *ch* is a titlecase character.

int **Py_UNICODE_ISLINEBREAK**(*Py_UNICODE ch*)

> Return 1 or 0 depending on whether *ch* is a linebreak character.

int **Py_UNICODE_ISDECIMAL**(*Py_UNICODE ch*)

> Return 1 or 0 depending on whether *ch* is a decimal character.

int **Py_UNICODE_ISDIGIT**(*Py_UNICODE ch*)

> Return 1 or 0 depending on whether *ch* is a digit character.

int **Py_UNICODE_ISNUMERIC**(*Py_UNICODE ch*)

> Return 1 or 0 depending on whether *ch* is a numeric character.

int **Py_UNICODE_ISALPHA**(*Py_UNICODE ch*)

> Return 1 or 0 depending on whether *ch* is an alphabetic character.

int **Py_UNICODE_ISALNUM**(*Py_UNICODE ch*)

> Return 1 or 0 depending on whether *ch* is an alphanumeric character.

int **Py_UNICODE_ISPRINTABLE**(*Py_UNICODE ch*)

> Return 1 or 0 depending on whether *ch* is a printable character. Nonprintable characters are those characters defined in the Unicode character database as "Other" or "Separator", excepting the ASCII space (0x20) which is considered printable. (Note that printable characters in this context are those which should not be escaped when repr() is invoked on a string. It has no bearing on the handling of strings written to sys.stdout or sys.stderr.)

These APIs can be used for fast direct character conversions:

Py_UNICODE **Py_UNICODE_TOLOWER**(*Py_UNICODE ch*)

> Return the character *ch* converted to lower case.
>
> Deprecated since version 3.3: This function uses simple case mappings.

Py_UNICODE **Py_UNICODE_TOUPPER**(*Py_UNICODE ch*)

> Return the character *ch* converted to upper case.
>
> Deprecated since version 3.3: This function uses simple case mappings.

Py_UNICODE **Py_UNICODE_TOTITLE**(*Py_UNICODE ch*)

> Return the character *ch* converted to title case.
>
> Deprecated since version 3.3: This function uses simple case mappings.

int **Py_UNICODE_TODECIMAL**(*Py_UNICODE ch*)

> Return the character *ch* converted to a decimal positive integer. Return -1 if this is not possible. This macro does not raise exceptions.

int **Py_UNICODE_TODIGIT**(*Py_UNICODE ch*)

> Return the character *ch* converted to a single digit integer. Return -1 if this is not possible. This macro does not raise exceptions.

double **Py_UNICODE_TONUMERIC**(*Py_UNICODE ch*)

> Return the character *ch* converted to a double. Return -1.0 if this is not possible. This macro does not raise exceptions.

These APIs can be used to work with surrogates:

Py_UNICODE_IS_SURROGATE(ch)
> Check if *ch* is a surrogate (0xD800 <= ch <= 0xDFFF).

Py_UNICODE_IS_HIGH_SURROGATE(ch)
> Check if *ch* is a high surrogate (0xD800 <= ch <= 0xDBFF).

Py_UNICODE_IS_LOW_SURROGATE(ch)
> Check if *ch* is a low surrogate (0xDC00 <= ch <= 0xDFFF).

Py_UNICODE_JOIN_SURROGATES(high, low)
> Join two surrogate characters and return a single Py_UCS4 value. *high* and *low* are respectively the leading and trailing surrogates in a surrogate pair.

Creating and accessing Unicode strings

To create Unicode objects and access their basic sequence properties, use these APIs:

PyObject* **PyUnicode_New**(Py_ssize_t *size*, *Py_UCS4 maxchar*)
> Create a new Unicode object. *maxchar* should be the true maximum code point to be placed in the string. As an approximation, it can be rounded up to the nearest value in the sequence 127, 255, 65535, 1114111.
>
> This is the recommended way to allocate a new Unicode object. Objects created using this function are not resizable.
>
> New in version 3.3.

PyObject* **PyUnicode_FromKindAndData**(int *kind*, const void **buffer*, Py_ssize_t *size*)
> Create a new Unicode object with the given *kind* (possible values are *PyUnicode_1BYTE_KIND* etc., as returned by *PyUnicode_KIND()*). The *buffer* must point to an array of *size* units of 1, 2 or 4 bytes per character, as given by the kind.
>
> New in version 3.3.

PyObject* **PyUnicode_FromStringAndSize**(const char **u*, Py_ssize_t *size*)
> Create a Unicode object from the char buffer *u*. The bytes will be interpreted as being UTF-8 encoded. The buffer is copied into the new object. If the buffer is not *NULL*, the return value might be a shared object, i.e. modification of the data is not allowed.
>
> If *u* is *NULL*, this function behaves like *PyUnicode_FromUnicode()* with the buffer set to *NULL*. This usage is deprecated in favor of *PyUnicode_New()*.

PyObject ***PyUnicode_FromString**(const char **u*)
> Create a Unicode object from a UTF-8 encoded null-terminated char buffer *u*.

PyObject* **PyUnicode_FromFormat**(const char **format*, ...)
> Take a C **printf**()-style *format* string and a variable number of arguments, calculate the size of the resulting Python unicode string and return a string with the values formatted into it. The variable arguments must be C types and must correspond exactly to the format characters in the *format* ASCII-encoded string. The following format characters are allowed:

Format Characters	Type	Comment
%%	*n/a*	The literal % character.
%c	int	A single character, represented as a C int.
%d	int	Exactly equivalent to `printf("%d")`.
%u	unsigned int	Exactly equivalent to `printf("%u")`.
%ld	long	Exactly equivalent to `printf("%ld")`.
%li	long	Exactly equivalent to `printf("%li")`.
%lu	unsigned long	Exactly equivalent to `printf("%lu")`.
%lld	long long	Exactly equivalent to `printf("%lld")`.
%lli	long long	Exactly equivalent to `printf("%lli")`.
%llu	unsigned long long	Exactly equivalent to `printf("%llu")`.
%zd	Py_ssize_t	Exactly equivalent to `printf("%zd")`.
%zi	Py_ssize_t	Exactly equivalent to `printf("%zi")`.
%zu	size_t	Exactly equivalent to `printf("%zu")`.
%i	int	Exactly equivalent to `printf("%i")`.
%x	int	Exactly equivalent to `printf("%x")`.
%s	char*	A null-terminated C character array.
%p	void*	The hex representation of a C pointer. Mostly equivalent to `printf("%p")` except that it is guaranteed to start with the literal 0x regardless of what the platform's `printf` yields.
%A	PyObject*	The result of calling `ascii()`.
%U	PyObject*	A unicode object.
%V	PyObject*, char *	A unicode object (which may be *NULL*) and a null-terminated C character array as a second parameter (which will be used, if the first parameter is *NULL*).
%S	PyObject*	The result of calling *PyObject_Str()*.
%R	PyObject*	The result of calling *PyObject_Repr()*.

An unrecognized format character causes all the rest of the format string to be copied as-is to the result string, and any extra arguments discarded.

Note: The width formatter unit is number of characters rather than bytes. The precision formatter unit is number of bytes for "%s" and "%V" (if the PyObject* argument is NULL), and a number of characters for "%A", "%U", "%S", "%R" and "%V" (if the PyObject* argument is not NULL).

Changed in version 3.2: Support for "%lld" and "%llu" added.

Changed in version 3.3: Support for "%li", "%lli" and "%zi" added.

Changed in version 3.4: Support width and precision formatter for "%s", "%A", "%U", "%V", "%S", "%R" added.

*PyObject** **PyUnicode_FromFormatV**(const char *format*, va_list *vargs*)
Identical to *PyUnicode_FromFormat()* except that it takes exactly two arguments.

*PyObject** **PyUnicode_FromEncodedObject**(*PyObject* *obj*, const char *encoding*, const char *errors*)
Return value: New reference. Decode an encoded object *obj* to a Unicode object.

`bytes`, `bytearray` and other *bytes-like objects* are decoded according to the given *encoding* and using the error handling defined by *errors*. Both can be *NULL* to have the interface use the default values (see *Built-in Codecs* for details).

All other objects, including Unicode objects, cause a `TypeError` to be set.

The API returns *NULL* if there was an error. The caller is responsible for decref'ing the returned objects.

Py_ssize_t **PyUnicode_GetLength**(*PyObject* *unicode*)

Return the length of the Unicode object, in code points.

New in version 3.3.

Py_ssize_t **PyUnicode_CopyCharacters**(*PyObject* **to*, Py_ssize_t *to_start*, *PyObject* **from*, Py_ssize_t *from_start*, Py_ssize_t *how_many*)

Copy characters from one Unicode object into another. This function performs character conversion when necessary and falls back to `memcpy()` if possible. Returns `-1` and sets an exception on error, otherwise returns the number of copied characters.

New in version 3.3.

Py_ssize_t **PyUnicode_Fill**(*PyObject* **unicode*, Py_ssize_t *start*, Py_ssize_t *length*, *Py_UCS4* *fill_char*)

Fill a string with a character: write *fill_char* into `unicode[start:start+length]`.

Fail if *fill_char* is bigger than the string maximum character, or if the string has more than 1 reference.

Return the number of written character, or return `-1` and raise an exception on error.

New in version 3.3.

int **PyUnicode_WriteChar**(*PyObject* **unicode*, Py_ssize_t *index*, *Py_UCS4* *character*)

Write a character to a string. The string must have been created through *PyUnicode_New()*. Since Unicode strings are supposed to be immutable, the string must not be shared, or have been hashed yet.

This function checks that *unicode* is a Unicode object, that the index is not out of bounds, and that the object can be modified safely (i.e. that it its reference count is one).

New in version 3.3.

Py_UCS4 **PyUnicode_ReadChar**(*PyObject* **unicode*, Py_ssize_t *index*)

Read a character from a string. This function checks that *unicode* is a Unicode object and the index is not out of bounds, in contrast to the macro version *PyUnicode_READ_CHAR()*.

New in version 3.3.

PyObject* **PyUnicode_Substring**(*PyObject* **str*, Py_ssize_t *start*, Py_ssize_t *end*)

Return a substring of *str*, from character index *start* (included) to character index *end* (excluded). Negative indices are not supported.

New in version 3.3.

Py_UCS4* **PyUnicode_AsUCS4**(*PyObject* **u*, *Py_UCS4* **buffer*, Py_ssize_t *buflen*, int *copy_null*)

Copy the string *u* into a UCS4 buffer, including a null character, if *copy_null* is set. Returns *NULL* and sets an exception on error (in particular, a `SystemError` if *buflen* is smaller than the length of *u*). *buffer* is returned on success.

New in version 3.3.

Py_UCS4* **PyUnicode_AsUCS4Copy**(*PyObject* **u*)

Copy the string *u* into a new UCS4 buffer that is allocated using *PyMem_Malloc()*. If this fails, *NULL* is returned with a `MemoryError` set. The returned buffer always has an extra null code point appended.

New in version 3.3.

Deprecated Py_UNICODE APIs

Deprecated since version 3.3, will be removed in version 4.0.

These API functions are deprecated with the implementation of PEP 393. Extension modules can continue using them, as they will not be removed in Python 3.x, but need to be aware that their use can now cause performance and memory hits.

PyObject* **PyUnicode_FromUnicode**(const *Py_UNICODE* *u, Py_ssize_t *size*)

Return value: New reference. Create a Unicode object from the Py_UNICODE buffer *u* of the given size. *u* may be *NULL* which causes the contents to be undefined. It is the user's responsibility to fill in the needed data. The buffer is copied into the new object.

If the buffer is not *NULL*, the return value might be a shared object. Therefore, modification of the resulting Unicode object is only allowed when *u* is *NULL*.

If the buffer is *NULL*, *PyUnicode_READY()* must be called once the string content has been filled before using any of the access macros such as *PyUnicode_KIND()*.

Please migrate to using *PyUnicode_FromKindAndData()*, *PyUnicode_FromWideChar()* or *PyUnicode_New()*.

Py_UNICODE* **PyUnicode_AsUnicode**(*PyObject* *unicode)

Return a read-only pointer to the Unicode object's internal *Py_UNICODE* buffer, or *NULL* on error. This will create the *Py_UNICODE** representation of the object if it is not yet available. The buffer is always terminated with an extra null code point. Note that the resulting *Py_UNICODE* string may also contain embedded null code points, which would cause the string to be truncated when used in most C functions.

Please migrate to using *PyUnicode_AsUCS4()*, *PyUnicode_AsWideChar()*, *PyUnicode_ReadChar()* or similar new APIs.

PyObject* **PyUnicode_TransformDecimalToASCII**(*Py_UNICODE* *s, Py_ssize_t *size*)

Create a Unicode object by replacing all decimal digits in *Py_UNICODE* buffer of the given *size* by ASCII digits 0–9 according to their decimal value. Return *NULL* if an exception occurs.

Py_UNICODE* **PyUnicode_AsUnicodeAndSize**(*PyObject* *unicode, Py_ssize_t *size)

Like *PyUnicode_AsUnicode()*, but also saves the *Py_UNICODE()* array length (excluding the extra null terminator) in *size*. Note that the resulting *Py_UNICODE** string may contain embedded null code points, which would cause the string to be truncated when used in most C functions.

New in version 3.3.

Py_UNICODE* **PyUnicode_AsUnicodeCopy**(*PyObject* *unicode)

Create a copy of a Unicode string ending with a null code point. Return *NULL* and raise a `MemoryError` exception on memory allocation failure, otherwise return a new allocated buffer (use *PyMem_Free()* to free the buffer). Note that the resulting *Py_UNICODE** string may contain embedded null code points, which would cause the string to be truncated when used in most C functions.

New in version 3.2.

Please migrate to using *PyUnicode_AsUCS4Copy()* or similar new APIs.

Py_ssize_t **PyUnicode_GetSize**(*PyObject* *unicode)

Return the size of the deprecated *Py_UNICODE* representation, in code units (this includes surrogate pairs as 2 units).

Please migrate to using *PyUnicode_GetLength()*.

PyObject* **PyUnicode_FromObject**(*PyObject* *obj)

Return value: New reference. Copy an instance of a Unicode subtype to a new true Unicode object if necessary. If *obj* is already a true Unicode object (not a subtype), return the reference with incremented refcount.

Objects other than Unicode or its subtypes will cause a `TypeError`.

Locale Encoding

The current locale encoding can be used to decode text from the operating system.

*PyObject** **PyUnicode_DecodeLocaleAndSize**(const char *str*, Py_ssize_t *len*, const char *errors*)
> Decode a string from the current locale encoding. The supported error handlers are "strict" and "surrogateescape" (PEP 383). The decoder uses "strict" error handler if *errors* is NULL. *str* must end with a null character but cannot contain embedded null characters.
>
> Use *PyUnicode_DecodeFSDefaultAndSize()* to decode a string from Py_FileSystemDefaultEncoding (the locale encoding read at Python startup).
>
> **See also:**
>
> The *Py_DecodeLocale()* function.
>
> New in version 3.3.
>
> Changed in version 3.6.5: The function now also uses the current locale encoding for the surrogateescape error handler. Previously, *Py_DecodeLocale()* was used for the surrogateescape, and the current locale encoding was used for strict.

*PyObject** **PyUnicode_DecodeLocale**(const char *str*, const char *errors*)
> Similar to *PyUnicode_DecodeLocaleAndSize()*, but compute the string length using strlen().
>
> New in version 3.3.

*PyObject** **PyUnicode_EncodeLocale**(*PyObject* *unicode*, const char *errors*)
> Encode a Unicode object to the current locale encoding. The supported error handlers are "strict" and "surrogateescape" (PEP 383). The encoder uses "strict" error handler if *errors* is NULL. Return a bytes object. *unicode* cannot contain embedded null characters.
>
> Use *PyUnicode_EncodeFSDefault()* to encode a string to Py_FileSystemDefaultEncoding (the locale encoding read at Python startup).
>
> **See also:**
>
> The *Py_EncodeLocale()* function.
>
> New in version 3.3.
>
> Changed in version 3.6.5: The function now also uses the current locale encoding for the surrogateescape error handler. Previously, *Py_EncodeLocale()* was used for the surrogateescape, and the current locale encoding was used for strict.

File System Encoding

To encode and decode file names and other environment strings, Py_FileSystemDefaultEncoding should be used as the encoding, and Py_FileSystemDefaultEncodeErrors should be used as the error handler (PEP 383 and PEP 529). To encode file names to bytes during argument parsing, the "O&" converter should be used, passing *PyUnicode_FSConverter()* as the conversion function:

int **PyUnicode_FSConverter**(*PyObject** *obj*, void* *result*)
> ParseTuple converter: encode str objects – obtained directly or through the os.PathLike interface – to bytes using *PyUnicode_EncodeFSDefault()*; bytes objects are output as-is. *result* must be a *PyBytesObject** which must be released when it is no longer used.
>
> New in version 3.1.
>
> Changed in version 3.6: Accepts a *path-like object*.

To decode file names to str during argument parsing, the "O&" converter should be used, passing *PyUnicode_FSDecoder()* as the conversion function:

---

int **PyUnicode_FSDecoder**(*PyObject* obj*, void* *result*)
> ParseTuple converter: decode **bytes** objects – obtained either directly or indirectly through the **os.**
> **PathLike** interface – to **str** using *PyUnicode_DecodeFSDefaultAndSize()*; **str** objects are output
> as-is. *result* must be a *PyUnicodeObject** which must be released when it is no longer used.
>
> New in version 3.2.
>
> Changed in version 3.6: Accepts a *path-like object*.

PyObject* **PyUnicode_DecodeFSDefaultAndSize**(const char *s, Py_ssize_t *size*)
> Decode   a   string   using   **Py_FileSystemDefaultEncoding**   and   the
> **Py_FileSystemDefaultEncodeErrors** error handler.
>
> If **Py_FileSystemDefaultEncoding** is not set, fall back to the locale encoding.
>
> **Py_FileSystemDefaultEncoding** is initialized at startup from the locale encoding and cannot
> be modified later.   If you need to decode a string from the current locale encoding, use
> *PyUnicode_DecodeLocaleAndSize()*.
>
> **See also:**
>
> The *Py_DecodeLocale()* function.
>
> Changed in version 3.6: Use **Py_FileSystemDefaultEncodeErrors** error handler.

PyObject* **PyUnicode_DecodeFSDefault**(const char *s)
> Decode   a   null-terminated   string   using   **Py_FileSystemDefaultEncoding**   and   the
> **Py_FileSystemDefaultEncodeErrors** error handler.
>
> If **Py_FileSystemDefaultEncoding** is not set, fall back to the locale encoding.
>
> Use *PyUnicode_DecodeFSDefaultAndSize()* if you know the string length.
>
> Changed in version 3.6: Use **Py_FileSystemDefaultEncodeErrors** error handler.

PyObject* **PyUnicode_EncodeFSDefault**(*PyObject *unicode*)
> Encode   a   Unicode   object   to   **Py_FileSystemDefaultEncoding**   with   the
> **Py_FileSystemDefaultEncodeErrors** error handler, and return **bytes**.   Note that the resulting
> **bytes** object may contain null bytes.
>
> If **Py_FileSystemDefaultEncoding** is not set, fall back to the locale encoding.
>
> **Py_FileSystemDefaultEncoding** is initialized at startup from the locale encoding and can-
> not be modified later.   If you need to encode a string to the current locale encoding, use
> *PyUnicode_EncodeLocale()*.
>
> **See also:**
>
> The *Py_EncodeLocale()* function.
>
> New in version 3.2.
>
> Changed in version 3.6: Use **Py_FileSystemDefaultEncodeErrors** error handler.

wchar_t Support

wchar_t support for platforms which support it:

PyObject* **PyUnicode_FromWideChar**(const wchar_t *w, Py_ssize_t *size*)
> *Return value: New reference.* Create a Unicode object from the **wchar_t** buffer *w* of the given *size*.
> Passing **-1** as the *size* indicates that the function must itself compute the length, using wcslen. Return
> *NULL* on failure.

Py_ssize_t **PyUnicode_AsWideChar**(*PyUnicodeObject *unicode*, wchar_t *w*, Py_ssize_t *size*)
> Copy the Unicode object contents into the `wchar_t` buffer *w*. At most *size* `wchar_t` characters are copied (excluding a possibly trailing null termination character). Return the number of `wchar_t` characters copied or `-1` in case of an error. Note that the resulting `wchar_t*` string may or may not be null-terminated. It is the responsibility of the caller to make sure that the `wchar_t*` string is null-terminated in case this is required by the application. Also, note that the `wchar_t*` string might contain null characters, which would cause the string to be truncated when used with most C functions.

wchar_t* **PyUnicode_AsWideCharString**(*PyObject *unicode*, Py_ssize_t **size*)
> Convert the Unicode object to a wide character string. The output string always ends with a null character. If *size* is not *NULL*, write the number of wide characters (excluding the trailing null termination character) into **size*.
>
> Returns a buffer allocated by `PyMem_Alloc()` (use *PyMem_Free()* to free it) on success. On error, returns *NULL*, **size* is undefined and raises a `MemoryError`. Note that the resulting `wchar_t` string might contain null characters, which would cause the string to be truncated when used with most C functions.
>
> New in version 3.2.

Built-in Codecs

Python provides a set of built-in codecs which are written in C for speed. All of these codecs are directly usable via the following functions.

Many of the following APIs take two arguments encoding and errors, and they have the same semantics as the ones of the built-in `str()` string object constructor.

Setting encoding to *NULL* causes the default encoding to be used which is ASCII. The file system calls should use *PyUnicode_FSConverter()* for encoding file names. This uses the variable `Py_FileSystemDefaultEncoding` internally. This variable should be treated as read-only: on some systems, it will be a pointer to a static string, on others, it will change at run-time (such as when the application invokes setlocale).

Error handling is set by errors which may also be set to *NULL* meaning to use the default handling defined for the codec. Default error handling for all built-in codecs is "strict" (`ValueError` is raised).

The codecs all use a similar interface. Only deviation from the following generic ones are documented for simplicity.

Generic Codecs

These are the generic codec APIs:

*PyObject** **PyUnicode_Decode**(const char **s*, Py_ssize_t *size*, const char **encoding*, const char **errors*)
> *Return value: New reference.* Create a Unicode object by decoding *size* bytes of the encoded string *s*. *encoding* and *errors* have the same meaning as the parameters of the same name in the `str()` built-in function. The codec to be used is looked up using the Python codec registry. Return *NULL* if an exception was raised by the codec.

*PyObject** **PyUnicode_AsEncodedString**(*PyObject *unicode*, const char **encoding*, const char **errors*)
> *Return value: New reference.* Encode a Unicode object and return the result as Python bytes object. *encoding* and *errors* have the same meaning as the parameters of the same name in the Unicode `encode()` method. The codec to be used is looked up using the Python codec registry. Return *NULL* if an exception was raised by the codec.

PyObject* **PyUnicode_Encode**(const *Py_UNICODE* *s, Py_ssize_t *size*, const char *encoding, const char *errors)

> *Return value: New reference.* Encode the *Py_UNICODE* buffer *s* of the given *size* and return a Python bytes object. *encoding* and *errors* have the same meaning as the parameters of the same name in the Unicode **encode()** method. The codec to be used is looked up using the Python codec registry. Return *NULL* if an exception was raised by the codec.
>
> Deprecated since version 3.3, will be removed in version 4.0: Part of the old-style *Py_UNICODE* API; please migrate to using *PyUnicode_AsEncodedString()*.

UTF-8 Codecs

These are the UTF-8 codec APIs:

PyObject* **PyUnicode_DecodeUTF8**(const char *s, Py_ssize_t *size*, const char *errors)

> *Return value: New reference.* Create a Unicode object by decoding *size* bytes of the UTF-8 encoded string *s*. Return *NULL* if an exception was raised by the codec.

PyObject* **PyUnicode_DecodeUTF8Stateful**(const char *s, Py_ssize_t *size*, const char *errors, Py_ssize_t *consumed)

> *Return value: New reference.* If *consumed* is *NULL*, behave like *PyUnicode_DecodeUTF8()*. If *consumed* is not *NULL*, trailing incomplete UTF-8 byte sequences will not be treated as an error. Those bytes will not be decoded and the number of bytes that have been decoded will be stored in *consumed*.

PyObject* **PyUnicode_AsUTF8String**(*PyObject* *unicode)

> *Return value: New reference.* Encode a Unicode object using UTF-8 and return the result as Python bytes object. Error handling is "strict". Return *NULL* if an exception was raised by the codec.

char* **PyUnicode_AsUTF8AndSize**(*PyObject* *unicode, Py_ssize_t *size)

> Return a pointer to the UTF-8 encoding of the Unicode object, and store the size of the encoded representation (in bytes) in *size*. The *size* argument can be *NULL*; in this case no size will be stored. The returned buffer always has an extra null byte appended (not included in *size*), regardless of whether there are any other null code points.
>
> In the case of an error, *NULL* is returned with an exception set and no *size* is stored.
>
> This caches the UTF-8 representation of the string in the Unicode object, and subsequent calls will return a pointer to the same buffer. The caller is not responsible for deallocating the buffer.
>
> New in version 3.3.

char* **PyUnicode_AsUTF8**(*PyObject* *unicode)

> As *PyUnicode_AsUTF8AndSize()*, but does not store the size.
>
> New in version 3.3.

PyObject* **PyUnicode_EncodeUTF8**(const *Py_UNICODE* *s, Py_ssize_t *size*, const char *errors)

> *Return value: New reference.* Encode the *Py_UNICODE* buffer *s* of the given *size* using UTF-8 and return a Python bytes object. Return *NULL* if an exception was raised by the codec.
>
> Deprecated since version 3.3, will be removed in version 4.0: Part of the old-style *Py_UNICODE* API; please migrate to using *PyUnicode_AsUTF8String()*, *PyUnicode_AsUTF8AndSize()* or *PyUnicode_AsEncodedString()*.

UTF-32 Codecs

These are the UTF-32 codec APIs:

PyObject* **PyUnicode_DecodeUTF32**(const char *s, Py_ssize_t *size*, const char *errors, int *byteorder)

Decode *size* bytes from a UTF-32 encoded buffer string and return the corresponding Unicode object. *errors* (if non-*NULL*) defines the error handling. It defaults to "strict".

If *byteorder* is non-*NULL*, the decoder starts decoding using the given byte order:

```
*byteorder == -1: little endian
*byteorder == 0:  native order
*byteorder == 1:  big endian
```

If *byteorder is zero, and the first four bytes of the input data are a byte order mark (BOM), the decoder switches to this byte order and the BOM is not copied into the resulting Unicode string. If *byteorder is -1 or 1, any byte order mark is copied to the output.

After completion, **byteorder* is set to the current byte order at the end of input data.

If *byteorder* is *NULL*, the codec starts in native order mode.

Return *NULL* if an exception was raised by the codec.

PyObject* **PyUnicode_DecodeUTF32Stateful**(const char *s, Py_ssize_t *size*, const char *errors, int *byteorder, Py_ssize_t *consumed)

If *consumed* is *NULL*, behave like *PyUnicode_DecodeUTF32()*. If *consumed* is not *NULL*, *PyUnicode_DecodeUTF32Stateful()* will not treat trailing incomplete UTF-32 byte sequences (such as a number of bytes not divisible by four) as an error. Those bytes will not be decoded and the number of bytes that have been decoded will be stored in *consumed*.

PyObject* **PyUnicode_AsUTF32String**(*PyObject* *unicode)

Return a Python byte string using the UTF-32 encoding in native byte order. The string always starts with a BOM mark. Error handling is "strict". Return *NULL* if an exception was raised by the codec.

PyObject* **PyUnicode_EncodeUTF32**(const *Py_UNICODE* *s, Py_ssize_t *size*, const char *errors, int *byteorder*)

Return a Python bytes object holding the UTF-32 encoded value of the Unicode data in *s*. Output is written according to the following byte order:

```
byteorder == -1: little endian
byteorder == 0:  native byte order (writes a BOM mark)
byteorder == 1:  big endian
```

If byteorder is 0, the output string will always start with the Unicode BOM mark (U+FEFF). In the other two modes, no BOM mark is prepended.

If *Py_UNICODE_WIDE* is not defined, surrogate pairs will be output as a single code point.

Return *NULL* if an exception was raised by the codec.

Deprecated since version 3.3, will be removed in version 4.0: Part of the old-style *Py_UNICODE* API; please migrate to using *PyUnicode_AsUTF32String()* or *PyUnicode_AsEncodedString()*.

UTF-16 Codecs

These are the UTF-16 codec APIs:

PyObject* **PyUnicode_DecodeUTF16**(const char *s, Py_ssize_t *size*, const char *errors, int *byteorder)

Return value: New reference. Decode *size* bytes from a UTF-16 encoded buffer string and return the corresponding Unicode object. *errors* (if non-*NULL*) defines the error handling. It defaults to "strict".

If *byteorder* is non-*NULL*, the decoder starts decoding using the given byte order:

```
*byteorder == -1: little endian
*byteorder == 0:  native order
*byteorder == 1:  big endian
```

If *byteorder is zero, and the first two bytes of the input data are a byte order mark (BOM), the decoder switches to this byte order and the BOM is not copied into the resulting Unicode string. If *byteorder is -1 or 1, any byte order mark is copied to the output (where it will result in either a \ufeff or a \ufffe character).

After completion, *byteorder* is set to the current byte order at the end of input data.

If *byteorder* is *NULL*, the codec starts in native order mode.

Return *NULL* if an exception was raised by the codec.

*PyObject** **PyUnicode_DecodeUTF16Stateful**(const char *s, Py_ssize_t *size*, const char *errors, int *byteorder, Py_ssize_t *consumed)
   Return value: New reference. If *consumed* is *NULL*, behave like *PyUnicode_DecodeUTF16()*. If *consumed* is not *NULL*, *PyUnicode_DecodeUTF16Stateful()* will not treat trailing incomplete UTF-16 byte sequences (such as an odd number of bytes or a split surrogate pair) as an error. Those bytes will not be decoded and the number of bytes that have been decoded will be stored in *consumed*.

*PyObject** **PyUnicode_AsUTF16String**(*PyObject* *unicode*)
   Return value: New reference. Return a Python byte string using the UTF-16 encoding in native byte order. The string always starts with a BOM mark. Error handling is "strict". Return *NULL* if an exception was raised by the codec.

*PyObject** **PyUnicode_EncodeUTF16**(const *Py_UNICODE* *s, Py_ssize_t *size*, const char *errors, int *byteorder*)
   Return value: New reference. Return a Python bytes object holding the UTF-16 encoded value of the Unicode data in *s*. Output is written according to the following byte order:

```
byteorder == -1: little endian
byteorder == 0:  native byte order (writes a BOM mark)
byteorder == 1:  big endian
```

If byteorder is 0, the output string will always start with the Unicode BOM mark (U+FEFF). In the other two modes, no BOM mark is prepended.

If *Py_UNICODE_WIDE* is defined, a single *Py_UNICODE* value may get represented as a surrogate pair. If it is not defined, each *Py_UNICODE* values is interpreted as a UCS-2 character.

Return *NULL* if an exception was raised by the codec.

Deprecated since version 3.3, will be removed in version 4.0: Part of the old-style *Py_UNICODE* API; please migrate to using *PyUnicode_AsUTF16String()* or *PyUnicode_AsEncodedString()*.

UTF-7 Codecs

These are the UTF-7 codec APIs:

*PyObject** **PyUnicode_DecodeUTF7**(const char *s, Py_ssize_t *size*, const char *errors)
   Create a Unicode object by decoding *size* bytes of the UTF-7 encoded string *s*. Return *NULL* if an exception was raised by the codec.

*PyObject** **PyUnicode_DecodeUTF7Stateful**(const char *s, Py_ssize_t *size*, const char *errors, Py_ssize_t *consumed)
   If *consumed* is *NULL*, behave like *PyUnicode_DecodeUTF7()*. If *consumed* is not *NULL*, trailing incomplete UTF-7 base-64 sections will not be treated as an error. Those bytes will not be decoded and the number of bytes that have been decoded will be stored in *consumed*.

PyObject* **PyUnicode_EncodeUTF7**(const *Py_UNICODE* *s, Py_ssize_t *size*, int *base64SetO*, int *base64WhiteSpace*, const char *errors)

Encode the *Py_UNICODE* buffer of the given size using UTF-7 and return a Python bytes object. Return *NULL* if an exception was raised by the codec.

If *base64SetO* is nonzero, "Set O" (punctuation that has no otherwise special meaning) will be encoded in base-64. If *base64WhiteSpace* is nonzero, whitespace will be encoded in base-64. Both are set to zero for the Python "utf-7" codec.

Deprecated since version 3.3, will be removed in version 4.0: Part of the old-style *Py_UNICODE* API; please migrate to using *PyUnicode_AsEncodedString()*.

Unicode-Escape Codecs

These are the "Unicode Escape" codec APIs:

PyObject* **PyUnicode_DecodeUnicodeEscape**(const char *s, Py_ssize_t *size*, const char *errors)

Return value: New reference. Create a Unicode object by decoding *size* bytes of the Unicode-Escape encoded string *s*. Return *NULL* if an exception was raised by the codec.

PyObject* **PyUnicode_AsUnicodeEscapeString**(*PyObject* *unicode)

Return value: New reference. Encode a Unicode object using Unicode-Escape and return the result as a bytes object. Error handling is "strict". Return *NULL* if an exception was raised by the codec.

PyObject* **PyUnicode_EncodeUnicodeEscape**(const *Py_UNICODE* *s, Py_ssize_t *size*)

Return value: New reference. Encode the *Py_UNICODE* buffer of the given *size* using Unicode-Escape and return a bytes object. Return *NULL* if an exception was raised by the codec.

Deprecated since version 3.3, will be removed in version 4.0: Part of the old-style *Py_UNICODE* API; please migrate to using *PyUnicode_AsUnicodeEscapeString()*.

Raw-Unicode-Escape Codecs

These are the "Raw Unicode Escape" codec APIs:

PyObject* **PyUnicode_DecodeRawUnicodeEscape**(const char *s, Py_ssize_t *size*, const char *errors)

Return value: New reference. Create a Unicode object by decoding *size* bytes of the Raw-Unicode-Escape encoded string *s*. Return *NULL* if an exception was raised by the codec.

PyObject* **PyUnicode_AsRawUnicodeEscapeString**(*PyObject* *unicode)

Return value: New reference. Encode a Unicode object using Raw-Unicode-Escape and return the result as a bytes object. Error handling is "strict". Return *NULL* if an exception was raised by the codec.

PyObject* **PyUnicode_EncodeRawUnicodeEscape**(const *Py_UNICODE* *s, Py_ssize_t *size*, const char *errors)

Return value: New reference. Encode the *Py_UNICODE* buffer of the given *size* using Raw-Unicode-Escape and return a bytes object. Return *NULL* if an exception was raised by the codec.

Deprecated since version 3.3, will be removed in version 4.0: Part of the old-style *Py_UNICODE* API; please migrate to using *PyUnicode_AsRawUnicodeEscapeString()* or *PyUnicode_AsEncodedString()*.

Latin-1 Codecs

These are the Latin-1 codec APIs: Latin-1 corresponds to the first 256 Unicode ordinals and only these are accepted by the codecs during encoding.

PyObject* **PyUnicode_DecodeLatin1**(const char **s*, Py_ssize_t *size*, const char **errors*)
> *Return value: New reference.* Create a Unicode object by decoding *size* bytes of the Latin-1 encoded string *s*. Return *NULL* if an exception was raised by the codec.

PyObject* **PyUnicode_AsLatin1String**(*PyObject *unicode*)
> *Return value: New reference.* Encode a Unicode object using Latin-1 and return the result as Python bytes object. Error handling is "strict". Return *NULL* if an exception was raised by the codec.

PyObject* **PyUnicode_EncodeLatin1**(const *Py_UNICODE *s*, Py_ssize_t *size*, const char **errors*)
> *Return value: New reference.* Encode the *Py_UNICODE* buffer of the given *size* using Latin-1 and return a Python bytes object. Return *NULL* if an exception was raised by the codec.
>
> Deprecated since version 3.3, will be removed in version 4.0: Part of the old-style *Py_UNICODE* API; please migrate to using *PyUnicode_AsLatin1String()* or *PyUnicode_AsEncodedString()*.

ASCII Codecs

These are the ASCII codec APIs. Only 7-bit ASCII data is accepted. All other codes generate errors.

PyObject* **PyUnicode_DecodeASCII**(const char **s*, Py_ssize_t *size*, const char **errors*)
> *Return value: New reference.* Create a Unicode object by decoding *size* bytes of the ASCII encoded string *s*. Return *NULL* if an exception was raised by the codec.

PyObject* **PyUnicode_AsASCIIString**(*PyObject *unicode*)
> *Return value: New reference.* Encode a Unicode object using ASCII and return the result as Python bytes object. Error handling is "strict". Return *NULL* if an exception was raised by the codec.

PyObject* **PyUnicode_EncodeASCII**(const *Py_UNICODE *s*, Py_ssize_t *size*, const char **errors*)
> *Return value: New reference.* Encode the *Py_UNICODE* buffer of the given *size* using ASCII and return a Python bytes object. Return *NULL* if an exception was raised by the codec.
>
> Deprecated since version 3.3, will be removed in version 4.0: Part of the old-style *Py_UNICODE* API; please migrate to using *PyUnicode_AsASCIIString()* or *PyUnicode_AsEncodedString()*.

Character Map Codecs

This codec is special in that it can be used to implement many different codecs (and this is in fact what was done to obtain most of the standard codecs included in the **encodings** package). The codec uses mapping to encode and decode characters. The mapping objects provided must support the **__getitem__**() mapping interface; dictionaries and sequences work well.

These are the mapping codec APIs:

PyObject* **PyUnicode_DecodeCharmap**(const char **data*, Py_ssize_t *size*, *PyObject *mapping*, const char **errors*)
> *Return value: New reference.* Create a Unicode object by decoding *size* bytes of the encoded string *s* using the given *mapping* object. Return *NULL* if an exception was raised by the codec.
>
> If *mapping* is *NULL*, Latin-1 decoding will be applied. Else *mapping* must map bytes ordinals (integers in the range from 0 to 255) to Unicode strings, integers (which are then interpreted as Unicode ordinals) or None. Unmapped data bytes – ones which cause a **LookupError**, as well as ones which get mapped to None, 0xFFFE or '\ufffe', are treated as undefined mappings and cause an error.

PyObject* **PyUnicode_AsCharmapString**(*PyObject *unicode*, *PyObject *mapping*)
> *Return value: New reference.* Encode a Unicode object using the given *mapping* object and return the result as a bytes object. Error handling is "strict". Return *NULL* if an exception was raised by the codec.

The *mapping* object must map Unicode ordinal integers to bytes objects, integers in the range from 0 to 255 or `None`. Unmapped character ordinals (ones which cause a `LookupError`) as well as mapped to `None` are treated as "undefined mapping" and cause an error.

PyObject* **PyUnicode_EncodeCharmap**(const *Py_UNICODE *s*, Py_ssize_t *size*, *PyObject *mapping*, const char **errors*)

    Return value: New reference. Encode the *Py_UNICODE* buffer of the given *size* using the given *mapping* object and return the result as a bytes object. Return *NULL* if an exception was raised by the codec.

    Deprecated since version 3.3, will be removed in version 4.0: Part of the old-style *Py_UNICODE* API; please migrate to using *PyUnicode_AsCharmapString()* or *PyUnicode_AsEncodedString()*.

The following codec API is special in that maps Unicode to Unicode.

PyObject* **PyUnicode_Translate**(*PyObject *unicode*, *PyObject *mapping*, const char **errors*)

    Return value: New reference. Translate a Unicode object using the given *mapping* object and return the resulting Unicode object. Return *NULL* if an exception was raised by the codec.

    The *mapping* object must map Unicode ordinal integers to Unicode strings, integers (which are then interpreted as Unicode ordinals) or `None` (causing deletion of the character). Unmapped character ordinals (ones which cause a `LookupError`) are left untouched and are copied as-is.

PyObject* **PyUnicode_TranslateCharmap**(const *Py_UNICODE *s*, Py_ssize_t *size*, *PyObject *mapping*, const char **errors*)

    Return value: New reference. Translate a *Py_UNICODE* buffer of the given *size* by applying a character *mapping* table to it and return the resulting Unicode object. Return *NULL* when an exception was raised by the codec.

    Deprecated since version 3.3, will be removed in version 4.0: Part of the old-style *Py_UNICODE* API; please migrate to using *PyUnicode_Translate()*. or *generic codec based API*

MBCS codecs for Windows

These are the MBCS codec APIs. They are currently only available on Windows and use the Win32 MBCS converters to implement the conversions. Note that MBCS (or DBCS) is a class of encodings, not just one. The target encoding is defined by the user settings on the machine running the codec.

PyObject* **PyUnicode_DecodeMBCS**(const char **s*, Py_ssize_t *size*, const char **errors*)

    Return value: New reference. Create a Unicode object by decoding *size* bytes of the MBCS encoded string *s*. Return *NULL* if an exception was raised by the codec.

PyObject* **PyUnicode_DecodeMBCSStateful**(const char **s*, int *size*, const char **errors*, int **consumed*)

    If *consumed* is *NULL*, behave like *PyUnicode_DecodeMBCS()*. If *consumed* is not *NULL*, *PyUnicode_DecodeMBCSStateful()* will not decode trailing lead byte and the number of bytes that have been decoded will be stored in *consumed*.

PyObject* **PyUnicode_AsMBCSString**(*PyObject *unicode*)

    Return value: New reference. Encode a Unicode object using MBCS and return the result as Python bytes object. Error handling is "strict". Return *NULL* if an exception was raised by the codec.

PyObject* **PyUnicode_EncodeCodePage**(int *code_page*, *PyObject *unicode*, const char **errors*)

    Encode the Unicode object using the specified code page and return a Python bytes object. Return *NULL* if an exception was raised by the codec. Use `CP_ACP` code page to get the MBCS encoder.

    New in version 3.3.

PyObject* **PyUnicode_EncodeMBCS**(const *Py_UNICODE *s*, Py_ssize_t *size*, const char **errors*)

    Return value: New reference. Encode the *Py_UNICODE* buffer of the given *size* using MBCS and return a Python bytes object. Return *NULL* if an exception was raised by the codec.

Deprecated since version 3.3, will be removed in version 4.0: Part of the old-style *Py_UNICODE* API; please migrate to using *PyUnicode_AsMBCSString()*, *PyUnicode_EncodeCodePage()* or *PyUnicode_AsEncodedString()*.

Methods & Slots

Methods and Slot Functions

The following APIs are capable of handling Unicode objects and strings on input (we refer to them as strings in the descriptions) and return Unicode objects or integers as appropriate.

They all return *NULL* or `-1` if an exception occurs.

PyObject* **PyUnicode_Concat**(*PyObject* *left, *PyObject* *right)
  Return value: New reference. Concat two strings giving a new Unicode string.

PyObject* **PyUnicode_Split**(*PyObject* *s, *PyObject* *sep, Py_ssize_t *maxsplit*)
  Return value: New reference. Split a string giving a list of Unicode strings. If *sep* is *NULL*, splitting will be done at all whitespace substrings. Otherwise, splits occur at the given separator. At most *maxsplit* splits will be done. If negative, no limit is set. Separators are not included in the resulting list.

PyObject* **PyUnicode_Splitlines**(*PyObject* *s, int *keepend*)
  Return value: New reference. Split a Unicode string at line breaks, returning a list of Unicode strings. CRLF is considered to be one line break. If *keepend* is 0, the Line break characters are not included in the resulting strings.

PyObject* **PyUnicode_Translate**(*PyObject* *str, *PyObject* *table, const char *errors)
  Translate a string by applying a character mapping table to it and return the resulting Unicode object.

  The mapping table must map Unicode ordinal integers to Unicode ordinal integers or **None** (causing deletion of the character).

  Mapping tables need only provide the **__getitem__**() interface; dictionaries and sequences work well. Unmapped character ordinals (ones which cause a **LookupError**) are left untouched and are copied as-is.

  errors has the usual meaning for codecs. It may be *NULL* which indicates to use the default error handling.

PyObject* **PyUnicode_Join**(*PyObject* *separator, *PyObject* *seq)
  Return value: New reference. Join a sequence of strings using the given *separator* and return the resulting Unicode string.

Py_ssize_t **PyUnicode_Tailmatch**(*PyObject* *str, *PyObject* *substr, Py_ssize_t *start*, Py_ssize_t *end*, int *direction*)
  Return 1 if *substr* matches `str[start:end]` at the given tail end (*direction* == `-1` means to do a prefix match, *direction* == 1 a suffix match), 0 otherwise. Return `-1` if an error occurred.

Py_ssize_t **PyUnicode_Find**(*PyObject* *str, *PyObject* *substr, Py_ssize_t *start*, Py_ssize_t *end*, int *direction*)
  Return the first position of *substr* in `str[start:end]` using the given *direction* (*direction* == 1 means to do a forward search, *direction* == `-1` a backward search). The return value is the index of the first match; a value of `-1` indicates that no match was found, and `-2` indicates that an error occurred and an exception has been set.

Py_ssize_t **PyUnicode_FindChar**(*PyObject* *str, *Py_UCS4 ch*, Py_ssize_t *start*, Py_ssize_t *end*, int *direction*)
  Return the first position of the character *ch* in `str[start:end]` using the given *direction* (*direction* == 1 means to do a forward search, *direction* == `-1` a backward search). The return value is the

index of the first match; a value of -1 indicates that no match was found, and -2 indicates that an error occurred and an exception has been set.

New in version 3.3.

Py_ssize_t **PyUnicode_Count**(*PyObject* *str, *PyObject* *substr, Py_ssize_t *start*, Py_ssize_t *end*)
> Return the number of non-overlapping occurrences of *substr* in str[start:end]. Return -1 if an error occurred.

PyObject* **PyUnicode_Replace**(*PyObject* *str, *PyObject* *substr, *PyObject* *replstr, Py_ssize_t *maxcount*)
> *Return value: New reference.* Replace at most *maxcount* occurrences of *substr* in *str* with *replstr* and return the resulting Unicode object. *maxcount* == -1 means replace all occurrences.

int **PyUnicode_Compare**(*PyObject* *left, *PyObject* *right)
> Compare two strings and return -1, 0, 1 for less than, equal, and greater than, respectively.

> This function returns -1 upon failure, so one should call *PyErr_Occurred()* to check for errors.

int **PyUnicode_CompareWithASCIIString**(*PyObject* *uni, const char *string)
> Compare a unicode object, *uni*, with *string* and return -1, 0, 1 for less than, equal, and greater than, respectively. It is best to pass only ASCII-encoded strings, but the function interprets the input string as ISO-8859-1 if it contains non-ASCII characters.

> This function does not raise exceptions.

PyObject* **PyUnicode_RichCompare**(*PyObject* *left, *PyObject* *right, int *op*)
> Rich compare two unicode strings and return one of the following:

> * NULL in case an exception was raised
> * Py_True or Py_False for successful comparisons
> * Py_NotImplemented in case the type combination is unknown

> Possible values for *op* are Py_GT, Py_GE, Py_EQ, Py_NE, Py_LT, and Py_LE.

PyObject* **PyUnicode_Format**(*PyObject* *format, *PyObject* *args)
> *Return value: New reference.* Return a new string object from *format* and *args*; this is analogous to format % args.

int **PyUnicode_Contains**(*PyObject* *container, *PyObject* *element)
> Check whether *element* is contained in *container* and return true or false accordingly.

> *element* has to coerce to a one element Unicode string. -1 is returned if there was an error.

void **PyUnicode_InternInPlace**(*PyObject* **string)
> Intern the argument *string in place. The argument must be the address of a pointer variable pointing to a Python unicode string object. If there is an existing interned string that is the same as *string, it sets *string to it (decrementing the reference count of the old string object and incrementing the reference count of the interned string object), otherwise it leaves *string alone and interns it (incrementing its reference count). (Clarification: even though there is a lot of talk about reference counts, think of this function as reference-count-neutral; you own the object after the call if and only if you owned it before the call.)

PyObject* **PyUnicode_InternFromString**(const char *v)
> A combination of *PyUnicode_FromString()* and *PyUnicode_InternInPlace()*, returning either a new unicode string object that has been interned, or a new ("owned") reference to an earlier interned string object with the same value.

8.3.4 Tuple Objects

PyTupleObject
> This subtype of *PyObject* represents a Python tuple object.

PyTypeObject **PyTuple_Type**
> This instance of *PyTypeObject* represents the Python tuple type; it is the same object as **tuple** in the Python layer.

int **PyTuple_Check**(*PyObject* *p)
> Return true if *p* is a tuple object or an instance of a subtype of the tuple type.

int **PyTuple_CheckExact**(*PyObject* *p)
> Return true if *p* is a tuple object, but not an instance of a subtype of the tuple type.

*PyObject** **PyTuple_New**(Py_ssize_t *len*)
> *Return value: New reference.* Return a new tuple object of size *len*, or *NULL* on failure.

*PyObject** **PyTuple_Pack**(Py_ssize_t *n*, ...)
> *Return value: New reference.* Return a new tuple object of size *n*, or *NULL* on failure. The tuple values are initialized to the subsequent *n* C arguments pointing to Python objects. **PyTuple_Pack(2, a, b)** is equivalent to **Py_BuildValue("(OO)", a, b)**.

Py_ssize_t **PyTuple_Size**(*PyObject* *p)
> Take a pointer to a tuple object, and return the size of that tuple.

Py_ssize_t **PyTuple_GET_SIZE**(*PyObject* *p)
> Return the size of the tuple *p*, which must be non-*NULL* and point to a tuple; no error checking is performed.

*PyObject** **PyTuple_GetItem**(*PyObject* *p, Py_ssize_t *pos*)
> *Return value: Borrowed reference.* Return the object at position *pos* in the tuple pointed to by *p*. If *pos* is out of bounds, return *NULL* and sets an **IndexError** exception.

*PyObject** **PyTuple_GET_ITEM**(*PyObject* *p, Py_ssize_t *pos*)
> *Return value: Borrowed reference.* Like *PyTuple_GetItem()*, but does no checking of its arguments.

*PyObject** **PyTuple_GetSlice**(*PyObject* *p, Py_ssize_t *low*, Py_ssize_t *high*)
> *Return value: New reference.* Take a slice of the tuple pointed to by *p* from *low* to *high* and return it as a new tuple.

int **PyTuple_SetItem**(*PyObject* *p, Py_ssize_t *pos*, *PyObject* *o)
> Insert a reference to object *o* at position *pos* of the tuple pointed to by *p*. Return 0 on success.

> **Note:** This function "steals" a reference to *o*.

---

void **PyTuple_SET_ITEM**(*PyObject* *p, Py_ssize_t *pos*, *PyObject* *o)
> Like *PyTuple_SetItem()*, but does no error checking, and should *only* be used to fill in brand new tuples.

> **Note:** This function "steals" a reference to *o*.

---

int **_PyTuple_Resize**(*PyObject* **p, Py_ssize_t *newsize*)
> Can be used to resize a tuple. *newsize* will be the new length of the tuple. Because tuples are *supposed* to be immutable, this should only be used if there is only one reference to the object. Do *not* use this if the tuple may already be known to some other part of the code. The tuple will always grow or shrink at the end. Think of this as destroying the old tuple and creating a new one, only more efficiently. Returns 0 on success. Client code should never assume that the resulting value of *p will be the same

as before calling this function. If the object referenced by *p is replaced, the original *p is destroyed. On failure, returns -1 and sets *p to *NULL*, and raises `MemoryError` or `SystemError`.

int **PyTuple_ClearFreeList**()
Clear the free list. Return the total number of freed items.

8.3.5 Struct Sequence Objects

Struct sequence objects are the C equivalent of `namedtuple()` objects, i.e. a sequence whose items can also be accessed through attributes. To create a struct sequence, you first have to create a specific struct sequence type.

*PyTypeObject** **PyStructSequence_NewType**(*PyStructSequence_Desc *desc*)
Create a new struct sequence type from the data in *desc*, described below. Instances of the resulting type can be created with *PyStructSequence_New()*.

void **PyStructSequence_InitType**(*PyTypeObject *type*, *PyStructSequence_Desc *desc*)
Initializes a struct sequence type *type* from *desc* in place.

int **PyStructSequence_InitType2**(*PyTypeObject *type*, *PyStructSequence_Desc *desc*)
The same as `PyStructSequence_InitType`, but returns 0 on success and -1 on failure.

New in version 3.4.

PyStructSequence_Desc
Contains the meta information of a struct sequence type to create.

Field	C Type	Meaning
name	char *	name of the struct sequence type
doc	char *	pointer to docstring for the type or NULL to omit
fields	PyStructSequence_Field *	pointer to *NULL*-terminated array with field names of the new type
n_in_sequence	int	number of fields visible to the Python side (if used as tuple)

PyStructSequence_Field
Describes a field of a struct sequence. As a struct sequence is modeled as a tuple, all fields are typed as *PyObject*. The index in the `fields` array of the *PyStructSequence_Desc* determines which field of the struct sequence is described.

Field	C Type	Meaning
name	char *	name for the field or *NULL* to end the list of named fields, set to PyStructSequence_UnnamedField to leave unnamed
doc	char *	field docstring or *NULL* to omit

char* **PyStructSequence_UnnamedField**
Special value for a field name to leave it unnamed.

*PyObject** **PyStructSequence_New**(*PyTypeObject *type*)
Creates an instance of *type*, which must have been created with *PyStructSequence_NewType()*.

*PyObject** **PyStructSequence_GetItem**(*PyObject *p*, Py_ssize_t *pos*)
Return the object at position *pos* in the struct sequence pointed to by *p*. No bounds checking is performed.

PyObject* **PyStructSequence_GET_ITEM**(*PyObject *p*, Py_ssize_t *pos*)
> Macro equivalent of *PyStructSequence_GetItem()*.

void **PyStructSequence_SetItem**(*PyObject *p*, Py_ssize_t *pos*, *PyObject *o*)
> Sets the field at index *pos* of the struct sequence *p* to value *o*. Like *PyTuple_SET_ITEM()*, this should only be used to fill in brand new instances.

Note: This function "steals" a reference to *o*.

PyObject* **PyStructSequence_SET_ITEM**(*PyObject *p*, Py_ssize_t **pos*, *PyObject *o*)
> Macro equivalent of *PyStructSequence_SetItem()*.

Note: This function "steals" a reference to *o*.

8.3.6 List Objects

PyListObject
> This subtype of *PyObject* represents a Python list object.

PyTypeObject **PyList_Type**
> This instance of *PyTypeObject* represents the Python list type. This is the same object as **list** in the Python layer.

int **PyList_Check**(*PyObject *p*)
> Return true if *p* is a list object or an instance of a subtype of the list type.

int **PyList_CheckExact**(*PyObject *p*)
> Return true if *p* is a list object, but not an instance of a subtype of the list type.

PyObject* **PyList_New**(Py_ssize_t *len*)
> *Return value: New reference.* Return a new list of length *len* on success, or *NULL* on failure.

Note: If *len* is greater than zero, the returned list object's items are set to NULL. Thus you cannot use abstract API functions such as *PySequence_SetItem()* or expose the object to Python code before setting all items to a real object with *PyList_SetItem()*.

Py_ssize_t **PyList_Size**(*PyObject *list*)
> Return the length of the list object in *list*; this is equivalent to **len(list)** on a list object.

Py_ssize_t **PyList_GET_SIZE**(*PyObject *list*)
> Macro form of *PyList_Size()* without error checking.

PyObject* **PyList_GetItem**(*PyObject *list*, Py_ssize_t *index*)
> *Return value: Borrowed reference.* Return the object at position *index* in the list pointed to by *list*. The position must be positive, indexing from the end of the list is not supported. If *index* is out of bounds, return *NULL* and set an **IndexError** exception.

PyObject* **PyList_GET_ITEM**(*PyObject *list*, Py_ssize_t *i*)
> *Return value: Borrowed reference.* Macro form of *PyList_GetItem()* without error checking.

int **PyList_SetItem**(*PyObject *list*, Py_ssize_t *index*, *PyObject *item*)
> Set the item at index *index* in list to *item*. Return 0 on success or **-1** on failure.

> **Note:** This function "steals" a reference to *item* and discards a reference to an item already in the list at the affected position.

void **PyList_SET_ITEM**(*PyObject* *list*, Py_ssize_t *i*, *PyObject* *o*)
> Macro form of *PyList_SetItem()* without error checking. This is normally only used to fill in new lists where there is no previous content.

> **Note:** This macro "steals" a reference to *item*, and, unlike *PyList_SetItem()*, does *not* discard a reference to any item that is being replaced; any reference in *list* at position *i* will be leaked.

int **PyList_Insert**(*PyObject* *list*, Py_ssize_t *index*, *PyObject* *item*)
> Insert the item *item* into list *list* in front of index *index*. Return 0 if successful; return −1 and set an exception if unsuccessful. Analogous to `list.insert(index, item)`.

int **PyList_Append**(*PyObject* *list*, *PyObject* *item*)
> Append the object *item* at the end of list *list*. Return 0 if successful; return −1 and set an exception if unsuccessful. Analogous to `list.append(item)`.

*PyObject** **PyList_GetSlice**(*PyObject* *list*, Py_ssize_t *low*, Py_ssize_t *high*)
> *Return value: New reference.* Return a list of the objects in *list* containing the objects *between low* and *high*. Return *NULL* and set an exception if unsuccessful. Analogous to `list[low:high]`. Negative indices, as when slicing from Python, are not supported.

int **PyList_SetSlice**(*PyObject* *list*, Py_ssize_t *low*, Py_ssize_t *high*, *PyObject* *itemlist*)
> Set the slice of *list* between *low* and *high* to the contents of *itemlist*. Analogous to `list[low:high] = itemlist`. The *itemlist* may be *NULL*, indicating the assignment of an empty list (slice deletion). Return 0 on success, −1 on failure. Negative indices, as when slicing from Python, are not supported.

int **PyList_Sort**(*PyObject* *list*)
> Sort the items of *list* in place. Return 0 on success, −1 on failure. This is equivalent to `list.sort()`.

int **PyList_Reverse**(*PyObject* *list*)
> Reverse the items of *list* in place. Return 0 on success, −1 on failure. This is the equivalent of `list.reverse()`.

*PyObject** **PyList_AsTuple**(*PyObject* *list*)
> *Return value: New reference.* Return a new tuple object containing the contents of *list*; equivalent to `tuple(list)`.

int **PyList_ClearFreeList**()
> Clear the free list. Return the total number of freed items.
>
> New in version 3.3.

8.4 Container Objects

8.4.1 Dictionary Objects

PyDictObject
> This subtype of *PyObject* represents a Python dictionary object.

PyTypeObject **PyDict_Type**
> This instance of *PyTypeObject* represents the Python dictionary type. This is the same object as `dict` in the Python layer.

int **PyDict_Check**(*PyObject* **p*)

> Return true if *p* is a dict object or an instance of a subtype of the dict type.

int **PyDict_CheckExact**(*PyObject* **p*)

> Return true if *p* is a dict object, but not an instance of a subtype of the dict type.

PyObject* **PyDict_New**()

> *Return value: New reference.* Return a new empty dictionary, or *NULL* on failure.

PyObject* **PyDictProxy_New**(*PyObject* **mapping*)

> *Return value: New reference.* Return a types.MappingProxyType object for a mapping which enforces read-only behavior. This is normally used to create a view to prevent modification of the dictionary for non-dynamic class types.

void **PyDict_Clear**(*PyObject* **p*)

> Empty an existing dictionary of all key-value pairs.

int **PyDict_Contains**(*PyObject* **p*, *PyObject* **key*)

> Determine if dictionary *p* contains *key*. If an item in *p* is matches *key*, return 1, otherwise return 0. On error, return -1. This is equivalent to the Python expression key in p.

PyObject* **PyDict_Copy**(*PyObject* **p*)

> *Return value: New reference.* Return a new dictionary that contains the same key-value pairs as *p*.

int **PyDict_SetItem**(*PyObject* **p*, *PyObject* **key*, *PyObject* **val*)

> Insert *value* into the dictionary *p* with a key of *key*. *key* must be *hashable*; if it isn't, **TypeError** will be raised. Return 0 on success or -1 on failure.

int **PyDict_SetItemString**(*PyObject* **p*, const char **key*, *PyObject* **val*)

> Insert *value* into the dictionary *p* using *key* as a key. *key* should be a **char***. The key object is created using PyUnicode_FromString(key). Return 0 on success or -1 on failure.

int **PyDict_DelItem**(*PyObject* **p*, *PyObject* **key*)

> Remove the entry in dictionary *p* with key *key*. *key* must be hashable; if it isn't, **TypeError** is raised. Return 0 on success or -1 on failure.

int **PyDict_DelItemString**(*PyObject* **p*, const char **key*)

> Remove the entry in dictionary *p* which has a key specified by the string *key*. Return 0 on success or -1 on failure.

PyObject* **PyDict_GetItem**(*PyObject* **p*, *PyObject* **key*)

> *Return value: Borrowed reference.* Return the object from dictionary *p* which has a key *key*. Return *NULL* if the key *key* is not present, but *without* setting an exception.

PyObject* **PyDict_GetItemWithError**(*PyObject* **p*, *PyObject* **key*)

> Variant of *PyDict_GetItem()* that does not suppress exceptions. Return *NULL* **with** an exception set if an exception occurred. Return *NULL* **without** an exception set if the key wasn't present.

PyObject* **PyDict_GetItemString**(*PyObject* **p*, const char **key*)

> *Return value: Borrowed reference.* This is the same as *PyDict_GetItem()*, but *key* is specified as a **char***, rather than a *PyObject**.

PyObject* **PyDict_SetDefault**(*PyObject* **p*, *PyObject* **key*, *PyObject* **default*)

> *Return value: Borrowed reference.* This is the same as the Python-level dict.setdefault(). If present, it returns the value corresponding to *key* from the dictionary *p*. If the key is not in the dict, it is inserted with value *defaultobj* and *defaultobj* is returned. This function evaluates the hash function of *key* only once, instead of evaluating it independently for the lookup and the insertion.
>
> New in version 3.4.

PyObject* **PyDict_Items**(*PyObject* **p*)

> *Return value: New reference.* Return a *PyListObject* containing all the items from the dictionary.

PyObject* **PyDict_Keys**(*PyObject* *p)

> *Return value: New reference.* Return a *PyListObject* containing all the keys from the dictionary.

PyObject* **PyDict_Values**(*PyObject* *p)

> *Return value: New reference.* Return a *PyListObject* containing all the values from the dictionary *p*.

Py_ssize_t **PyDict_Size**(*PyObject* *p)

> Return the number of items in the dictionary. This is equivalent to `len(p)` on a dictionary.

int **PyDict_Next**(*PyObject* *p, Py_ssize_t *ppos, *PyObject* **pkey, *PyObject* **pvalue)

> Iterate over all key-value pairs in the dictionary *p*. The `Py_ssize_t` referred to by *ppos* must be initialized to 0 prior to the first call to this function to start the iteration; the function returns true for each pair in the dictionary, and false once all pairs have been reported. The parameters *pkey* and *pvalue* should either point to *PyObject** variables that will be filled in with each key and value, respectively, or may be *NULL*. Any references returned through them are borrowed. *ppos* should not be altered during iteration. Its value represents offsets within the internal dictionary structure, and since the structure is sparse, the offsets are not consecutive.
>
> For example:

```
PyObject *key, *value;
Py_ssize_t pos = 0;

while (PyDict_Next(self->dict, &pos, &key, &value)) {
    /* do something interesting with the values... */
    ...
}
```

> The dictionary *p* should not be mutated during iteration. It is safe to modify the values of the keys as you iterate over the dictionary, but only so long as the set of keys does not change. For example:

```
PyObject *key, *value;
Py_ssize_t pos = 0;

while (PyDict_Next(self->dict, &pos, &key, &value)) {
    long i = PyLong_AsLong(value);
    if (i == -1 && PyErr_Occurred()) {
        return -1;
    }
    PyObject *o = PyLong_FromLong(i + 1);
    if (o == NULL)
        return -1;
    if (PyDict_SetItem(self->dict, key, o) < 0) {
        Py_DECREF(o);
        return -1;
    }
    Py_DECREF(o);
}
```

int **PyDict_Merge**(*PyObject* *a, *PyObject* *b, int *override*)

> Iterate over mapping object *b* adding key-value pairs to dictionary *a*. *b* may be a dictionary, or any object supporting *PyMapping_Keys()* and *PyObject_GetItem()*. If *override* is true, existing pairs in *a* will be replaced if a matching key is found in *b*, otherwise pairs will only be added if there is not a matching key in *a*. Return 0 on success or -1 if an exception was raised.

int **PyDict_Update**(*PyObject* *a, *PyObject* *b)

> This is the same as **PyDict_Merge**(a, b, 1) in C, and is similar to `a.update(b)` in Python except that *PyDict_Update()* doesn't fall back to the iterating over a sequence of key value pairs if the second argument has no "keys" attribute. Return 0 on success or -1 if an exception was raised.

int **PyDict_MergeFromSeq2**(*PyObject* **a*, *PyObject* **seq2*, int *override*)

Update or merge into dictionary *a*, from the key-value pairs in *seq2*. *seq2* must be an iterable object producing iterable objects of length 2, viewed as key-value pairs. In case of duplicate keys, the last wins if *override* is true, else the first wins. Return 0 on success or −1 if an exception was raised. Equivalent Python (except for the return value):

```
def PyDict_MergeFromSeq2(a, seq2, override):
    for key, value in seq2:
        if override or key not in a:
            a[key] = value
```

int **PyDict_ClearFreeList**()

Clear the free list. Return the total number of freed items.

New in version 3.3.

8.4.2 Set Objects

This section details the public API for **set** and **frozenset** objects. Any functionality not listed below is best accessed using the either the abstract object protocol (including *PyObject_CallMethod()*, *PyObject_RichCompareBool()*, *PyObject_Hash()*, *PyObject_Repr()*, *PyObject_IsTrue()*, *PyObject_Print()*, and *PyObject_GetIter()*) or the abstract number protocol (including *PyNumber_And()*, *PyNumber_Subtract()*, *PyNumber_Or()*, *PyNumber_Xor()*, *PyNumber_InPlaceAnd()*, *PyNumber_InPlaceSubtract()*, *PyNumber_InPlaceOr()*, and *PyNumber_InPlaceXor()*).

PySetObject

This subtype of *PyObject* is used to hold the internal data for both **set** and **frozenset** objects. It is like a *PyDictObject* in that it is a fixed size for small sets (much like tuple storage) and will point to a separate, variable sized block of memory for medium and large sized sets (much like list storage). None of the fields of this structure should be considered public and are subject to change. All access should be done through the documented API rather than by manipulating the values in the structure.

PyTypeObject **PySet_Type**

This is an instance of *PyTypeObject* representing the Python **set** type.

PyTypeObject **PyFrozenSet_Type**

This is an instance of *PyTypeObject* representing the Python **frozenset** type.

The following type check macros work on pointers to any Python object. Likewise, the constructor functions work with any iterable Python object.

int **PySet_Check**(*PyObject* **p*)

Return true if *p* is a **set** object or an instance of a subtype.

int **PyFrozenSet_Check**(*PyObject* **p*)

Return true if *p* is a **frozenset** object or an instance of a subtype.

int **PyAnySet_Check**(*PyObject* **p*)

Return true if *p* is a **set** object, a **frozenset** object, or an instance of a subtype.

int **PyAnySet_CheckExact**(*PyObject* **p*)

Return true if *p* is a **set** object or a **frozenset** object but not an instance of a subtype.

int **PyFrozenSet_CheckExact**(*PyObject* **p*)

Return true if *p* is a **frozenset** object but not an instance of a subtype.

PyObject* **PySet_New**(*PyObject* **iterable*)

Return value: New reference. Return a new **set** containing objects returned by the *iterable*. The *iterable* may be *NULL* to create a new empty set. Return the new set on success or *NULL* on failure.

Raise `TypeError` if *iterable* is not actually iterable. The constructor is also useful for copying a set (c=set(s)).

PyObject* **PyFrozenSet_New**(*PyObject* *iterable)
> *Return value: New reference.* Return a new `frozenset` containing objects returned by the *iterable*. The *iterable* may be *NULL* to create a new empty frozenset. Return the new set on success or *NULL* on failure. Raise `TypeError` if *iterable* is not actually iterable.

The following functions and macros are available for instances of **set** or **frozenset** or instances of their subtypes.

Py_ssize_t **PySet_Size**(*PyObject* *anyset)
> Return the length of a **set** or **frozenset** object. Equivalent to `len(anyset)`. Raises a `PyExc_SystemError` if *anyset* is not a **set**, **frozenset**, or an instance of a subtype.

Py_ssize_t **PySet_GET_SIZE**(*PyObject* *anyset)
> Macro form of *PySet_Size()* without error checking.

int **PySet_Contains**(*PyObject* *anyset, *PyObject* *key)
> Return 1 if found, 0 if not found, and -1 if an error is encountered. Unlike the Python `__contains__()` method, this function does not automatically convert unhashable sets into temporary frozensets. Raise a `TypeError` if the *key* is unhashable. Raise `PyExc_SystemError` if *anyset* is not a **set**, **frozenset**, or an instance of a subtype.

int **PySet_Add**(*PyObject* *set, *PyObject* *key)
> Add *key* to a **set** instance. Also works with **frozenset** instances (like *PyTuple_SetItem()* it can be used to fill-in the values of brand new frozensets before they are exposed to other code). Return 0 on success or -1 on failure. Raise a `TypeError` if the *key* is unhashable. Raise a `MemoryError` if there is no room to grow. Raise a `SystemError` if *set* is not an instance of **set** or its subtype.

The following functions are available for instances of **set** or its subtypes but not for instances of **frozenset** or its subtypes.

int **PySet_Discard**(*PyObject* *set, *PyObject* *key)
> Return 1 if found and removed, 0 if not found (no action taken), and -1 if an error is encountered. Does not raise `KeyError` for missing keys. Raise a `TypeError` if the *key* is unhashable. Unlike the Python `discard()` method, this function does not automatically convert unhashable sets into temporary frozensets. Raise `PyExc_SystemError` if *set* is not an instance of **set** or its subtype.

PyObject* **PySet_Pop**(*PyObject* *set)
> *Return value: New reference.* Return a new reference to an arbitrary object in the *set*, and removes the object from the *set*. Return *NULL* on failure. Raise `KeyError` if the set is empty. Raise a `SystemError` if *set* is not an instance of **set** or its subtype.

int **PySet_Clear**(*PyObject* *set)
> Empty an existing set of all elements.

int **PySet_ClearFreeList**()
> Clear the free list. Return the total number of freed items.

> New in version 3.3.

8.5 Function Objects

8.5.1 Function Objects

There are a few functions specific to Python functions.

PyFunctionObject
> The C structure used for functions.

PyTypeObject **PyFunction_Type**
> This is an instance of *PyTypeObject* and represents the Python function type. It is exposed to Python programmers as **types.FunctionType**.

int **PyFunction_Check**(*PyObject* *o*)
> Return true if *o* is a function object (has type *PyFunction_Type*). The parameter must not be *NULL*.

*PyObject** **PyFunction_New**(*PyObject* *code*, *PyObject* *globals*)
> *Return value: New reference.* Return a new function object associated with the code object *code*. *globals* must be a dictionary with the global variables accessible to the function.
>
> The function's docstring and name are retrieved from the code object. ___module___ is retrieved from *globals*. The argument defaults, annotations and closure are set to *NULL*. ___qualname___ is set to the same value as the function's name.

*PyObject** **PyFunction_NewWithQualName**(*PyObject* *code*, *PyObject* *globals*, *PyObject* *qualname*)
> *Return value: New reference.* As *PyFunction_New()*, but also allows setting the function object's **__qualname__** attribute. *qualname* should be a unicode object or NULL; if NULL, the **__qualname__** attribute is set to the same value as its **__name__** attribute.
>
> New in version 3.3.

*PyObject** **PyFunction_GetCode**(*PyObject* *op*)
> *Return value: Borrowed reference.* Return the code object associated with the function object *op*.

*PyObject** **PyFunction_GetGlobals**(*PyObject* *op*)
> *Return value: Borrowed reference.* Return the globals dictionary associated with the function object *op*.

*PyObject** **PyFunction_GetModule**(*PyObject* *op*)
> *Return value: Borrowed reference.* Return the ___module___ attribute of the function object *op*. This is normally a string containing the module name, but can be set to any other object by Python code.

*PyObject** **PyFunction_GetDefaults**(*PyObject* *op*)
> *Return value: Borrowed reference.* Return the argument default values of the function object *op*. This can be a tuple of arguments or *NULL*.

int **PyFunction_SetDefaults**(*PyObject* *op*, *PyObject* *defaults*)
> Set the argument default values for the function object *op*. *defaults* must be *Py_None* or a tuple.
>
> Raises **SystemError** and returns -1 on failure.

*PyObject** **PyFunction_GetClosure**(*PyObject* *op*)
> *Return value: Borrowed reference.* Return the closure associated with the function object *op*. This can be *NULL* or a tuple of cell objects.

int **PyFunction_SetClosure**(*PyObject* *op*, *PyObject* *closure*)
> Set the closure associated with the function object *op*. *closure* must be *Py_None* or a tuple of cell objects.
>
> Raises **SystemError** and returns -1 on failure.

PyObject ***PyFunction_GetAnnotations**(*PyObject* *op*)
> Return the annotations of the function object *op*. This can be a mutable dictionary or *NULL*.

int **PyFunction_SetAnnotations**(*PyObject* *op*, *PyObject* *annotations*)
> Set the annotations for the function object *op*. *annotations* must be a dictionary or *Py_None*.
>
> Raises **SystemError** and returns -1 on failure.

8.5.2 Instance Method Objects

An instance method is a wrapper for a *PyCFunction* and the new way to bind a *PyCFunction* to a class object. It replaces the former call PyMethod_New(func, NULL, class).

PyTypeObject **PyInstanceMethod_Type**
>   This instance of *PyTypeObject* represents the Python instance method type. It is not exposed to Python programs.

int **PyInstanceMethod_Check**(*PyObject* *o*)
>   Return true if *o* is an instance method object (has type *PyInstanceMethod_Type*). The parameter must not be *NULL*.

*PyObject** **PyInstanceMethod_New**(*PyObject* *func*)
>   Return a new instance method object, with *func* being any callable object *func* is the function that will be called when the instance method is called.

*PyObject** **PyInstanceMethod_Function**(*PyObject* *im*)
>   Return the function object associated with the instance method *im*.

*PyObject** **PyInstanceMethod_GET_FUNCTION**(*PyObject* *im*)
>   Macro version of *PyInstanceMethod_Function()* which avoids error checking.

8.5.3 Method Objects

Methods are bound function objects. Methods are always bound to an instance of a user-defined class. Unbound methods (methods bound to a class object) are no longer available.

PyTypeObject **PyMethod_Type**
>   This instance of *PyTypeObject* represents the Python method type. This is exposed to Python programs as types.MethodType.

int **PyMethod_Check**(*PyObject* *o*)
>   Return true if *o* is a method object (has type *PyMethod_Type*). The parameter must not be *NULL*.

*PyObject** **PyMethod_New**(*PyObject* *func*, *PyObject* *self*)
>   *Return value: New reference.* Return a new method object, with *func* being any callable object and *self* the instance the method should be bound. *func* is the function that will be called when the method is called. *self* must not be *NULL*.

*PyObject** **PyMethod_Function**(*PyObject* *meth*)
>   *Return value: Borrowed reference.* Return the function object associated with the method *meth*.

*PyObject** **PyMethod_GET_FUNCTION**(*PyObject* *meth*)
>   *Return value: Borrowed reference.* Macro version of *PyMethod_Function()* which avoids error checking.

*PyObject** **PyMethod_Self**(*PyObject* *meth*)
>   *Return value: Borrowed reference.* Return the instance associated with the method *meth*.

*PyObject** **PyMethod_GET_SELF**(*PyObject* *meth*)
>   *Return value: Borrowed reference.* Macro version of *PyMethod_Self()* which avoids error checking.

int **PyMethod_ClearFreeList**()
>   Clear the free list. Return the total number of freed items.

8.5.4 Cell Objects

"Cell" objects are used to implement variables referenced by multiple scopes. For each such variable, a cell object is created to store the value; the local variables of each stack frame that references the value contains

---

a reference to the cells from outer scopes which also use that variable. When the value is accessed, the value contained in the cell is used instead of the cell object itself. This de-referencing of the cell object requires support from the generated byte-code; these are not automatically de-referenced when accessed. Cell objects are not likely to be useful elsewhere.

PyCellObject
> The C structure used for cell objects.

PyTypeObject **PyCell_Type**
> The type object corresponding to cell objects.

int **PyCell_Check**(ob)
> Return true if *ob* is a cell object; *ob* must not be *NULL*.

PyObject* **PyCell_New**(*PyObject *ob*)
> *Return value: New reference.* Create and return a new cell object containing the value *ob*. The parameter may be *NULL*.

PyObject* **PyCell_Get**(*PyObject *cell*)
> *Return value: New reference.* Return the contents of the cell *cell*.

PyObject* **PyCell_GET**(*PyObject *cell*)
> *Return value: Borrowed reference.* Return the contents of the cell *cell*, but without checking that *cell* is non-*NULL* and a cell object.

int **PyCell_Set**(*PyObject *cell*, *PyObject *value*)
> Set the contents of the cell object *cell* to *value*. This releases the reference to any current content of the cell. *value* may be *NULL*. *cell* must be non-*NULL*; if it is not a cell object, -1 will be returned. On success, 0 will be returned.

void **PyCell_SET**(*PyObject *cell*, *PyObject *value*)
> Sets the value of the cell object *cell* to *value*. No reference counts are adjusted, and no checks are made for safety; *cell* must be non-*NULL* and must be a cell object.

8.5.5 Code Objects

Code objects are a low-level detail of the CPython implementation. Each one represents a chunk of executable code that hasn't yet been bound into a function.

PyCodeObject
> The C structure of the objects used to describe code objects. The fields of this type are subject to change at any time.

PyTypeObject **PyCode_Type**
> This is an instance of *PyTypeObject* representing the Python **code** type.

int **PyCode_Check**(*PyObject *co*)
> Return true if *co* is a **code** object.

int **PyCode_GetNumFree**(*PyCodeObject *co*)
> Return the number of free variables in *co*.

PyCodeObject* **PyCode_New**(int *argcount*, int *kwonlyargcount*, int *nlocals*, int *stacksize*, int *flags*, *PyObject *code*, *PyObject *consts*, *PyObject *names*, *PyObject *varnames*, *PyObject *freevars*, *PyObject *cellvars*, *PyObject *filename*, *PyObject *name*, int *firstlineno*, *PyObject *lnotab*)
> Return a new code object. If you need a dummy code object to create a frame, use *PyCode_NewEmpty()* instead. Calling *PyCode_New()* directly can bind you to a precise Python version since the definition of the bytecode changes often.

PyCodeObject* **PyCode_NewEmpty**(const char **filename*, const char **funcname*, int *firstlineno*)
> Return a new empty code object with the specified filename, function name, and first line number. It is illegal to `exec()` or `eval()` the resulting code object.

8.6 Other Objects

8.6.1 File Objects

These APIs are a minimal emulation of the Python 2 C API for built-in file objects, which used to rely on the buffered I/O (`FILE*`) support from the C standard library. In Python 3, files and streams use the new `io` module, which defines several layers over the low-level unbuffered I/O of the operating system. The functions described below are convenience C wrappers over these new APIs, and meant mostly for internal error reporting in the interpreter; third-party code is advised to access the `io` APIs instead.

PyFile_FromFd(int *fd*, const char **name*, const char **mode*, int *buffering*, const char **encoding*, const char **errors*, const char **newline*, int *closefd*)
> Create a Python file object from the file descriptor of an already opened file *fd*. The arguments *name*, *encoding*, *errors* and *newline* can be *NULL* to use the defaults; *buffering* can be *-1* to use the default. *name* is ignored and kept for backward compatibility. Return *NULL* on failure. For a more comprehensive description of the arguments, please refer to the `io.open()` function documentation.

> > **Warning:** Since Python streams have their own buffering layer, mixing them with OS-level file descriptors can produce various issues (such as unexpected ordering of data).

> Changed in version 3.2: Ignore *name* attribute.

int **PyObject_AsFileDescriptor**(*PyObject *p*)
> Return the file descriptor associated with *p* as an `int`. If the object is an integer, its value is returned. If not, the object's `fileno()` method is called if it exists; the method must return an integer, which is returned as the file descriptor value. Sets an exception and returns −1 on failure.

PyObject* **PyFile_GetLine**(*PyObject *p*, int *n*)
> *Return value: New reference.* Equivalent to `p.readline([n])`, this function reads one line from the object *p*. *p* may be a file object or any object with a `readline()` method. If *n* is 0, exactly one line is read, regardless of the length of the line. If *n* is greater than 0, no more than *n* bytes will be read from the file; a partial line can be returned. In both cases, an empty string is returned if the end of the file is reached immediately. If *n* is less than 0, however, one line is read regardless of length, but `EOFError` is raised if the end of the file is reached immediately.

int **PyFile_WriteObject**(*PyObject *obj*, *PyObject *p*, int *flags*)
> Write object *obj* to file object *p*. The only supported flag for *flags* is `Py_PRINT_RAW`; if given, the `str()` of the object is written instead of the `repr()`. Return 0 on success or −1 on failure; the appropriate exception will be set.

int **PyFile_WriteString**(const char **s*, *PyObject *p*)
> Write string *s* to file object *p*. Return 0 on success or −1 on failure; the appropriate exception will be set.

8.6.2 Module Objects

PyTypeObject **PyModule_Type**
> This instance of *PyTypeObject* represents the Python module type. This is exposed to Python programs as `types.ModuleType`.

---

int **PyModule_Check**(*PyObject* **p*)

    Return true if *p* is a module object, or a subtype of a module object.

int **PyModule_CheckExact**(*PyObject* **p*)

    Return true if *p* is a module object, but not a subtype of *PyModule_Type*.

PyObject* **PyModule_NewObject**(*PyObject* **name*)

    Return a new module object with the **__name__** attribute set to *name*. The module's **__name__**, **__doc__**, **__package__**, and **__loader__** attributes are filled in (all but **__name__** are set to None); the caller is responsible for providing a **__file__** attribute.

    New in version 3.3.

    Changed in version 3.4: **__package__** and **__loader__** are set to None.

PyObject* **PyModule_New**(const char **name*)

    Return value: New reference. Similar to *PyModule_NewObject()*, but the name is a UTF-8 encoded string instead of a Unicode object.

PyObject* **PyModule_GetDict**(*PyObject* **module*)

    Return value: Borrowed reference. Return the dictionary object that implements *module*'s namespace; this object is the same as the **__dict__** attribute of the module object. If *module* is not a module object (or a subtype of a module object), SystemError is raised and *NULL* is returned.

    It is recommended extensions use other **PyModule_*()** and **PyObject_*()** functions rather than directly manipulate a module's **__dict__**.

PyObject* **PyModule_GetNameObject**(*PyObject* **module*)

    Return *module*'s **__name__** value. If the module does not provide one, or if it is not a string, SystemError is raised and *NULL* is returned.

    New in version 3.3.

char* **PyModule_GetName**(*PyObject* **module*)

    Similar to *PyModule_GetNameObject()* but return the name encoded to 'utf-8'.

void* **PyModule_GetState**(*PyObject* **module*)

    Return the "state" of the module, that is, a pointer to the block of memory allocated at module creation time, or *NULL*. See *PyModuleDef.m_size*.

PyModuleDef* **PyModule_GetDef**(*PyObject* **module*)

    Return a pointer to the *PyModuleDef* struct from which the module was created, or *NULL* if the module wasn't created from a definition.

PyObject* **PyModule_GetFilenameObject**(*PyObject* **module*)

    Return the name of the file from which *module* was loaded using *module*'s **__file__** attribute. If this is not defined, or if it is not a unicode string, raise SystemError and return *NULL*; otherwise return a reference to a Unicode object.

    New in version 3.2.

char* **PyModule_GetFilename**(*PyObject* **module*)

    Similar to *PyModule_GetFilenameObject()* but return the filename encoded to 'utf-8'.

    Deprecated since version 3.2: *PyModule_GetFilename()* raises UnicodeEncodeError on unencodable filenames, use *PyModule_GetFilenameObject()* instead.

Initializing C modules

Modules objects are usually created from extension modules (shared libraries which export an initialization function), or compiled-in modules (where the initialization function is added using *PyImport_AppendInittab()*). See building or extending-with-embedding for details.

The initialization function can either pass a module definition instance to *PyModule_Create()*, and return the resulting module object, or request "multi-phase initialization" by returning the definition struct itself.

PyModuleDef

> The module definition struct, which holds all information needed to create a module object. There is usually only one statically initialized variable of this type for each module.

> PyModuleDef_Base **m_base**

>> Always initialize this member to PyModuleDef_HEAD_INIT.

> char* **m_name**

>> Name for the new module.

> char* **m_doc**

>> Docstring for the module; usually a docstring variable created with PyDoc_STRVAR() is used.

> Py_ssize_t **m_size**

>> Module state may be kept in a per-module memory area that can be retrieved with *PyModule_GetState()*, rather than in static globals. This makes modules safe for use in multiple sub-interpreters.

>> This memory area is allocated based on *m_size* on module creation, and freed when the module object is deallocated, after the **m_free** function has been called, if present.

>> Setting **m_size** to **-1** means that the module does not support sub-interpreters, because it has global state.

>> Setting it to a non-negative value means that the module can be re-initialized and specifies the additional amount of memory it requires for its state. Non-negative **m_size** is required for multi-phase initialization.

>> See PEP 3121 for more details.

> *PyMethodDef** **m_methods**

>> A pointer to a table of module-level functions, described by *PyMethodDef* values. Can be *NULL* if no functions are present.

> *PyModuleDef_Slot** **m_slots**

>> An array of slot definitions for multi-phase initialization, terminated by a {0, NULL} entry. When using single-phase initialization, *m_slots* must be *NULL*.

>> Changed in version 3.5: Prior to version 3.5, this member was always set to *NULL*, and was defined as:

>>> *inquiry* **m_reload**

> *traverseproc* **m_traverse**

>> A traversal function to call during GC traversal of the module object, or *NULL* if not needed.

> *inquiry* **m_clear**

>> A clear function to call during GC clearing of the module object, or *NULL* if not needed.

> freefunc **m_free**

>> A function to call during deallocation of the module object, or *NULL* if not needed.

Single-phase initialization

The module initialization function may create and return the module object directly. This is referred to as "single-phase initialization", and uses one of the following two module creation functions:

*PyObject** **PyModule_Create**(*PyModuleDef *def*)

> Create a new module object, given the definition in *def*. This behaves like *PyModule_Create2()* with *module_api_version* set to PYTHON_API_VERSION.

PyObject* **PyModule_Create2**(*PyModuleDef* *def, int *module_api_version*)

Create a new module object, given the definition in *def*, assuming the API version *module_api_version*. If that version does not match the version of the running interpreter, a `RuntimeWarning` is emitted.

> **Note:** Most uses of this function should be using *PyModule_Create()* instead; only use this if you are sure you need it.

Before it is returned from in the initialization function, the resulting module object is typically populated using functions like *PyModule_AddObject()*.

Multi-phase initialization

An alternate way to specify extensions is to request "multi-phase initialization". Extension modules created this way behave more like Python modules: the initialization is split between the *creation phase*, when the module object is created, and the *execution phase*, when it is populated. The distinction is similar to the `__new__()` and `__init__()` methods of classes.

Unlike modules created using single-phase initialization, these modules are not singletons: if the *sys.modules* entry is removed and the module is re-imported, a new module object is created, and the old module is subject to normal garbage collection – as with Python modules. By default, multiple modules created from the same definition should be independent: changes to one should not affect the others. This means that all state should be specific to the module object (using e.g. using *PyModule_GetState()*), or its contents (such as the module's `__dict__` or individual classes created with *PyType_FromSpec()*).

All modules created using multi-phase initialization are expected to support *sub-interpreters*. Making sure multiple modules are independent is typically enough to achieve this.

To request multi-phase initialization, the initialization function (PyInit_modulename) returns a *PyModuleDef* instance with non-empty *m_slots*. Before it is returned, the **PyModuleDef** instance must be initialized with the following function:

PyObject* **PyModuleDef_Init**(*PyModuleDef* *def)

Ensures a module definition is a properly initialized Python object that correctly reports its type and reference count.

Returns *def* cast to **PyObject***, or *NULL* if an error occurred.

New in version 3.5.

The *m_slots* member of the module definition must point to an array of **PyModuleDef_Slot** structures:

PyModuleDef_Slot

int **slot**

A slot ID, chosen from the available values explained below.

void* **value**

Value of the slot, whose meaning depends on the slot ID.

New in version 3.5.

The *m_slots* array must be terminated by a slot with id 0.

The available slot types are:

Py_mod_create

Specifies a function that is called to create the module object itself. The *value* pointer of this slot must point to a function of the signature:

PyObject* **create_module**(*PyObject* *spec, *PyModuleDef* *def)

The function receives a `ModuleSpec` instance, as defined in PEP 451, and the module definition. It should return a new module object, or set an error and return *NULL*.

This function should be kept minimal. In particular, it should not call arbitrary Python code, as trying to import the same module again may result in an infinite loop.

Multiple `Py_mod_create` slots may not be specified in one module definition.

If `Py_mod_create` is not specified, the import machinery will create a normal module object using *PyModule_New()*. The name is taken from *spec*, not the definition, to allow extension modules to dynamically adjust to their place in the module hierarchy and be imported under different names through symlinks, all while sharing a single module definition.

There is no requirement for the returned object to be an instance of *PyModule_Type*. Any type can be used, as long as it supports setting and getting import-related attributes. However, only `PyModule_Type` instances may be returned if the `PyModuleDef` has non-*NULL* `m_traverse`, `m_clear`, `m_free`; non-zero `m_size`; or slots other than `Py_mod_create`.

Py_mod_exec

> Specifies a function that is called to *execute* the module. This is equivalent to executing the code of a Python module: typically, this function adds classes and constants to the module. The signature of the function is:
>
> int **exec_module**(*PyObject* * *module*)
>
> If multiple `Py_mod_exec` slots are specified, they are processed in the order they appear in the *m_slots* array.

See PEP 489 for more details on multi-phase initialization.

Low-level module creation functions

The following functions are called under the hood when using multi-phase initialization. They can be used directly, for example when creating module objects dynamically. Note that both `PyModule_FromDefAndSpec` and `PyModule_ExecDef` must be called to fully initialize a module.

PyObject * **PyModule_FromDefAndSpec**(*PyModuleDef* *def, *PyObject* *spec)

> Create a new module object, given the definition in *module* and the ModuleSpec *spec*. This behaves like *PyModule_FromDefAndSpec2()* with *module_api_version* set to `PYTHON_API_VERSION`.
>
> New in version 3.5.

PyObject * **PyModule_FromDefAndSpec2**(*PyModuleDef* *def, *PyObject* *spec, int *module_api_version*)

> Create a new module object, given the definition in *module* and the ModuleSpec *spec*, assuming the API version *module_api_version*. If that version does not match the version of the running interpreter, a `RuntimeWarning` is emitted.

Note: Most uses of this function should be using *PyModule_FromDefAndSpec()* instead; only use this if you are sure you need it.

> New in version 3.5.

int **PyModule_ExecDef**(*PyObject* *module, *PyModuleDef* *def)

> Process any execution slots (*Py_mod_exec*) given in *def*.
>
> New in version 3.5.

int **PyModule_SetDocString**(*PyObject* *module, const char *docstring)

> Set the docstring for *module* to *docstring*. This function is called automatically when creating a module from `PyModuleDef`, using either `PyModule_Create` or `PyModule_FromDefAndSpec`.

New in version 3.5.

int **PyModule_AddFunctions**(*PyObject *module*, *PyMethodDef *functions*)

>   Add the functions from the *NULL* terminated *functions* array to *module*. Refer to the *PyMethodDef* documentation for details on individual entries (due to the lack of a shared module namespace, module level "functions" implemented in C typically receive the module as their first parameter, making them similar to instance methods on Python classes). This function is called automatically when creating a module from PyModuleDef, using either `PyModule_Create` or `PyModule_FromDefAndSpec`.

New in version 3.5.

Support functions

The module initialization function (if using single phase initialization) or a function called from a module execution slot (if using multi-phase initialization), can use the following functions to help initialize the module state:

int **PyModule_AddObject**(*PyObject *module*, const char **name*, *PyObject *value*)

>   Add an object to *module* as *name*. This is a convenience function which can be used from the module's initialization function. This steals a reference to *value*. Return -1 on error, 0 on success.

int **PyModule_AddIntConstant**(*PyObject *module*, const char **name*, long *value*)

>   Add an integer constant to *module* as *name*. This convenience function can be used from the module's initialization function. Return -1 on error, 0 on success.

int **PyModule_AddStringConstant**(*PyObject *module*, const char **name*, const char **value*)

>   Add a string constant to *module* as *name*. This convenience function can be used from the module's initialization function. The string *value* must be *NULL*-terminated. Return -1 on error, 0 on success.

int **PyModule_AddIntMacro**(*PyObject *module*, macro)

>   Add an int constant to *module*. The name and the value are taken from *macro*. For example **PyModule_AddIntMacro**(module, AF_INET) adds the int constant *AF_INET* with the value of *AF_INET* to *module*. Return -1 on error, 0 on success.

int **PyModule_AddStringMacro**(*PyObject *module*, macro)

>   Add a string constant to *module*.

Module lookup

Single-phase initialization creates singleton modules that can be looked up in the context of the current interpreter. This allows the module object to be retrieved later with only a reference to the module definition.

These functions will not work on modules created using multi-phase initialization, since multiple such modules can be created from a single definition.

PyObject* **PyState_FindModule**(*PyModuleDef *def*)

>   Returns the module object that was created from *def* for the current interpreter. This method requires that the module object has been attached to the interpreter state with *PyState_AddModule()* beforehand. In case the corresponding module object is not found or has not been attached to the interpreter state yet, it returns *NULL*.

int **PyState_AddModule**(*PyObject *module*, *PyModuleDef *def*)

>   Attaches the module object passed to the function to the interpreter state. This allows the module object to be accessible via *PyState_FindModule()*.

>   Only effective on modules created using single-phase initialization.

>   New in version 3.3.

int **PyState_RemoveModule**(*PyModuleDef* *def*)
>   Removes the module object created from *def* from the interpreter state.

>   New in version 3.3.

8.6.3 Iterator Objects

Python provides two general-purpose iterator objects. The first, a sequence iterator, works with an arbitrary sequence supporting the __getitem__() method. The second works with a callable object and a sentinel value, calling the callable for each item in the sequence, and ending the iteration when the sentinel value is returned.

PyTypeObject **PySeqIter_Type**
>   Type object for iterator objects returned by *PySeqIter_New()* and the one-argument form of the iter() built-in function for built-in sequence types.

int **PySeqIter_Check**(op)
>   Return true if the type of *op* is *PySeqIter_Type*.

*PyObject** **PySeqIter_New**(*PyObject* *seq*)
>   *Return value: New reference.* Return an iterator that works with a general sequence object, *seq*. The iteration ends when the sequence raises IndexError for the subscripting operation.

PyTypeObject **PyCallIter_Type**
>   Type object for iterator objects returned by *PyCallIter_New()* and the two-argument form of the iter() built-in function.

int **PyCallIter_Check**(op)
>   Return true if the type of *op* is *PyCallIter_Type*.

*PyObject** **PyCallIter_New**(*PyObject* *callable*, *PyObject* *sentinel*)
>   *Return value: New reference.* Return a new iterator. The first parameter, *callable*, can be any Python callable object that can be called with no parameters; each call to it should return the next item in the iteration. When *callable* returns a value equal to *sentinel*, the iteration will be terminated.

8.6.4 Descriptor Objects

"Descriptors" are objects that describe some attribute of an object. They are found in the dictionary of type objects.

PyTypeObject **PyProperty_Type**
>   The type object for the built-in descriptor types.

*PyObject** **PyDescr_NewGetSet**(*PyTypeObject* *type*, struct *PyGetSetDef* *getset*)
>   *Return value: New reference.*

*PyObject** **PyDescr_NewMember**(*PyTypeObject* *type*, struct *PyMemberDef* *meth*)
>   *Return value: New reference.*

*PyObject** **PyDescr_NewMethod**(*PyTypeObject* *type*, struct *PyMethodDef* *meth*)
>   *Return value: New reference.*

*PyObject** **PyDescr_NewWrapper**(*PyTypeObject* *type*, struct wrapperbase *wrapper*, void *wrapped*)
>   *Return value: New reference.*

*PyObject** **PyDescr_NewClassMethod**(*PyTypeObject* *type*, *PyMethodDef* *method*)
>   *Return value: New reference.*

int **PyDescr_IsData**(*PyObject* *descr*)
>   Return true if the descriptor objects *descr* describes a data attribute, or false if it describes a method. *descr* must be a descriptor object; there is no error checking.

---

*PyObject** **PyWrapper_New**(*PyObject* *, *PyObject* *)
    Return value: New reference.

8.6.5 Slice Objects

PyTypeObject **PySlice_Type**
    The type object for slice objects. This is the same as `slice` in the Python layer.

int **PySlice_Check**(*PyObject* *ob*)
    Return true if *ob* is a slice object; *ob* must not be *NULL*.

*PyObject** **PySlice_New**(*PyObject* *start*, *PyObject* *stop*, *PyObject* *step*)
    Return value: New reference. Return a new slice object with the given values. The *start*, *stop*, and *step* parameters are used as the values of the slice object attributes of the same names. Any of the values may be *NULL*, in which case the `None` will be used for the corresponding attribute. Return *NULL* if the new object could not be allocated.

int **PySlice_GetIndices**(*PyObject* *slice*, Py_ssize_t *length*, Py_ssize_t *start*, Py_ssize_t *stop*,
                    Py_ssize_t *step*)
    Retrieve the start, stop and step indices from the slice object *slice*, assuming a sequence of length *length*. Treats indices greater than *length* as errors.

    Returns 0 on success and -1 on error with no exception set (unless one of the indices was not `None` and failed to be converted to an integer, in which case -1 is returned with an exception set).

    You probably do not want to use this function.

    Changed in version 3.2: The parameter type for the *slice* parameter was `PySliceObject*` before.

int **PySlice_GetIndicesEx**(*PyObject* *slice*, Py_ssize_t *length*, Py_ssize_t *start*, Py_ssize_t *stop*,
                      Py_ssize_t *step*, Py_ssize_t *slicelength*)
    Usable replacement for *PySlice_GetIndices()*. Retrieve the start, stop, and step indices from the slice object *slice* assuming a sequence of length *length*, and store the length of the slice in *slicelength*. Out of bounds indices are clipped in a manner consistent with the handling of normal slices.

    Returns 0 on success and -1 on error with exception set.

    Changed in version 3.2: The parameter type for the *slice* parameter was `PySliceObject*` before.

8.6.6 Ellipsis Object

PyObject ***Py_Ellipsis**
    The Python `Ellipsis` object. This object has no methods. It needs to be treated just like any other object with respect to reference counts. Like *Py_None* it is a singleton object.

8.6.7 MemoryView objects

A `memoryview` object exposes the C level *buffer interface* as a Python object which can then be passed around like any other object.

PyObject ***PyMemoryView_FromObject**(*PyObject* *obj*)
    Create a memoryview object from an object that provides the buffer interface. If *obj* supports writable buffer exports, the memoryview object will be read/write, otherwise it may be either read-only or read/write at the discretion of the exporter.

PyObject ***PyMemoryView_FromMemory**(char *mem*, Py_ssize_t *size*, int *flags*)
    Create a memoryview object using *mem* as the underlying buffer. *flags* can be one of `PyBUF_READ` or `PyBUF_WRITE`.

New in version 3.3.

PyObject ***PyMemoryView_FromBuffer**(*Py_buffer* *view)
> Create a memoryview object wrapping the given buffer structure *view*. For simple byte buffers, *PyMemoryView_FromMemory()* is the preferred function.

PyObject ***PyMemoryView_GetContiguous**(*PyObject* *obj, int *buffertype*, char *order*)
> Create a memoryview object to a *contiguous* chunk of memory (in either 'C' or 'F'ortran *order*) from an object that defines the buffer interface. If memory is contiguous, the memoryview object points to the original memory. Otherwise, a copy is made and the memoryview points to a new bytes object.

int **PyMemoryView_Check**(*PyObject* *obj)
> Return true if the object *obj* is a memoryview object. It is not currently allowed to create subclasses of memoryview.

Py_buffer ***PyMemoryView_GET_BUFFER**(*PyObject* *mview)
> Return a pointer to the memoryview's private copy of the exporter's buffer. *mview* **must** be a memoryview instance; this macro doesn't check its type, you must do it yourself or you will risk crashes.

Py_buffer ***PyMemoryView_GET_BASE**(*PyObject* *mview)
> Return either a pointer to the exporting object that the memoryview is based on or *NULL* if the memoryview has been created by one of the functions *PyMemoryView_FromMemory()* or *PyMemoryView_FromBuffer()*. *mview* **must** be a memoryview instance.

8.6.8 Weak Reference Objects

Python supports *weak references* as first-class objects. There are two specific object types which directly implement weak references. The first is a simple reference object, and the second acts as a proxy for the original object as much as it can.

int **PyWeakref_Check**(ob)
> Return true if *ob* is either a reference or proxy object.

int **PyWeakref_CheckRef**(ob)
> Return true if *ob* is a reference object.

int **PyWeakref_CheckProxy**(ob)
> Return true if *ob* is a proxy object.

PyObject* **PyWeakref_NewRef**(*PyObject* *ob, *PyObject* *callback)
> *Return value: New reference.* Return a weak reference object for the object *ob*. This will always return a new reference, but is not guaranteed to create a new object; an existing reference object may be returned. The second parameter, *callback*, can be a callable object that receives notification when *ob* is garbage collected; it should accept a single parameter, which will be the weak reference object itself. *callback* may also be **None** or *NULL*. If *ob* is not a weakly-referencable object, or if *callback* is not callable, **None**, or *NULL*, this will return *NULL* and raise **TypeError**.

PyObject* **PyWeakref_NewProxy**(*PyObject* *ob, *PyObject* *callback)
> *Return value: New reference.* Return a weak reference proxy object for the object *ob*. This will always return a new reference, but is not guaranteed to create a new object; an existing proxy object may be returned. The second parameter, *callback*, can be a callable object that receives notification when *ob* is garbage collected; it should accept a single parameter, which will be the weak reference object itself. *callback* may also be **None** or *NULL*. If *ob* is not a weakly-referencable object, or if *callback* is not callable, **None**, or *NULL*, this will return *NULL* and raise **TypeError**.

PyObject* **PyWeakref_GetObject**(*PyObject* *ref)
> *Return value: Borrowed reference.* Return the referenced object from a weak reference, *ref*. If the referent is no longer live, returns **Py_None**.

Note: This function returns a **borrowed reference** to the referenced object. This means that you should always call `Py_INCREF()` on the object except if you know that it cannot be destroyed while you are still using it.

PyObject* **PyWeakref_GET_OBJECT**(*PyObject *ref*)
> *Return value: Borrowed reference.* Similar to *PyWeakref_GetObject()*, but implemented as a macro that does no error checking.

8.6.9 Capsules

Refer to using-capsules for more information on using these objects.

PyCapsule
> This subtype of *PyObject* represents an opaque value, useful for C extension modules who need to pass an opaque value (as a **void*** pointer) through Python code to other C code. It is often used to make a C function pointer defined in one module available to other modules, so the regular import mechanism can be used to access C APIs defined in dynamically loaded modules.

PyCapsule_Destructor
> The type of a destructor callback for a capsule. Defined as:

```
typedef void (*PyCapsule_Destructor)(PyObject *);
```

> See *PyCapsule_New()* for the semantics of PyCapsule_Destructor callbacks.

int **PyCapsule_CheckExact**(*PyObject *p*)
> Return true if its argument is a *PyCapsule*.

PyObject* **PyCapsule_New**(void **pointer*, const char **name*, *PyCapsule_Destructor destructor*)
> *Return value: New reference.* Create a *PyCapsule* encapsulating the *pointer*. The *pointer* argument may not be *NULL*.

> On failure, set an exception and return *NULL*.

> The *name* string may either be *NULL* or a pointer to a valid C string. If non-*NULL*, this string must outlive the capsule. (Though it is permitted to free it inside the *destructor*.)

> If the *destructor* argument is not *NULL*, it will be called with the capsule as its argument when it is destroyed.

> If this capsule will be stored as an attribute of a module, the *name* should be specified as **modulename. attributename**. This will enable other modules to import the capsule using *PyCapsule_Import()*.

void* **PyCapsule_GetPointer**(*PyObject *capsule*, const char **name*)
> Retrieve the *pointer* stored in the capsule. On failure, set an exception and return *NULL*.

> The *name* parameter must compare exactly to the name stored in the capsule. If the name stored in the capsule is *NULL*, the *name* passed in must also be *NULL*. Python uses the C function **strcmp()** to compare capsule names.

PyCapsule_Destructor **PyCapsule_GetDestructor**(*PyObject *capsule*)
> Return the current destructor stored in the capsule. On failure, set an exception and return *NULL*.

> It is legal for a capsule to have a *NULL* destructor. This makes a *NULL* return code somewhat ambiguous; use *PyCapsule_IsValid()* or *PyErr_Occurred()* to disambiguate.

void* **PyCapsule_GetContext**(*PyObject *capsule*)
> Return the current context stored in the capsule. On failure, set an exception and return *NULL*.

It is legal for a capsule to have a *NULL* context. This makes a *NULL* return code somewhat ambiguous; use *PyCapsule_IsValid()* or *PyErr_Occurred()* to disambiguate.

const char* **PyCapsule_GetName**(*PyObject* **capsule*)
> Return the current name stored in the capsule. On failure, set an exception and return *NULL*.

> It is legal for a capsule to have a *NULL* name. This makes a *NULL* return code somewhat ambiguous; use *PyCapsule_IsValid()* or *PyErr_Occurred()* to disambiguate.

void* **PyCapsule_Import**(const char **name*, int *no_block*)
> Import a pointer to a C object from a capsule attribute in a module. The *name* parameter should specify the full name to the attribute, as in **module.attribute**. The *name* stored in the capsule must match this string exactly. If *no_block* is true, import the module without blocking (using *PyImport_ImportModuleNoBlock()*). If *no_block* is false, import the module conventionally (using *PyImport_ImportModule()*).

> Return the capsule's internal *pointer* on success. On failure, set an exception and return *NULL*. However, if *PyCapsule_Import()* failed to import the module, and *no_block* was true, no exception is set.

int **PyCapsule_IsValid**(*PyObject* **capsule*, const char **name*)
> Determines whether or not *capsule* is a valid capsule. A valid capsule is non-*NULL*, passes *PyCapsule_CheckExact()*, has a non-*NULL* pointer stored in it, and its internal name matches the *name* parameter. (See *PyCapsule_GetPointer()* for information on how capsule names are compared.)

> In other words, if *PyCapsule_IsValid()* returns a true value, calls to any of the accessors (any function starting with **PyCapsule_Get()**) are guaranteed to succeed.

> Return a nonzero value if the object is valid and matches the name passed in. Return 0 otherwise. This function will not fail.

int **PyCapsule_SetContext**(*PyObject* **capsule*, void **context*)
> Set the context pointer inside *capsule* to *context*.

> Return 0 on success. Return nonzero and set an exception on failure.

int **PyCapsule_SetDestructor**(*PyObject* **capsule*, *PyCapsule_Destructor destructor*)
> Set the destructor inside *capsule* to *destructor*.

> Return 0 on success. Return nonzero and set an exception on failure.

int **PyCapsule_SetName**(*PyObject* **capsule*, const char **name*)
> Set the name inside *capsule* to *name*. If non-*NULL*, the name must outlive the capsule. If the previous *name* stored in the capsule was not *NULL*, no attempt is made to free it.

> Return 0 on success. Return nonzero and set an exception on failure.

int **PyCapsule_SetPointer**(*PyObject* **capsule*, void **pointer*)
> Set the void pointer inside *capsule* to *pointer*. The pointer may not be *NULL*.

> Return 0 on success. Return nonzero and set an exception on failure.

8.6.10 Generator Objects

Generator objects are what Python uses to implement generator iterators. They are normally created by iterating over a function that yields values, rather than explicitly calling *PyGen_New()* or *PyGen_NewWithQualName()*.

PyGenObject
> The C structure used for generator objects.

PyTypeObject **PyGen_Type**
> The type object corresponding to generator objects.

int **PyGen_Check**(*PyObject* **ob*)

> Return true if *ob* is a generator object; *ob* must not be *NULL*.

int **PyGen_CheckExact**(*PyObject* **ob*)

> Return true if *ob*'s type is *PyGen_Type*; *ob* must not be *NULL*.

PyObject* **PyGen_New**(*PyFrameObject* **frame*)

> *Return value: New reference.* Create and return a new generator object based on the *frame* object. A reference to *frame* is stolen by this function. The argument must not be *NULL*.

PyObject* **PyGen_NewWithQualName**(*PyFrameObject* **frame*, *PyObject* **name*, *PyObject* **qualname*)

> *Return value: New reference.* Create and return a new generator object based on the *frame* object, with __name__ and __qualname__ set to *name* and *qualname*. A reference to *frame* is stolen by this function. The *frame* argument must not be *NULL*.

8.6.11 Coroutine Objects

New in version 3.5.

Coroutine objects are what functions declared with an **async** keyword return.

PyCoroObject

> The C structure used for coroutine objects.

PyTypeObject **PyCoro_Type**

> The type object corresponding to coroutine objects.

int **PyCoro_CheckExact**(*PyObject* **ob*)

> Return true if *ob*'s type is *PyCoro_Type*; *ob* must not be *NULL*.

PyObject* **PyCoro_New**(*PyFrameObject* **frame*, *PyObject* **name*, *PyObject* **qualname*)

> *Return value: New reference.* Create and return a new coroutine object based on the *frame* object, with __name__ and __qualname__ set to *name* and *qualname*. A reference to *frame* is stolen by this function. The *frame* argument must not be *NULL*.

8.6.12 DateTime Objects

Various date and time objects are supplied by the **datetime** module. Before using any of these functions, the header file **datetime.h** must be included in your source (note that this is not included by **Python.h**), and the macro **PyDateTime_IMPORT** must be invoked, usually as part of the module initialisation function. The macro puts a pointer to a C structure into a static variable, **PyDateTimeAPI**, that is used by the following macros.

Type-check macros:

int **PyDate_Check**(*PyObject* **ob*)

> Return true if *ob* is of type **PyDateTime_DateType** or a subtype of **PyDateTime_DateType**. *ob* must not be *NULL*.

int **PyDate_CheckExact**(*PyObject* **ob*)

> Return true if *ob* is of type **PyDateTime_DateType**. *ob* must not be *NULL*.

int **PyDateTime_Check**(*PyObject* **ob*)

> Return true if *ob* is of type **PyDateTime_DateTimeType** or a subtype of **PyDateTime_DateTimeType**. *ob* must not be *NULL*.

int **PyDateTime_CheckExact**(*PyObject* **ob*)

> Return true if *ob* is of type **PyDateTime_DateTimeType**. *ob* must not be *NULL*.

int **PyTime_Check**(*PyObject* *ob*)

> Return true if *ob* is of type PyDateTime_TimeType or a subtype of PyDateTime_TimeType. *ob* must not be *NULL*.

int **PyTime_CheckExact**(*PyObject* *ob*)

> Return true if *ob* is of type PyDateTime_TimeType. *ob* must not be *NULL*.

int **PyDelta_Check**(*PyObject* *ob*)

> Return true if *ob* is of type PyDateTime_DeltaType or a subtype of PyDateTime_DeltaType. *ob* must not be *NULL*.

int **PyDelta_CheckExact**(*PyObject* *ob*)

> Return true if *ob* is of type PyDateTime_DeltaType. *ob* must not be *NULL*.

int **PyTZInfo_Check**(*PyObject* *ob*)

> Return true if *ob* is of type PyDateTime_TZInfoType or a subtype of PyDateTime_TZInfoType. *ob* must not be *NULL*.

int **PyTZInfo_CheckExact**(*PyObject* *ob*)

> Return true if *ob* is of type PyDateTime_TZInfoType. *ob* must not be *NULL*.

Macros to create objects:

PyObject* **PyDate_FromDate**(int *year*, int *month*, int *day*)

> *Return value: New reference.* Return a datetime.date object with the specified year, month and day.

PyObject* **PyDateTime_FromDateAndTime**(int *year*, int *month*, int *day*, int *hour*, int *minute*, int *second*, int *usecond*)

> *Return value: New reference.* Return a datetime.datetime object with the specified year, month, day, hour, minute, second and microsecond.

PyObject* **PyTime_FromTime**(int *hour*, int *minute*, int *second*, int *usecond*)

> *Return value: New reference.* Return a datetime.time object with the specified hour, minute, second and microsecond.

PyObject* **PyDelta_FromDSU**(int *days*, int *seconds*, int *useconds*)

> *Return value: New reference.* Return a datetime.timedelta object representing the given number of days, seconds and microseconds. Normalization is performed so that the resulting number of microseconds and seconds lie in the ranges documented for datetime.timedelta objects.

Macros to extract fields from date objects. The argument must be an instance of PyDateTime_Date, including subclasses (such as PyDateTime_DateTime). The argument must not be *NULL*, and the type is not checked:

int **PyDateTime_GET_YEAR**(PyDateTime_Date *o*)

> Return the year, as a positive int.

int **PyDateTime_GET_MONTH**(PyDateTime_Date *o*)

> Return the month, as an int from 1 through 12.

int **PyDateTime_GET_DAY**(PyDateTime_Date *o*)

> Return the day, as an int from 1 through 31.

Macros to extract fields from datetime objects. The argument must be an instance of PyDateTime_DateTime, including subclasses. The argument must not be *NULL*, and the type is not checked:

int **PyDateTime_DATE_GET_HOUR**(PyDateTime_DateTime *o*)

> Return the hour, as an int from 0 through 23.

int **PyDateTime_DATE_GET_MINUTE**(PyDateTime_DateTime *o*)

> Return the minute, as an int from 0 through 59.

int **PyDateTime_DATE_GET_SECOND**(PyDateTime_DateTime *o*)

> Return the second, as an int from 0 through 59.

int **PyDateTime_DATE_GET_MICROSECOND**(PyDateTime_DateTime *o*)
> Return the microsecond, as an int from 0 through 999999.

Macros to extract fields from time objects. The argument must be an instance of `PyDateTime_Time`, including subclasses. The argument must not be *NULL*, and the type is not checked:

int **PyDateTime_TIME_GET_HOUR**(PyDateTime_Time *o*)
> Return the hour, as an int from 0 through 23.

int **PyDateTime_TIME_GET_MINUTE**(PyDateTime_Time *o*)
> Return the minute, as an int from 0 through 59.

int **PyDateTime_TIME_GET_SECOND**(PyDateTime_Time *o*)
> Return the second, as an int from 0 through 59.

int **PyDateTime_TIME_GET_MICROSECOND**(PyDateTime_Time *o*)
> Return the microsecond, as an int from 0 through 999999.

Macros to extract fields from time delta objects. The argument must be an instance of `PyDateTime_Delta`, including subclasses. The argument must not be *NULL*, and the type is not checked:

int **PyDateTime_DELTA_GET_DAYS**(PyDateTime_Delta *o*)
> Return the number of days, as an int from -999999999 to 999999999.
>
> New in version 3.3.

int **PyDateTime_DELTA_GET_SECONDS**(PyDateTime_Delta *o*)
> Return the number of seconds, as an int from 0 through 86399.
>
> New in version 3.3.

int **PyDateTime_DELTA_GET_MICROSECONDS**(PyDateTime_Delta *o*)
> Return the number of microseconds, as an int from 0 through 999999.
>
> New in version 3.3.

Macros for the convenience of modules implementing the DB API:

*PyObject** **PyDateTime_FromTimestamp**(*PyObject* *args*)
> *Return value: New reference.* Create and return a new `datetime.datetime` object given an argument tuple suitable for passing to `datetime.datetime.fromtimestamp()`.

*PyObject** **PyDate_FromTimestamp**(*PyObject* *args*)
> *Return value: New reference.* Create and return a new `datetime.date` object given an argument tuple suitable for passing to `datetime.date.fromtimestamp()`.

INITIALIZATION, FINALIZATION, AND THREADS

9.1 Initializing and finalizing the interpreter

void **Py_Initialize**()

Initialize the Python interpreter. In an application embedding Python, this should be called before using any other Python/C API functions; with the exception of *Py_SetProgramName()*, *Py_SetPythonHome()* and *Py_SetPath()*. This initializes the table of loaded modules (sys.modules), and creates the fundamental modules builtins, __main__ and sys. It also initializes the module search path (sys.path). It does not set sys.argv; use *PySys_SetArgvEx()* for that. This is a no-op when called for a second time (without calling *Py_FinalizeEx()* first). There is no return value; it is a fatal error if the initialization fails.

Note: On Windows, changes the console mode from O_TEXT to O_BINARY, which will also affect non-Python uses of the console using the C Runtime.

---

void **Py_InitializeEx**(int *initsigs*)

This function works like *Py_Initialize()* if *initsigs* is 1. If *initsigs* is 0, it skips initialization registration of signal handlers, which might be useful when Python is embedded.

int **Py_IsInitialized**()

Return true (nonzero) when the Python interpreter has been initialized, false (zero) if not. After *Py_FinalizeEx()* is called, this returns false until *Py_Initialize()* is called again.

int **Py_FinalizeEx**()

Undo all initializations made by *Py_Initialize()* and subsequent use of Python/C API functions, and destroy all sub-interpreters (see *Py_NewInterpreter()* below) that were created and not yet destroyed since the last call to *Py_Initialize()*. Ideally, this frees all memory allocated by the Python interpreter. This is a no-op when called for a second time (without calling *Py_Initialize()* again first). Normally the return value is 0. If there were errors during finalization (flushing buffered data), -1 is returned.

This function is provided for a number of reasons. An embedding application might want to restart Python without having to restart the application itself. An application that has loaded the Python interpreter from a dynamically loadable library (or DLL) might want to free all memory allocated by Python before unloading the DLL. During a hunt for memory leaks in an application a developer might want to free all memory allocated by Python before exiting from the application.

Bugs and caveats: The destruction of modules and objects in modules is done in random order; this may cause destructors (__del__() methods) to fail when they depend on other objects (even functions) or modules. Dynamically loaded extension modules loaded by Python are not unloaded. Small amounts of memory allocated by the Python interpreter may not be freed (if you find a leak, please report it). Memory tied up in circular references between objects is not freed. Some memory allocated by extension modules may not be freed. Some extensions may not work properly if their initialization routine is called more than once; this can happen if an application calls *Py_Initialize()* and *Py_FinalizeEx()* more than once.

New in version 3.6.

void **Py_Finalize**()
This is a backwards-compatible version of *Py_FinalizeEx()* that disregards the return value.

9.2 Process-wide parameters

int **Py_SetStandardStreamEncoding**(const char *encoding*, const char *errors*)
This function should be called before *Py_Initialize()*, if it is called at all. It specifies which encoding and error handling to use with standard IO, with the same meanings as in **str.encode()**.

It overrides **PYTHONIOENCODING** values, and allows embedding code to control IO encoding when the environment variable does not work.

encoding and/or **errors** may be NULL to use **PYTHONIOENCODING** and/or default values (depending on other settings).

Note that **sys.stderr** always uses the "backslashreplace" error handler, regardless of this (or any other) setting.

If *Py_FinalizeEx()* is called, this function will need to be called again in order to affect subsequent calls to *Py_Initialize()*.

Returns 0 if successful, a nonzero value on error (e.g. calling after the interpreter has already been initialized).

New in version 3.4.

void **Py_SetProgramName**(wchar_t *name*)
This function should be called before *Py_Initialize()* is called for the first time, if it is called at all. It tells the interpreter the value of the **argv[0]** argument to the **main()** function of the program (converted to wide characters). This is used by *Py_GetPath()* and some other functions below to find the Python run-time libraries relative to the interpreter executable. The default value is 'python'. The argument should point to a zero-terminated wide character string in static storage whose contents will not change for the duration of the program's execution. No code in the Python interpreter will change the contents of this storage.

Use *Py_DecodeLocale()* to decode a bytes string to get a **wchar_*** string.

wchar* **Py_GetProgramName**()
Return the program name set with *Py_SetProgramName()*, or the default. The returned string points into static storage; the caller should not modify its value.

wchar_t* **Py_GetPrefix**()
Return the *prefix* for installed platform-independent files. This is derived through a number of complicated rules from the program name set with *Py_SetProgramName()* and some environment variables; for example, if the program name is '/usr/local/bin/python', the prefix is '/usr/local'. The returned string points into static storage; the caller should not modify its value. This corresponds to the **prefix** variable in the top-level **Makefile** and the **--prefix** argument to the **configure** script at build time. The value is available to Python code as **sys.prefix**. It is only useful on Unix. See also the next function.

wchar_t* **Py_GetExecPrefix**()
Return the *exec-prefix* for installed platform-*dependent* files. This is derived through a number of complicated rules from the program name set with *Py_SetProgramName()* and some environment variables; for example, if the program name is '/usr/local/bin/python', the exec-prefix is '/usr/local'. The returned string points into static storage; the caller should not modify its value. This

The Python/C API, Release 3.6.4

corresponds to the **exec_prefix** variable in the top-level **Makefile** and the **--exec-prefix** argument to the **configure** script at build time. The value is available to Python code as `sys.exec_prefix`. It is only useful on Unix.

Background: The exec-prefix differs from the prefix when platform dependent files (such as executables and shared libraries) are installed in a different directory tree. In a typical installation, platform dependent files may be installed in the `/usr/local/plat` subtree while platform independent may be installed in `/usr/local`.

Generally speaking, a platform is a combination of hardware and software families, e.g. Sparc machines running the Solaris 2.x operating system are considered the same platform, but Intel machines running Solaris 2.x are another platform, and Intel machines running Linux are yet another platform. Different major revisions of the same operating system generally also form different platforms. Non-Unix operating systems are a different story; the installation strategies on those systems are so different that the prefix and exec-prefix are meaningless, and set to the empty string. Note that compiled Python bytecode files are platform independent (but not independent from the Python version by which they were compiled!).

System administrators will know how to configure the **mount** or **automount** programs to share `/usr/local` between platforms while having `/usr/local/plat` be a different filesystem for each platform.

wchar_t* **Py_GetProgramFullPath**()
> Return the full program name of the Python executable; this is computed as a side-effect of deriving the default module search path from the program name (set by *Py_SetProgramName()* above). The returned string points into static storage; the caller should not modify its value. The value is available to Python code as `sys.executable`.

wchar_t* **Py_GetPath**()
> Return the default module search path; this is computed from the program name (set by *Py_SetProgramName()* above) and some environment variables. The returned string consists of a series of directory names separated by a platform dependent delimiter character. The delimiter character is `':'` on Unix and Mac OS X, `';'` on Windows. The returned string points into static storage; the caller should not modify its value. The list `sys.path` is initialized with this value on interpreter startup; it can be (and usually is) modified later to change the search path for loading modules.

void **Py_SetPath**(const wchar_t *)
> Set the default module search path. If this function is called before *Py_Initialize()*, then *Py_GetPath()* won't attempt to compute a default search path but uses the one provided instead. This is useful if Python is embedded by an application that has full knowledge of the location of all modules. The path components should be separated by the platform dependent delimiter character, which is `':'` on Unix and Mac OS X, `';'` on Windows.

> This also causes `sys.executable` to be set only to the raw program name (see *Py_SetProgramName()*) and for `sys.prefix` and `sys.exec_prefix` to be empty. It is up to the caller to modify these if required after calling *Py_Initialize()*.

> Use *Py_DecodeLocale()* to decode a bytes string to get a `wchar_*` string.

> The path argument is copied internally, so the caller may free it after the call completes.

const char* **Py_GetVersion**()
> Return the version of this Python interpreter. This is a string that looks something like

```
"3.0a5+ (py3k:63103M, May 12 2008, 00:53:55) \n[GCC 4.2.3]"
```

> The first word (up to the first space character) is the current Python version; the first three characters are the major and minor version separated by a period. The returned string points into static storage; the caller should not modify its value. The value is available to Python code as `sys.version`.

const char* **Py_GetPlatform**()
> Return the platform identifier for the current platform. On Unix, this is formed from the "official"

name of the operating system, converted to lower case, followed by the major revision number; e.g., for Solaris 2.x, which is also known as SunOS 5.x, the value is `'sunos5'`. On Mac OS X, it is `'darwin'`. On Windows, it is `'win'`. The returned string points into static storage; the caller should not modify its value. The value is available to Python code as `sys.platform`.

const char* **Py_GetCopyright**()

Return the official copyright string for the current Python version, for example

`'Copyright 1991-1995 Stichting Mathematisch Centrum, Amsterdam'`

The returned string points into static storage; the caller should not modify its value. The value is available to Python code as `sys.copyright`.

const char* **Py_GetCompiler**()

Return an indication of the compiler used to build the current Python version, in square brackets, for example:

```
"[GCC 2.7.2.2]"
```

The returned string points into static storage; the caller should not modify its value. The value is available to Python code as part of the variable `sys.version`.

const char* **Py_GetBuildInfo**()

Return information about the sequence number and build date and time of the current Python interpreter instance, for example

```
"#67, Aug  1 1997, 22:34:28"
```

The returned string points into static storage; the caller should not modify its value. The value is available to Python code as part of the variable `sys.version`.

void **PySys_SetArgvEx**(int *argc*, wchar_t **argv*, int *updatepath*)

Set `sys.argv` based on *argc* and *argv*. These parameters are similar to those passed to the program's **main()** function with the difference that the first entry should refer to the script file to be executed rather than the executable hosting the Python interpreter. If there isn't a script that will be run, the first entry in *argv* can be an empty string. If this function fails to initialize `sys.argv`, a fatal condition is signalled using *Py_FatalError()*.

If *updatepath* is zero, this is all the function does. If *updatepath* is non-zero, the function also modifies `sys.path` according to the following algorithm:

- If the name of an existing script is passed in `argv[0]`, the absolute path of the directory where the script is located is prepended to `sys.path`.
- Otherwise (that is, if *argc* is 0 or `argv[0]` doesn't point to an existing file name), an empty string is prepended to `sys.path`, which is the same as prepending the current working directory (`"."`).

Use *Py_DecodeLocale()* to decode a bytes string to get a `wchar_*` string.

Note: It is recommended that applications embedding the Python interpreter for purposes other than executing a single script pass 0 as *updatepath*, and update `sys.path` themselves if desired. See CVE-2008-5983.

On versions before 3.1.3, you can achieve the same effect by manually popping the first `sys.path` element after having called *PySys_SetArgv()*, for example using:

```
PyRun_SimpleString("import sys; sys.path.pop(0)\n");
```

New in version 3.1.3.

void **PySys_SetArgv**(int *argc*, wchar_t **argv*)

> This function works like *PySys_SetArgvEx()* with *updatepath* set to 1 unless the **python** interpreter was started with the -I.
>
> Use *Py_DecodeLocale()* to decode a bytes string to get a wchar_* string.
>
> Changed in version 3.4: The *updatepath* value depends on -I.

void **Py_SetPythonHome**(wchar_t **home*)

> Set the default "home" directory, that is, the location of the standard Python libraries. See PYTHONHOME for the meaning of the argument string.
>
> The argument should point to a zero-terminated character string in static storage whose contents will not change for the duration of the program's execution. No code in the Python interpreter will change the contents of this storage.
>
> Use *Py_DecodeLocale()* to decode a bytes string to get a wchar_* string.

w_char* **Py_GetPythonHome**()

> Return the default "home", that is, the value set by a previous call to *Py_SetPythonHome()*, or the value of the PYTHONHOME environment variable if it is set.

9.3 Thread State and the Global Interpreter Lock

The Python interpreter is not fully thread-safe. In order to support multi-threaded Python programs, there's a global lock, called the *global interpreter lock* or *GIL*, that must be held by the current thread before it can safely access Python objects. Without the lock, even the simplest operations could cause problems in a multi-threaded program: for example, when two threads simultaneously increment the reference count of the same object, the reference count could end up being incremented only once instead of twice.

Therefore, the rule exists that only the thread that has acquired the *GIL* may operate on Python objects or call Python/C API functions. In order to emulate concurrency of execution, the interpreter regularly tries to switch threads (see **sys.setswitchinterval()**). The lock is also released around potentially blocking I/O operations like reading or writing a file, so that other Python threads can run in the meantime.

The Python interpreter keeps some thread-specific bookkeeping information inside a data structure called *PyThreadState*. There's also one global variable pointing to the current *PyThreadState*: it can be retrieved using *PyThreadState_Get()*.

9.3.1 Releasing the GIL from extension code

Most extension code manipulating the *GIL* has the following simple structure:

```
Save the thread state in a local variable.
Release the global interpreter lock.
... Do some blocking I/O operation ...
Reacquire the global interpreter lock.
Restore the thread state from the local variable.
```

This is so common that a pair of macros exists to simplify it:

```
Py_BEGIN_ALLOW_THREADS
... Do some blocking I/O operation ...
Py_END_ALLOW_THREADS
```

The *Py_BEGIN_ALLOW_THREADS* macro opens a new block and declares a hidden local variable; the *Py_END_ALLOW_THREADS* macro closes the block. These two macros are still available when Python is compiled without thread support (they simply have an empty expansion).

When thread support is enabled, the block above expands to the following code:

```
PyThreadState *_save;

_save = PyEval_SaveThread();
...Do some blocking I/O operation...
PyEval_RestoreThread(_save);
```

Here is how these functions work: the global interpreter lock is used to protect the pointer to the current thread state. When releasing the lock and saving the thread state, the current thread state pointer must be retrieved before the lock is released (since another thread could immediately acquire the lock and store its own thread state in the global variable). Conversely, when acquiring the lock and restoring the thread state, the lock must be acquired before storing the thread state pointer.

Note: Calling system I/O functions is the most common use case for releasing the GIL, but it can also be useful before calling long-running computations which don't need access to Python objects, such as compression or cryptographic functions operating over memory buffers. For example, the standard `zlib` and `hashlib` modules release the GIL when compressing or hashing data.

9.3.2 Non-Python created threads

When threads are created using the dedicated Python APIs (such as the `threading` module), a thread state is automatically associated to them and the code showed above is therefore correct. However, when threads are created from C (for example by a third-party library with its own thread management), they don't hold the GIL, nor is there a thread state structure for them.

If you need to call Python code from these threads (often this will be part of a callback API provided by the aforementioned third-party library), you must first register these threads with the interpreter by creating a thread state data structure, then acquiring the GIL, and finally storing their thread state pointer, before you can start using the Python/C API. When you are done, you should reset the thread state pointer, release the GIL, and finally free the thread state data structure.

The *PyGILState_Ensure()* and *PyGILState_Release()* functions do all of the above automatically. The typical idiom for calling into Python from a C thread is:

```
PyGILState_STATE gstate;
gstate = PyGILState_Ensure();

/* Perform Python actions here. */
result = CallSomeFunction();
/* evaluate result or handle exception */

/* Release the thread. No Python API allowed beyond this point. */
PyGILState_Release(gstate);
```

Note that the `PyGILState_*()` functions assume there is only one global interpreter (created automatically by *Py_Initialize()*). Python supports the creation of additional interpreters (using *Py_NewInterpreter()*), but mixing multiple interpreters and the `PyGILState_*()` API is unsupported.

Another important thing to note about threads is their behaviour in the face of the C `fork()` call. On most systems with `fork()`, after a process forks only the thread that issued the fork will exist. That also means any locks held by other threads will never be released. Python solves this for `os.fork()` by acquiring the locks it uses internally before the fork, and releasing them afterwards. In addition, it resets any lock-objects in the child. When extending or embedding Python, there is no way to inform Python of additional (non-Python) locks that need to be acquired before or reset after a fork. OS facilities such as `pthread_atfork()` would need to be used to accomplish the same thing. Additionally, when extending or embedding Python, calling `fork()` directly rather than through `os.fork()` (and returning to or calling into Python) may result in a deadlock by one of Python's internal locks being held by a thread that is defunct after the fork. *PyOS_AfterFork()* tries to reset the necessary locks, but is not always able to.

9.3.3 High-level API

These are the most commonly used types and functions when writing C extension code, or when embedding the Python interpreter:

PyInterpreterState

> This data structure represents the state shared by a number of cooperating threads. Threads belonging to the same interpreter share their module administration and a few other internal items. There are no public members in this structure.
>
> Threads belonging to different interpreters initially share nothing, except process state like available memory, open file descriptors and such. The global interpreter lock is also shared by all threads, regardless of to which interpreter they belong.

PyThreadState

> This data structure represents the state of a single thread. The only public data member is *PyInterpreterState* *`interp`, which points to this thread's interpreter state.

void **PyEval_InitThreads**()

> Initialize and acquire the global interpreter lock. It should be called in the main thread before creating a second thread or engaging in any other thread operations such as `PyEval_ReleaseThread(tstate)`. It is not needed before calling *PyEval_SaveThread()* or *PyEval_RestoreThread()*.
>
> This is a no-op when called for a second time.
>
> Changed in version 3.2: This function cannot be called before *Py_Initialize()* anymore.

Note: When only the main thread exists, no GIL operations are needed. This is a common situation (most Python programs do not use threads), and the lock operations slow the interpreter down a bit. Therefore, the lock is not created initially. This situation is equivalent to having acquired the lock: when there is only a single thread, all object accesses are safe. Therefore, when this function initializes the global interpreter lock, it also acquires it. Before the Python `_thread` module creates a new thread, knowing that either it has the lock or the lock hasn't been created yet, it calls *PyEval_InitThreads()*. When this call returns, it is guaranteed that the lock has been created and that the calling thread has acquired it.

It is **not** safe to call this function when it is unknown which thread (if any) currently has the global interpreter lock.

This function is not available when thread support is disabled at compile time.

---

int **PyEval_ThreadsInitialized**()

> Returns a non-zero value if *PyEval_InitThreads()* has been called. This function can be called without holding the GIL, and therefore can be used to avoid calls to the locking API when running single-threaded. This function is not available when thread support is disabled at compile time.

PyThreadState* **PyEval_SaveThread**()

> Release the global interpreter lock (if it has been created and thread support is enabled) and reset the thread state to *NULL*, returning the previous thread state (which is not *NULL*). If the lock has been created, the current thread must have acquired it. (This function is available even when thread support is disabled at compile time.)

void **PyEval_RestoreThread**(*PyThreadState* *tstate*)

>   Acquire the global interpreter lock (if it has been created and thread support is enabled) and set the thread state to *tstate*, which must not be *NULL*. If the lock has been created, the current thread must not have acquired it, otherwise deadlock ensues. (This function is available even when thread support is disabled at compile time.)

*PyThreadState** **PyThreadState_Get**()

>   Return the current thread state. The global interpreter lock must be held. When the current thread state is *NULL*, this issues a fatal error (so that the caller needn't check for *NULL*).

*PyThreadState** **PyThreadState_Swap**(*PyThreadState* *tstate*)

>   Swap the current thread state with the thread state given by the argument *tstate*, which may be *NULL*. The global interpreter lock must be held and is not released.

void **PyEval_ReInitThreads**()

>   This function is called from *PyOS_AfterFork()* to ensure that newly created child processes don't hold locks referring to threads which are not running in the child process.

The following functions use thread-local storage, and are not compatible with sub-interpreters:

PyGILState_STATE **PyGILState_Ensure**()

>   Ensure that the current thread is ready to call the Python C API regardless of the current state of Python, or of the global interpreter lock. This may be called as many times as desired by a thread as long as each call is matched with a call to *PyGILState_Release()*. In general, other thread-related APIs may be used between *PyGILState_Ensure()* and *PyGILState_Release()* calls as long as the thread state is restored to its previous state before the Release(). For example, normal usage of the *Py_BEGIN_ALLOW_THREADS* and *Py_END_ALLOW_THREADS* macros is acceptable.
>
>   The return value is an opaque "handle" to the thread state when *PyGILState_Ensure()* was called, and must be passed to *PyGILState_Release()* to ensure Python is left in the same state. Even though recursive calls are allowed, these handles *cannot* be shared - each unique call to *PyGILState_Ensure()* must save the handle for its call to *PyGILState_Release()*.
>
>   When the function returns, the current thread will hold the GIL and be able to call arbitrary Python code. Failure is a fatal error.

void **PyGILState_Release**(PyGILState_STATE)

>   Release any resources previously acquired. After this call, Python's state will be the same as it was prior to the corresponding *PyGILState_Ensure()* call (but generally this state will be unknown to the caller, hence the use of the GILState API).
>
>   Every call to *PyGILState_Ensure()* must be matched by a call to *PyGILState_Release()* on the same thread.

*PyThreadState** **PyGILState_GetThisThreadState**()

>   Get the current thread state for this thread. May return NULL if no GILState API has been used on the current thread. Note that the main thread always has such a thread-state, even if no auto-thread-state call has been made on the main thread. This is mainly a helper/diagnostic function.

int **PyGILState_Check**()

>   Return 1 if the current thread is holding the GIL and 0 otherwise. This function can be called from any thread at any time. Only if it has had its Python thread state initialized and currently is holding the GIL will it return 1. This is mainly a helper/diagnostic function. It can be useful for example in callback contexts or memory allocation functions when knowing that the GIL is locked can allow the caller to perform sensitive actions or otherwise behave differently.
>
>   New in version 3.4.

The following macros are normally used without a trailing semicolon; look for example usage in the Python source distribution.

Py_BEGIN_ALLOW_THREADS

This macro expands to { PyThreadState *_save; _save = PyEval_SaveThread();. Note that it contains an opening brace; it must be matched with a following *Py_END_ALLOW_THREADS* macro. See above for further discussion of this macro. It is a no-op when thread support is disabled at compile time.

Py_END_ALLOW_THREADS

This macro expands to PyEval_RestoreThread(_save); }. Note that it contains a closing brace; it must be matched with an earlier *Py_BEGIN_ALLOW_THREADS* macro. See above for further discussion of this macro. It is a no-op when thread support is disabled at compile time.

Py_BLOCK_THREADS

This macro expands to PyEval_RestoreThread(_save);: it is equivalent to *Py_END_ALLOW_THREADS* without the closing brace. It is a no-op when thread support is disabled at compile time.

Py_UNBLOCK_THREADS

This macro expands to _save = PyEval_SaveThread();: it is equivalent to *Py_BEGIN_ALLOW_THREADS* without the opening brace and variable declaration. It is a no-op when thread support is disabled at compile time.

9.3.4 Low-level API

All of the following functions are only available when thread support is enabled at compile time, and must be called only when the global interpreter lock has been created.

*PyInterpreterState** **PyInterpreterState_New()**

Create a new interpreter state object. The global interpreter lock need not be held, but may be held if it is necessary to serialize calls to this function.

void **PyInterpreterState_Clear**(*PyInterpreterState *interp*)

Reset all information in an interpreter state object. The global interpreter lock must be held.

void **PyInterpreterState_Delete**(*PyInterpreterState *interp*)

Destroy an interpreter state object. The global interpreter lock need not be held. The interpreter state must have been reset with a previous call to *PyInterpreterState_Clear()*.

*PyThreadState** **PyThreadState_New**(*PyInterpreterState *interp*)

Create a new thread state object belonging to the given interpreter object. The global interpreter lock need not be held, but may be held if it is necessary to serialize calls to this function.

void **PyThreadState_Clear**(*PyThreadState *tstate*)

Reset all information in a thread state object. The global interpreter lock must be held.

void **PyThreadState_Delete**(*PyThreadState *tstate*)

Destroy a thread state object. The global interpreter lock need not be held. The thread state must have been reset with a previous call to *PyThreadState_Clear()*.

*PyObject** **PyThreadState_GetDict()**

Return value: Borrowed reference. Return a dictionary in which extensions can store thread-specific state information. Each extension should use a unique key to use to store state in the dictionary. It is okay to call this function when no current thread state is available. If this function returns *NULL*, no exception has been raised and the caller should assume no current thread state is available.

int **PyThreadState_SetAsyncExc**(long *id*, *PyObject *exc*)

Asynchronously raise an exception in a thread. The *id* argument is the thread id of the target thread; *exc* is the exception object to be raised. This function does not steal any references to *exc*. To prevent naive misuse, you must write your own C extension to call this. Must be called with the GIL held. Returns the number of thread states modified; this is normally one, but will be zero if the thread id isn't found. If *exc* is NULL, the pending exception (if any) for the thread is cleared. This raises no exceptions.

void **PyEval_AcquireThread**(*PyThreadState* *tstate)

> Acquire the global interpreter lock and set the current thread state to *tstate*, which should not be *NULL*. The lock must have been created earlier. If this thread already has the lock, deadlock ensues.

> *PyEval_RestoreThread()* is a higher-level function which is always available (even when thread support isn't enabled or when threads have not been initialized).

void **PyEval_ReleaseThread**(*PyThreadState* *tstate)

> Reset the current thread state to *NULL* and release the global interpreter lock. The lock must have been created earlier and must be held by the current thread. The *tstate* argument, which must not be *NULL*, is only used to check that it represents the current thread state — if it isn't, a fatal error is reported.

> *PyEval_SaveThread()* is a higher-level function which is always available (even when thread support isn't enabled or when threads have not been initialized).

void **PyEval_AcquireLock**()

> Acquire the global interpreter lock. The lock must have been created earlier. If this thread already has the lock, a deadlock ensues.

> Deprecated since version 3.2: This function does not update the current thread state. Please use *PyEval_RestoreThread()* or *PyEval_AcquireThread()* instead.

void **PyEval_ReleaseLock**()

> Release the global interpreter lock. The lock must have been created earlier.

> Deprecated since version 3.2: This function does not update the current thread state. Please use *PyEval_SaveThread()* or *PyEval_ReleaseThread()* instead.

9.4 Sub-interpreter support

While in most uses, you will only embed a single Python interpreter, there are cases where you need to create several independent interpreters in the same process and perhaps even in the same thread. Sub-interpreters allow you to do that. You can switch between sub-interpreters using the *PyThreadState_Swap()* function. You can create and destroy them using the following functions:

PyThreadState* **Py_NewInterpreter**()

> Create a new sub-interpreter. This is an (almost) totally separate environment for the execution of Python code. In particular, the new interpreter has separate, independent versions of all imported modules, including the fundamental modules builtins, __main__ and sys. The table of loaded modules (sys.modules) and the module search path (sys.path) are also separate. The new environment has no sys.argv variable. It has new standard I/O stream file objects sys.stdin, sys.stdout and sys.stderr (however these refer to the same underlying file descriptors).

> The return value points to the first thread state created in the new sub-interpreter. This thread state is made in the current thread state. Note that no actual thread is created; see the discussion of thread states below. If creation of the new interpreter is unsuccessful, *NULL* is returned; no exception is set since the exception state is stored in the current thread state and there may not be a current thread state. (Like all other Python/C API functions, the global interpreter lock must be held before calling this function and is still held when it returns; however, unlike most other Python/C API functions, there needn't be a current thread state on entry.)

> Extension modules are shared between (sub-)interpreters as follows: the first time a particular extension is imported, it is initialized normally, and a (shallow) copy of its module's dictionary is squirreled away. When the same extension is imported by another (sub-)interpreter, a new module is initialized and filled with the contents of this copy; the extension's init function is not called. Note that this is different from what happens when an extension is imported after the interpreter has been completely re-initialized

by calling *Py_FinalizeEx()* and *Py_Initialize()*; in that case, the extension's `initmodule` function *is* called again.

void **Py_EndInterpreter**(*PyThreadState *tstate*)

Destroy the (sub-)interpreter represented by the given thread state. The given thread state must be the current thread state. See the discussion of thread states below. When the call returns, the current thread state is *NULL*. All thread states associated with this interpreter are destroyed. (The global interpreter lock must be held before calling this function and is still held when it returns.) *Py_FinalizeEx()* will destroy all sub-interpreters that haven't been explicitly destroyed at that point.

9.4.1 Bugs and caveats

Because sub-interpreters (and the main interpreter) are part of the same process, the insulation between them isn't perfect — for example, using low-level file operations like `os.close()` they can (accidentally or maliciously) affect each other's open files. Because of the way extensions are shared between (sub-)interpreters, some extensions may not work properly; this is especially likely when the extension makes use of (static) global variables, or when the extension manipulates its module's dictionary after its initialization. It is possible to insert objects created in one sub-interpreter into a namespace of another sub-interpreter; this should be done with great care to avoid sharing user-defined functions, methods, instances or classes between sub-interpreters, since import operations executed by such objects may affect the wrong (sub-)interpreter's dictionary of loaded modules.

Also note that combining this functionality with `PyGILState_*()` APIs is delicate, because these APIs assume a bijection between Python thread states and OS-level threads, an assumption broken by the presence of sub-interpreters. It is highly recommended that you don't switch sub-interpreters between a pair of matching *PyGILState_Ensure()* and *PyGILState_Release()* calls. Furthermore, extensions (such as `ctypes`) using these APIs to allow calling of Python code from non-Python created threads will probably be broken when using sub-interpreters.

9.5 Asynchronous Notifications

A mechanism is provided to make asynchronous notifications to the main interpreter thread. These notifications take the form of a function pointer and a void pointer argument.

int **Py_AddPendingCall**(int (**func*)(void *), void **arg*)

Schedule a function to be called from the main interpreter thread. On success, `0` is returned and *func* is queued for being called in the main thread. On failure, `-1` is returned without setting any exception.

When successfully queued, *func* will be *eventually* called from the main interpreter thread with the argument *arg*. It will be called asynchronously with respect to normally running Python code, but with both these conditions met:

- on a *bytecode* boundary;
- with the main thread holding the *global interpreter lock* (*func* can therefore use the full C API).

func must return `0` on success, or `-1` on failure with an exception set. *func* won't be interrupted to perform another asynchronous notification recursively, but it can still be interrupted to switch threads if the global interpreter lock is released.

This function doesn't need a current thread state to run, and it doesn't need the global interpreter lock.

> **Warning:** This is a low-level function, only useful for very special cases. There is no guarantee that *func* will be called as quick as possible. If the main thread is busy executing a system call, *func*

> won't be called before the system call returns. This function is generally **not** suitable for calling Python code from arbitrary C threads. Instead, use the *PyGILState API*.

New in version 3.1.

9.6 Profiling and Tracing

The Python interpreter provides some low-level support for attaching profiling and execution tracing facilities. These are used for profiling, debugging, and coverage analysis tools.

This C interface allows the profiling or tracing code to avoid the overhead of calling through Python-level callable objects, making a direct C function call instead. The essential attributes of the facility have not changed; the interface allows trace functions to be installed per-thread, and the basic events reported to the trace function are the same as had been reported to the Python-level trace functions in previous versions.

int (***Py_tracefunc**)(*PyObject *obj*, *PyFrameObject *frame*, int *what*, *PyObject *arg*)
> The type of the trace function registered using *PyEval_SetProfile()* and *PyEval_SetTrace()*. The first parameter is the object passed to the registration function as *obj*, *frame* is the frame object to which the event pertains, *what* is one of the constants PyTrace_CALL, PyTrace_EXCEPTION, PyTrace_LINE, PyTrace_RETURN, PyTrace_C_CALL, PyTrace_C_EXCEPTION, or PyTrace_C_RETURN, and *arg* depends on the value of *what*:

Value of *what*	Meaning of *arg*
PyTrace_CALL	Always *Py_None*.
PyTrace_EXCEPTION	Exception information as returned by sys.exc_info().
PyTrace_LINE	Always *Py_None*.
PyTrace_RETURN	Value being returned to the caller, or *NULL* if caused by an exception.
PyTrace_C_CALL	Function object being called.
PyTrace_C_EXCEPTION	Function object being called.
PyTrace_C_RETURN	Function object being called.

int **PyTrace_CALL**
> The value of the *what* parameter to a *Py_tracefunc* function when a new call to a function or method is being reported, or a new entry into a generator. Note that the creation of the iterator for a generator function is not reported as there is no control transfer to the Python bytecode in the corresponding frame.

int **PyTrace_EXCEPTION**
> The value of the *what* parameter to a *Py_tracefunc* function when an exception has been raised. The callback function is called with this value for *what* when after any bytecode is processed after which the exception becomes set within the frame being executed. The effect of this is that as exception propagation causes the Python stack to unwind, the callback is called upon return to each frame as the exception propagates. Only trace functions receives these events; they are not needed by the profiler.

int **PyTrace_LINE**
> The value passed as the *what* parameter to a trace function (but not a profiling function) when a line-number event is being reported.

int **PyTrace_RETURN**
> The value for the *what* parameter to *Py_tracefunc* functions when a call is about to return.

int **PyTrace_C_CALL**
> The value for the *what* parameter to *Py_tracefunc* functions when a C function is about to be called.

int **PyTrace_C_EXCEPTION**
> The value for the *what* parameter to *Py_tracefunc* functions when a C function has raised an exception.

int **PyTrace_C_RETURN**
> The value for the *what* parameter to *Py_tracefunc* functions when a C function has returned.

void **PyEval_SetProfile**(*Py_tracefunc func*, *PyObject *obj*)
> Set the profiler function to *func*. The *obj* parameter is passed to the function as its first parameter, and may be any Python object, or *NULL*. If the profile function needs to maintain state, using a different value for *obj* for each thread provides a convenient and thread-safe place to store it. The profile function is called for all monitored events except PyTrace_LINE and PyTrace_EXCEPTION.

void **PyEval_SetTrace**(*Py_tracefunc func*, *PyObject *obj*)
> Set the tracing function to *func*. This is similar to *PyEval_SetProfile()*, except the tracing function does receive line-number events and does not receive any event related to C function objects being called. Any trace function registered using *PyEval_SetTrace()* will not receive PyTrace_C_CALL, PyTrace_C_EXCEPTION or PyTrace_C_RETURN as a value for the *what* parameter.

PyObject* **PyEval_GetCallStats**(*PyObject *self*)
> Return a tuple of function call counts. There are constants defined for the positions within the tuple:

Name	Value
PCALL_ALL	0
PCALL_FUNCTION	1
PCALL_FAST_FUNCTION	2
PCALL_FASTER_FUNCTION	3
PCALL_METHOD	4
PCALL_BOUND_METHOD	5
PCALL_CFUNCTION	6
PCALL_TYPE	7
PCALL_GENERATOR	8
PCALL_OTHER	9
PCALL_POP	10

> PCALL_FAST_FUNCTION means no argument tuple needs to be created. PCALL_FASTER_FUNCTION means that the fast-path frame setup code is used.

> If there is a method call where the call can be optimized by changing the argument tuple and calling the function directly, it gets recorded twice.

> This function is only present if Python is compiled with CALL_PROFILE defined.

9.7 Advanced Debugger Support

These functions are only intended to be used by advanced debugging tools.

PyInterpreterState* **PyInterpreterState_Head**()
> Return the interpreter state object at the head of the list of all such objects.

PyInterpreterState* **PyInterpreterState_Next**(*PyInterpreterState *interp*)
> Return the next interpreter state object after *interp* from the list of all such objects.

PyThreadState * **PyInterpreterState_ThreadHead**(*PyInterpreterState *interp*)
> Return the pointer to the first *PyThreadState* object in the list of threads associated with the interpreter *interp*.

*PyThreadState** **PyThreadState_Next**(*PyThreadState* *tstate*)

Return the next thread state object after *tstate* from the list of all such objects belonging to the same *PyInterpreterState* object.

MEMORY MANAGEMENT

10.1 Overview

Memory management in Python involves a private heap containing all Python objects and data structures. The management of this private heap is ensured internally by the *Python memory manager*. The Python memory manager has different components which deal with various dynamic storage management aspects, like sharing, segmentation, preallocation or caching.

At the lowest level, a raw memory allocator ensures that there is enough room in the private heap for storing all Python-related data by interacting with the memory manager of the operating system. On top of the raw memory allocator, several object-specific allocators operate on the same heap and implement distinct memory management policies adapted to the peculiarities of every object type. For example, integer objects are managed differently within the heap than strings, tuples or dictionaries because integers imply different storage requirements and speed/space tradeoffs. The Python memory manager thus delegates some of the work to the object-specific allocators, but ensures that the latter operate within the bounds of the private heap.

It is important to understand that the management of the Python heap is performed by the interpreter itself and that the user has no control over it, even if she regularly manipulates object pointers to memory blocks inside that heap. The allocation of heap space for Python objects and other internal buffers is performed on demand by the Python memory manager through the Python/C API functions listed in this document.

To avoid memory corruption, extension writers should never try to operate on Python objects with the functions exported by the C library: `malloc()`, `calloc()`, `realloc()` and `free()`. This will result in mixed calls between the C allocator and the Python memory manager with fatal consequences, because they implement different algorithms and operate on different heaps. However, one may safely allocate and release memory blocks with the C library allocator for individual purposes, as shown in the following example:

```
PyObject *res;
char *buf = (char *) malloc(BUFSIZ); /* for I/O */

if (buf == NULL)
    return PyErr_NoMemory();
...Do some I/O operation involving buf...
res = PyBytes_FromString(buf);
free(buf); /* malloc'ed */
return res;
```

In this example, the memory request for the I/O buffer is handled by the C library allocator. The Python memory manager is involved only in the allocation of the string object returned as a result.

In most situations, however, it is recommended to allocate memory from the Python heap specifically because the latter is under control of the Python memory manager. For example, this is required when the interpreter is extended with new object types written in C. Another reason for using the Python heap is the desire to *inform* the Python memory manager about the memory needs of the extension module. Even when the requested memory is used exclusively for internal, highly-specific purposes, delegating all memory requests to the Python memory manager causes the interpreter to have a more accurate image of its memory footprint as a whole. Consequently, under certain circumstances, the Python memory manager may or may not trigger appropriate actions, like garbage collection, memory compaction or other preventive procedures. Note that by using the C library allocator as shown in the previous example, the allocated memory for the I/O buffer escapes completely the Python memory manager.

See also:

The PYTHONMALLOC environment variable can be used to configure the memory allocators used by Python.

The PYTHONMALLOCSTATS environment variable can be used to print statistics of the *pymalloc memory allocator* every time a new pymalloc object arena is created, and on shutdown.

10.2 Raw Memory Interface

The following function sets are wrappers to the system allocator. These functions are thread-safe, the *GIL* does not need to be held.

The default raw memory block allocator uses the following functions: `malloc()`, `calloc()`, `realloc()` and `free()`; call `malloc(1)` (or `calloc(1, 1)`) when requesting zero bytes.

New in version 3.4.

void* **PyMem_RawMalloc**(size_t *n*)
> Allocates *n* bytes and returns a pointer of type void* to the allocated memory, or *NULL* if the request fails.
>
> Requesting zero bytes returns a distinct non-*NULL* pointer if possible, as if `PyMem_RawMalloc(1)` had been called instead. The memory will not have been initialized in any way.

void* **PyMem_RawCalloc**(size_t *nelem*, size_t *elsize*)
> Allocates *nelem* elements each whose size in bytes is *elsize* and returns a pointer of type void* to the allocated memory, or *NULL* if the request fails. The memory is initialized to zeros.
>
> Requesting zero elements or elements of size zero bytes returns a distinct non-*NULL* pointer if possible, as if `PyMem_RawCalloc(1, 1)` had been called instead.
>
> New in version 3.5.

void* **PyMem_RawRealloc**(void **p*, size_t *n*)
> Resizes the memory block pointed to by *p* to *n* bytes. The contents will be unchanged to the minimum of the old and the new sizes.
>
> If *p* is *NULL*, the call is equivalent to `PyMem_RawMalloc(n)`; else if *n* is equal to zero, the memory block is resized but is not freed, and the returned pointer is non-*NULL*.
>
> Unless *p* is *NULL*, it must have been returned by a previous call to *PyMem_RawMalloc()*, *PyMem_RawRealloc()* or *PyMem_RawCalloc()*.
>
> If the request fails, *PyMem_RawRealloc()* returns *NULL* and *p* remains a valid pointer to the previous memory area.

void **PyMem_RawFree**(void **p*)
> Frees the memory block pointed to by *p*, which must have been returned by a previous call to *PyMem_RawMalloc()*, *PyMem_RawRealloc()* or *PyMem_RawCalloc()*. Otherwise, or if `PyMem_RawFree(p)` has been called before, undefined behavior occurs.
>
> If *p* is *NULL*, no operation is performed.

10.3 Memory Interface

The following function sets, modeled after the ANSI C standard, but specifying behavior when requesting zero bytes, are available for allocating and releasing memory from the Python heap.

By default, these functions use *pymalloc memory allocator*.

> **Warning:** The *GIL* must be held when using these functions.

Changed in version 3.6: The default allocator is now pymalloc instead of system `malloc()`.

void* **PyMem_Malloc**(size_t *n*)

Allocates *n* bytes and returns a pointer of type `void*` to the allocated memory, or *NULL* if the request fails.

Requesting zero bytes returns a distinct non-*NULL* pointer if possible, as if `PyMem_Malloc(1)` had been called instead. The memory will not have been initialized in any way.

void* **PyMem_Calloc**(size_t *nelem*, size_t *elsize*)

Allocates *nelem* elements each whose size in bytes is *elsize* and returns a pointer of type `void*` to the allocated memory, or *NULL* if the request fails. The memory is initialized to zeros.

Requesting zero elements or elements of size zero bytes returns a distinct non-*NULL* pointer if possible, as if `PyMem_Calloc(1, 1)` had been called instead.

New in version 3.5.

void* **PyMem_Realloc**(void **p*, size_t *n*)

Resizes the memory block pointed to by *p* to *n* bytes. The contents will be unchanged to the minimum of the old and the new sizes.

If *p* is *NULL*, the call is equivalent to `PyMem_Malloc(n)`; else if *n* is equal to zero, the memory block is resized but is not freed, and the returned pointer is non-*NULL*.

Unless *p* is *NULL*, it must have been returned by a previous call to *PyMem_Malloc()*, *PyMem_Realloc()* or *PyMem_Calloc()*.

If the request fails, *PyMem_Realloc()* returns *NULL* and *p* remains a valid pointer to the previous memory area.

void **PyMem_Free**(void **p*)

Frees the memory block pointed to by *p*, which must have been returned by a previous call to *PyMem_Malloc()*, *PyMem_Realloc()* or *PyMem_Calloc()*. Otherwise, or if `PyMem_Free(p)` has been called before, undefined behavior occurs.

If *p* is *NULL*, no operation is performed.

The following type-oriented macros are provided for convenience. Note that *TYPE* refers to any C type.

TYPE* **PyMem_New**(TYPE, size_t *n*)

Same as *PyMem_Malloc()*, but allocates `(n * sizeof(TYPE))` bytes of memory. Returns a pointer cast to TYPE*. The memory will not have been initialized in any way.

TYPE* **PyMem_Resize**(void **p*, TYPE, size_t *n*)

Same as *PyMem_Realloc()*, but the memory block is resized to `(n * sizeof(TYPE))` bytes. Returns a pointer cast to TYPE*. On return, *p* will be a pointer to the new memory area, or *NULL* in the event of failure.

This is a C preprocessor macro; *p* is always reassigned. Save the original value of *p* to avoid losing memory when handling errors.

void **PyMem_Del**(void *p)
> Same as *PyMem_Free()*.

In addition, the following macro sets are provided for calling the Python memory allocator directly, without involving the C API functions listed above. However, note that their use does not preserve binary compatibility across Python versions and is therefore deprecated in extension modules.

- PyMem_MALLOC(size)
- PyMem_NEW(type, size)
- PyMem_REALLOC(ptr, size)
- PyMem_RESIZE(ptr, type, size)
- PyMem_FREE(ptr)
- PyMem_DEL(ptr)

10.4 Object allocators

The following function sets, modeled after the ANSI C standard, but specifying behavior when requesting zero bytes, are available for allocating and releasing memory from the Python heap.

By default, these functions use *pymalloc memory allocator*.

Warning: The *GIL* must be held when using these functions.

---

void* **PyObject_Malloc**(size_t n)
> Allocates n bytes and returns a pointer of type **void*** to the allocated memory, or *NULL* if the request fails.

> Requesting zero bytes returns a distinct non-*NULL* pointer if possible, as if PyObject_Malloc(1) had been called instead. The memory will not have been initialized in any way.

void* **PyObject_Calloc**(size_t *nelem*, size_t *elsize*)
> Allocates *nelem* elements each whose size in bytes is *elsize* and returns a pointer of type **void*** to the allocated memory, or *NULL* if the request fails. The memory is initialized to zeros.

> Requesting zero elements or elements of size zero bytes returns a distinct non-*NULL* pointer if possible, as if PyObject_Calloc(1, 1) had been called instead.

> New in version 3.5.

void* **PyObject_Realloc**(void *p, size_t n)
> Resizes the memory block pointed to by p to n bytes. The contents will be unchanged to the minimum of the old and the new sizes.

> If p is *NULL*, the call is equivalent to PyObject_Malloc(n); else if n is equal to zero, the memory block is resized but is not freed, and the returned pointer is non-*NULL*.

> Unless p is *NULL*, it must have been returned by a previous call to *PyObject_Malloc()*, *PyObject_Realloc()* or *PyObject_Calloc()*.

> If the request fails, *PyObject_Realloc()* returns *NULL* and p remains a valid pointer to the previous memory area.

void **PyObject_Free**(void *p)
> Frees the memory block pointed to by p, which must have been returned by a previous call to *PyObject_Malloc()*, *PyObject_Realloc()* or *PyObject_Calloc()*. Otherwise, or if PyObject_Free(p) has been called before, undefined behavior occurs.

If *p* is *NULL*, no operation is performed.

10.5 Customize Memory Allocators

New in version 3.4.

PyMemAllocatorEx

Structure used to describe a memory block allocator. The structure has four fields:

Field	Meaning
void *ctx	user context passed as first argument
void* malloc(void *ctx, size_t size)	allocate a memory block
void* calloc(void *ctx, size_t nelem, size_t elsize)	allocate a memory block initialized with zeros
void* realloc(void *ctx, void *ptr, size_t new_size)	allocate or resize a memory block
void free(void *ctx, void *ptr)	free a memory block

Changed in version 3.5: The `PyMemAllocator` structure was renamed to *PyMemAllocatorEx* and a new calloc field was added.

PyMemAllocatorDomain

Enum used to identify an allocator domain. Domains:

PYMEM_DOMAIN_RAW

Functions:

- *PyMem_RawMalloc()*
- *PyMem_RawRealloc()*
- *PyMem_RawCalloc()*
- *PyMem_RawFree()*

PYMEM_DOMAIN_MEM

Functions:

- *PyMem_Malloc()*,
- *PyMem_Realloc()*
- *PyMem_Calloc()*
- *PyMem_Free()*

PYMEM_DOMAIN_OBJ

Functions:

- *PyObject_Malloc()*
- *PyObject_Realloc()*
- *PyObject_Calloc()*
- *PyObject_Free()*

void **PyMem_GetAllocator**(*PyMemAllocatorDomain domain*, *PyMemAllocatorEx *allocator*)
Get the memory block allocator of the specified domain.

void **PyMem_SetAllocator**(*PyMemAllocatorDomain domain*, *PyMemAllocatorEx *allocator*)
Set the memory block allocator of the specified domain.

The new allocator must return a distinct non-NULL pointer when requesting zero bytes.

For the *PYMEM_DOMAIN_RAW* domain, the allocator must be thread-safe: the *GIL* is not held when the allocator is called.

If the new allocator is not a hook (does not call the previous allocator), the *PyMem_SetupDebugHooks()* function must be called to reinstall the debug hooks on top on the new allocator.

void **PyMem_SetupDebugHooks**(void)

> Setup hooks to detect bugs in the Python memory allocator functions.
>
> Newly allocated memory is filled with the byte 0xCB, freed memory is filled with the byte 0xDB.
>
> Runtime checks:
>
> - Detect API violations, ex: *PyObject_Free()* called on a buffer allocated by *PyMem_Malloc()*
> - Detect write before the start of the buffer (buffer underflow)
> - Detect write after the end of the buffer (buffer overflow)
> - Check that the *GIL* is held when allocator functions of *PYMEM_DOMAIN_OBJ* (ex: *PyObject_Malloc()*) and *PYMEM_DOMAIN_MEM* (ex: *PyMem_Malloc()*) domains are called
>
> On error, the debug hooks use the **tracemalloc** module to get the traceback where a memory block was allocated. The traceback is only displayed if **tracemalloc** is tracing Python memory allocations and the memory block was traced.
>
> These hooks are installed by default if Python is compiled in debug mode. The **PYTHONMALLOC** environment variable can be used to install debug hooks on a Python compiled in release mode.
>
> Changed in version 3.6: This function now also works on Python compiled in release mode. On error, the debug hooks now use **tracemalloc** to get the traceback where a memory block was allocated. The debug hooks now also check if the GIL is held when functions of *PYMEM_DOMAIN_OBJ* and *PYMEM_DOMAIN_MEM* domains are called.

10.6 The pymalloc allocator

Python has a *pymalloc* allocator optimized for small objects (smaller or equal to 512 bytes) with a short lifetime. It uses memory mappings called "arenas" with a fixed size of 256 KB. It falls back to *PyMem_RawMalloc()* and *PyMem_RawRealloc()* for allocations larger than 512 bytes.

pymalloc is the default allocator of the *PYMEM_DOMAIN_MEM* (ex: *PyMem_Malloc()*) and *PYMEM_DOMAIN_OBJ* (ex: *PyObject_Malloc()*) domains.

The arena allocator uses the following functions:

- **VirtualAlloc()** and **VirtualFree()** on Windows,
- **mmap()** and **munmap()** if available,
- **malloc()** and **free()** otherwise.

10.6.1 Customize pymalloc Arena Allocator

New in version 3.4.

PyObjectArenaAllocator

> Structure used to describe an arena allocator. The structure has three fields:

Field	Meaning
void *ctx	user context passed as first argument
void* alloc(void *ctx, size_t size)	allocate an arena of size bytes
void free(void *ctx, size_t size, void *ptr)	free an arena

PyObject_GetArenaAllocator(*PyObjectArenaAllocator* *allocator*)
> Get the arena allocator.

PyObject_SetArenaAllocator(*PyObjectArenaAllocator* *allocator*)
> Set the arena allocator.

10.7 Examples

Here is the example from section *Overview*, rewritten so that the I/O buffer is allocated from the Python heap by using the first function set:

```
PyObject *res;
char *buf = (char *) PyMem_Malloc(BUFSIZ); /* for I/O */

if (buf == NULL)
    return PyErr_NoMemory();
/* ...Do some I/O operation involving buf... */
res = PyBytes_FromString(buf);
PyMem_Free(buf); /* allocated with PyMem_Malloc */
return res;
```

The same code using the type-oriented function set:

```
PyObject *res;
char *buf = PyMem_New(char, BUFSIZ); /* for I/O */

if (buf == NULL)
    return PyErr_NoMemory();
/* ...Do some I/O operation involving buf... */
res = PyBytes_FromString(buf);
PyMem_Del(buf); /* allocated with PyMem_New */
return res;
```

Note that in the two examples above, the buffer is always manipulated via functions belonging to the same set. Indeed, it is required to use the same memory API family for a given memory block, so that the risk of mixing different allocators is reduced to a minimum. The following code sequence contains two errors, one of which is labeled as *fatal* because it mixes two different allocators operating on different heaps.

```
char *buf1 = PyMem_New(char, BUFSIZ);
char *buf2 = (char *) malloc(BUFSIZ);
char *buf3 = (char *) PyMem_Malloc(BUFSIZ);
...
PyMem_Del(buf3);   /* Wrong -- should be PyMem_Free() */
free(buf2);        /* Right -- allocated via malloc() */
free(buf1);        /* Fatal -- should be PyMem_Del() */
```

In addition to the functions aimed at handling raw memory blocks from the Python heap, objects in Python are allocated and released with *PyObject_New()*, *PyObject_NewVar()* and *PyObject_Del()*.

These will be explained in the next chapter on defining and implementing new object types in C.

OBJECT IMPLEMENTATION SUPPORT

This chapter describes the functions, types, and macros used when defining new object types.

11.1 Allocating Objects on the Heap

PyObject* **_PyObject_New**(*PyTypeObject* *type)
> *Return value: New reference.*

PyVarObject* **_PyObject_NewVar**(*PyTypeObject* *type, Py_ssize_t *size*)
> *Return value: New reference.*

PyObject* **PyObject_Init**(*PyObject* *op, *PyTypeObject* *type)
> *Return value: Borrowed reference.* Initialize a newly-allocated object *op* with its type and initial reference. Returns the initialized object. If *type* indicates that the object participates in the cyclic garbage detector, it is added to the detector's set of observed objects. Other fields of the object are not affected.

PyVarObject* **PyObject_InitVar**(*PyVarObject* *op, *PyTypeObject* *type, Py_ssize_t *size*)
> *Return value: Borrowed reference.* This does everything *PyObject_Init()* does, and also initializes the length information for a variable-size object.

TYPE* **PyObject_New**(TYPE, *PyTypeObject* *type)
> *Return value: New reference.* Allocate a new Python object using the C structure type *TYPE* and the Python type object *type*. Fields not defined by the Python object header are not initialized; the object's reference count will be one. The size of the memory allocation is determined from the *tp_basicsize* field of the type object.

TYPE* **PyObject_NewVar**(TYPE, *PyTypeObject* *type, Py_ssize_t *size*)
> *Return value: New reference.* Allocate a new Python object using the C structure type *TYPE* and the Python type object *type*. Fields not defined by the Python object header are not initialized. The allocated memory allows for the *TYPE* structure plus *size* fields of the size given by the *tp_itemsize* field of *type*. This is useful for implementing objects like tuples, which are able to determine their size at construction time. Embedding the array of fields into the same allocation decreases the number of allocations, improving the memory management efficiency.

void **PyObject_Del**(*PyObject* *op)
> Releases memory allocated to an object using *PyObject_New()* or *PyObject_NewVar()*. This is normally called from the *tp_dealloc* handler specified in the object's type. The fields of the object should not be accessed after this call as the memory is no longer a valid Python object.

PyObject **_Py_NoneStruct**
> Object which is visible in Python as **None**. This should only be accessed using the *Py_None* macro, which evaluates to a pointer to this object.

See also:

PyModule_Create() To allocate and create extension modules.

11.2 Common Object Structures

There are a large number of structures which are used in the definition of object types for Python. This section describes these structures and how they are used.

All Python objects ultimately share a small number of fields at the beginning of the object's representation in memory. These are represented by the *PyObject* and *PyVarObject* types, which are defined, in turn, by the expansions of some macros also used, whether directly or indirectly, in the definition of all other Python objects.

PyObject

All object types are extensions of this type. This is a type which contains the information Python needs to treat a pointer to an object as an object. In a normal "release" build, it contains only the object's reference count and a pointer to the corresponding type object. Nothing is actually declared to be a *PyObject*, but every pointer to a Python object can be cast to a *PyObject**. Access to the members must be done by using the macros *Py_REFCNT* and *Py_TYPE*.

PyVarObject

This is an extension of *PyObject* that adds the **ob_size** field. This is only used for objects that have some notion of *length*. This type does not often appear in the Python/C API. Access to the members must be done by using the macros *Py_REFCNT*, *Py_TYPE*, and *Py_SIZE*.

PyObject_HEAD

This is a macro used when declaring new types which represent objects without a varying length. The PyObject_HEAD macro expands to:

```
PyObject ob_base;
```

See documentation of *PyObject* above.

PyObject_VAR_HEAD

This is a macro used when declaring new types which represent objects with a length that varies from instance to instance. The PyObject_VAR_HEAD macro expands to:

```
PyVarObject ob_base;
```

See documentation of *PyVarObject* above.

Py_TYPE(o)

This macro is used to access the **ob_type** member of a Python object. It expands to:

```
(((PyObject*)(o))->ob_type)
```

Py_REFCNT(o)

This macro is used to access the **ob_refcnt** member of a Python object. It expands to:

```
(((PyObject*)(o))->ob_refcnt)
```

Py_SIZE(o)

This macro is used to access the **ob_size** member of a Python object. It expands to:

```
(((PyVarObject*)(o))->ob_size)
```

PyObject_HEAD_INIT(type)

This is a macro which expands to initialization values for a new *PyObject* type. This macro expands to:

```
_PyObject_EXTRA_INIT
1, type,
```

PyVarObject_HEAD_INIT(type, size)

This is a macro which expands to initialization values for a new *PyVarObject* type, including the
ob_size field. This macro expands to:

```
_PyObject_EXTRA_INIT
1, type, size,
```

PyCFunction

Type of the functions used to implement most Python callables in C. Functions of this type take two
PyObject* parameters and return one such value. If the return value is *NULL*, an exception shall have
been set. If not *NULL*, the return value is interpreted as the return value of the function as exposed
in Python. The function must return a new reference.

PyCFunctionWithKeywords

Type of the functions used to implement Python callables in C that take keyword arguments: they
take three *PyObject** parameters and return one such value. See *PyCFunction* above for the meaning
of the return value.

PyMethodDef

Structure used to describe a method of an extension type. This structure has four fields:

Field	C Type	Meaning
ml_name	char *	name of the method
ml_meth	PyCFunction	pointer to the C implementation
ml_flags	int	flag bits indicating how the call should be constructed
ml_doc	char *	points to the contents of the docstring

The **ml_meth** is a C function pointer. The functions may be of different types, but they always return
PyObject*. If the function is not of the *PyCFunction*, the compiler will require a cast in the method
table. Even though *PyCFunction* defines the first parameter as *PyObject**, it is common that the method
implementation uses the specific C type of the *self* object.

The **ml_flags** field is a bitfield which can include the following flags. The individual flags indicate either
a calling convention or a binding convention. Of the calling convention flags, only *METH_VARARGS* and
METH_KEYWORDS can be combined. Any of the calling convention flags can be combined with a binding flag.

METH_VARARGS

This is the typical calling convention, where the methods have the type *PyCFunction*. The function expects two *PyObject** values. The first one is the *self* object for methods; for module functions, it is the
module object. The second parameter (often called *args*) is a tuple object representing all arguments.
This parameter is typically processed using *PyArg_ParseTuple()* or *PyArg_UnpackTuple()*.

METH_KEYWORDS

Methods with these flags must be of type *PyCFunctionWithKeywords*. The function expects three
parameters: *self*, *args*, and a dictionary of all the keyword arguments. The flag must be combined with
METH_VARARGS, and the parameters are typically processed using *PyArg_ParseTupleAndKeywords()*.

METH_NOARGS

Methods without parameters don't need to check whether arguments are given if they are listed with
the *METH_NOARGS* flag. They need to be of type *PyCFunction*. The first parameter is typically named
self and will hold a reference to the module or object instance. In all cases the second parameter will
be *NULL*.

METH_O

Methods with a single object argument can be listed with the *METH_O* flag, instead of invoking

PyArg_ParseTuple() with a "O" argument. They have the type *PyCFunction*, with the *self* parameter, and a *PyObject** parameter representing the single argument.

These two constants are not used to indicate the calling convention but the binding when use with methods of classes. These may not be used for functions defined for modules. At most one of these flags may be set for any given method.

METH_CLASS
> The method will be passed the type object as the first parameter rather than an instance of the type. This is used to create *class methods*, similar to what is created when using the **classmethod()** built-in function.

METH_STATIC
> The method will be passed *NULL* as the first parameter rather than an instance of the type. This is used to create *static methods*, similar to what is created when using the **staticmethod()** built-in function.

One other constant controls whether a method is loaded in place of another definition with the same method name.

METH_COEXIST
> The method will be loaded in place of existing definitions. Without *METH_COEXIST*, the default is to skip repeated definitions. Since slot wrappers are loaded before the method table, the existence of a *sq_contains* slot, for example, would generate a wrapped method named __contains__() and preclude the loading of a corresponding PyCFunction with the same name. With the flag defined, the PyCFunction will be loaded in place of the wrapper object and will co-exist with the slot. This is helpful because calls to PyCFunctions are optimized more than wrapper object calls.

PyMemberDef
> Structure which describes an attribute of a type which corresponds to a C struct member. Its fields are:

Field	C Type	Meaning
name	char *	name of the member
type	int	the type of the member in the C struct
offset	Py_ssize_t	the offset in bytes that the member is located on the type's object struct
flags	int	flag bits indicating if the field should be read-only or writable
doc	char *	points to the contents of the docstring

type can be one of many **T_** macros corresponding to various C types. When the member is accessed in Python, it will be converted to the equivalent Python type.

Macro name	C type
T_SHORT	short
T_INT	int
T_LONG	long
T_FLOAT	float
T_DOUBLE	double
T_STRING	char *
T_OBJECT	PyObject *
T_OBJECT_EX	PyObject *
T_CHAR	char
T_BYTE	char
T_UBYTE	unsigned char
T_UINT	unsigned int
T_USHORT	unsigned short
T_ULONG	unsigned long
T_BOOL	char
T_LONGLONG	long long
T_ULONGLONG	unsigned long long
T_PYSSIZET	Py_ssize_t

`T_OBJECT` and `T_OBJECT_EX` differ in that `T_OBJECT` returns `None` if the member is *NULL* and `T_OBJECT_EX` raises an `AttributeError`. Try to use `T_OBJECT_EX` over `T_OBJECT` because `T_OBJECT_EX` handles use of the `del` statement on that attribute more correctly than `T_OBJECT`.

`flags` can be 0 for write and read access or `READONLY` for read-only access. Using `T_STRING` for `type` implies `READONLY`. Only `T_OBJECT` and `T_OBJECT_EX` members can be deleted. (They are set to *NULL*).

PyGetSetDef

Structure to define property-like access for a type. See also description of the *PyTypeObject.tp_getset* slot.

Field	C Type	Meaning
name	char *	attribute name
get	getter	C Function to get the attribute
set	setter	optional C function to set or delete the attribute, if omitted the attribute is readonly
doc	char *	optional docstring
clo-sure	void *	optional function pointer, providing additional data for getter and setter

The `get` function takes one *PyObject** parameter (the instance) and a function pointer (the associated `closure`):

```
typedef PyObject *(*getter)(PyObject *, void *);
```

It should return a new reference on success or *NULL* with a set exception on failure.

`set` functions take two *PyObject** parameters (the instance and the value to be set) and a function pointer (the associated `closure`):

```
typedef int (*setter)(PyObject *, PyObject *, void *);
```

In case the attribute should be deleted the second parameter is *NULL*. Should return 0 on success or -1 with a set exception on failure.

11.3 Type Objects

Perhaps one of the most important structures of the Python object system is the structure that defines a new type: the *PyTypeObject* structure. Type objects can be handled using any of the `PyObject_*()` or `PyType_*()` functions, but do not offer much that's interesting to most Python applications. These objects are fundamental to how objects behave, so they are very important to the interpreter itself and to any extension module that implements new types.

Type objects are fairly large compared to most of the standard types. The reason for the size is that each type object stores a large number of values, mostly C function pointers, each of which implements a small part of the type's functionality. The fields of the type object are examined in detail in this section. The fields will be described in the order in which they occur in the structure.

Typedefs: unaryfunc, binaryfunc, ternaryfunc, inquiry, intargfunc, intintargfunc, intobjargproc, intintobjargproc, objobjargproc, destructor, freefunc, printfunc, getattrfunc, getattrofunc, setattrfunc, setattrofunc, reprfunc, hashfunc

The structure definition for *PyTypeObject* can be found in **Include/object.h**. For convenience of reference, this repeats the definition found there:

```
typedef struct _typeobject {
    PyObject_VAR_HEAD
    const char *tp_name; /* For printing, in format "<module>.<name>" */
    Py_ssize_t tp_basicsize, tp_itemsize; /* For allocation */

    /* Methods to implement standard operations */

    destructor tp_dealloc;
    printfunc tp_print;
    getattrfunc tp_getattr;
    setattrfunc tp_setattr;
    PyAsyncMethods *tp_as_async; /* formerly known as tp_compare (Python 2)
                                     or tp_reserved (Python 3) */
    reprfunc tp_repr;

    /* Method suites for standard classes */

    PyNumberMethods *tp_as_number;
    PySequenceMethods *tp_as_sequence;
    PyMappingMethods *tp_as_mapping;

    /* More standard operations (here for binary compatibility) */

    hashfunc tp_hash;
    ternaryfunc tp_call;
    reprfunc tp_str;
    getattrofunc tp_getattro;
    setattrofunc tp_setattro;

    /* Functions to access object as input/output buffer */
    PyBufferProcs *tp_as_buffer;

    /* Flags to define presence of optional/expanded features */
    unsigned long tp_flags;

    const char *tp_doc; /* Documentation string */

    /* call function for all accessible objects */
```

```
    traverseproc tp_traverse;

    /* delete references to contained objects */
    inquiry tp_clear;

    /* rich comparisons */
    richcmpfunc tp_richcompare;

    /* weak reference enabler */
    Py_ssize_t tp_weaklistoffset;

    /* Iterators */
    getiterfunc tp_iter;
    iternextfunc tp_iternext;

    /* Attribute descriptor and subclassing stuff */
    struct PyMethodDef *tp_methods;
    struct PyMemberDef *tp_members;
    struct PyGetSetDef *tp_getset;
    struct _typeobject *tp_base;
    PyObject *tp_dict;
    descrgetfunc tp_descr_get;
    descrsetfunc tp_descr_set;
    Py_ssize_t tp_dictoffset;
    initproc tp_init;
    allocfunc tp_alloc;
    newfunc tp_new;
    freefunc tp_free; /* Low-level free-memory routine */
    inquiry tp_is_gc; /* For PyObject_IS_GC */
    PyObject *tp_bases;
    PyObject *tp_mro; /* method resolution order */
    PyObject *tp_cache;
    PyObject *tp_subclasses;
    PyObject *tp_weaklist;
    destructor tp_del;

    /* Type attribute cache version tag. Added in version 2.6 */
    unsigned int tp_version_tag;

    destructor tp_finalize;

} PyTypeObject;
```

The type object structure extends the *PyVarObject* structure. The **ob_size** field is used for dynamic types (created by **type_new()**, usually called from a class statement). Note that *PyType_Type* (the metatype) initializes *tp_itemsize*, which means that its instances (i.e. type objects) *must* have the **ob_size** field.

PyObject* **PyObject._ob_next**
PyObject* **PyObject._ob_prev**

These fields are only present when the macro **Py_TRACE_REFS** is defined. Their initialization to *NULL* is taken care of by the **PyObject_HEAD_INIT** macro. For statically allocated objects, these fields always remain *NULL*. For dynamically allocated objects, these two fields are used to link the object into a doubly-linked list of *all* live objects on the heap. This could be used for various debugging purposes; currently the only use is to print the objects that are still alive at the end of a run when the environment variable **PYTHONDUMPREFS** is set.

These fields are not inherited by subtypes.

Py_ssize_t **PyObject.ob_refcnt**

This is the type object's reference count, initialized to 1 by the `PyObject_HEAD_INIT` macro. Note that for statically allocated type objects, the type's instances (objects whose `ob_type` points back to the type) do *not* count as references. But for dynamically allocated type objects, the instances *do* count as references.

This field is not inherited by subtypes.

*PyTypeObject** `PyObject.ob_type`

This is the type's type, in other words its metatype. It is initialized by the argument to the `PyObject_HEAD_INIT` macro, and its value should normally be `&PyType_Type`. However, for dynamically loadable extension modules that must be usable on Windows (at least), the compiler complains that this is not a valid initializer. Therefore, the convention is to pass *NULL* to the `PyObject_HEAD_INIT` macro and to initialize this field explicitly at the start of the module's initialization function, before doing anything else. This is typically done like this:

```
Foo_Type.ob_type = &PyType_Type;
```

This should be done before any instances of the type are created. *PyType_Ready()* checks if `ob_type` is *NULL*, and if so, initializes it to the `ob_type` field of the base class. *PyType_Ready()* will not change this field if it is non-zero.

This field is inherited by subtypes.

Py_ssize_t `PyVarObject.ob_size`

For statically allocated type objects, this should be initialized to zero. For dynamically allocated type objects, this field has a special internal meaning.

This field is not inherited by subtypes.

const char* `PyTypeObject.tp_name`

Pointer to a NUL-terminated string containing the name of the type. For types that are accessible as module globals, the string should be the full module name, followed by a dot, followed by the type name; for built-in types, it should be just the type name. If the module is a submodule of a package, the full package name is part of the full module name. For example, a type named T defined in module M in subpackage Q in package P should have the *tp_name* initializer `"P.Q.M.T"`.

For dynamically allocated type objects, this should just be the type name, and the module name explicitly stored in the type dict as the value for key `'__module__'`.

For statically allocated type objects, the tp_name field should contain a dot. Everything before the last dot is made accessible as the `__module__` attribute, and everything after the last dot is made accessible as the `__name__` attribute.

If no dot is present, the entire *tp_name* field is made accessible as the `__name__` attribute, and the `__module__` attribute is undefined (unless explicitly set in the dictionary, as explained above). This means your type will be impossible to pickle. Additionally, it will not be listed in module documentations created with pydoc.

This field is not inherited by subtypes.

Py_ssize_t `PyTypeObject.tp_basicsize`
Py_ssize_t `PyTypeObject.tp_itemsize`

These fields allow calculating the size in bytes of instances of the type.

There are two kinds of types: types with fixed-length instances have a zero *tp_itemsize* field, types with variable-length instances have a non-zero *tp_itemsize* field. For a type with fixed-length instances, all instances have the same size, given in *tp_basicsize*.

For a type with variable-length instances, the instances must have an `ob_size` field, and the instance size is *tp_basicsize* plus N times *tp_itemsize*, where N is the "length" of the object. The value of N is typically stored in the instance's `ob_size` field. There are exceptions: for example, ints use a negative `ob_size` to indicate a negative number, and N is `abs(ob_size)` there. Also, the presence of an **ob_size** field in the instance layout doesn't mean that the instance structure is variable-length (for example, the structure for the list type has fixed-length instances, yet those instances have a meaningful **ob_size** field).

The basic size includes the fields in the instance declared by the macro *PyObject_HEAD* or *PyObject_VAR_HEAD* (whichever is used to declare the instance struct) and this in turn includes the **_ob_prev** and **_ob_next** fields if they are present. This means that the only correct way to get an initializer for the *tp_basicsize* is to use the **sizeof** operator on the struct used to declare the instance layout. The basic size does not include the GC header size.

These fields are inherited separately by subtypes. If the base type has a non-zero *tp_itemsize*, it is generally not safe to set *tp_itemsize* to a different non-zero value in a subtype (though this depends on the implementation of the base type).

A note about alignment: if the variable items require a particular alignment, this should be taken care of by the value of *tp_basicsize*. Example: suppose a type implements an array of **double**. *tp_itemsize* is **sizeof(double)**. It is the programmer's responsibility that *tp_basicsize* is a multiple of **sizeof(double)** (assuming this is the alignment requirement for **double**).

destructor **PyTypeObject.tp_dealloc**
> A pointer to the instance destructor function. This function must be defined unless the type guarantees that its instances will never be deallocated (as is the case for the singletons **None** and **Ellipsis**).
>
> The destructor function is called by the *Py_DECREF()* and *Py_XDECREF()* macros when the new reference count is zero. At this point, the instance is still in existence, but there are no references to it. The destructor function should free all references which the instance owns, free all memory buffers owned by the instance (using the freeing function corresponding to the allocation function used to allocate the buffer), and finally (as its last action) call the type's *tp_free* function. If the type is not subtypable (doesn't have the *Py_TPFLAGS_BASETYPE* flag bit set), it is permissible to call the object deallocator directly instead of via *tp_free*. The object deallocator should be the one used to allocate the instance; this is normally *PyObject_Del()* if the instance was allocated using *PyObject_New()* or **PyObject_VarNew()**, or *PyObject_GC_Del()* if the instance was allocated using *PyObject_GC_New()* or *PyObject_GC_NewVar()*.
>
> This field is inherited by subtypes.

printfunc **PyTypeObject.tp_print**
> Reserved slot, formerly used for print formatting in Python 2.x.

getattrfunc **PyTypeObject.tp_getattr**
> An optional pointer to the get-attribute-string function.
>
> This field is deprecated. When it is defined, it should point to a function that acts the same as the *tp_getattro* function, but taking a C string instead of a Python string object to give the attribute name. The signature is

```
PyObject * tp_getattr(PyObject *o, char *attr_name);
```

> This field is inherited by subtypes together with *tp_getattro*: a subtype inherits both *tp_getattr* and *tp_getattro* from its base type when the subtype's *tp_getattr* and *tp_getattro* are both *NULL*.

setattrfunc **PyTypeObject.tp_setattr**
> An optional pointer to the function for setting and deleting attributes.
>
> This field is deprecated. When it is defined, it should point to a function that acts the same as the *tp_setattro* function, but taking a C string instead of a Python string object to give the attribute name. The signature is

```
PyObject * tp_setattr(PyObject *o, char *attr_name, PyObject *v);
```

The *v* argument is set to *NULL* to delete the attribute. This field is inherited by subtypes together with `tp_setattro`: a subtype inherits both `tp_setattr` and `tp_setattro` from its base type when the subtype's `tp_setattr` and `tp_setattro` are both *NULL*.

*PyAsyncMethods** **tp_as_async**

Pointer to an additional structure that contains fields relevant only to objects which implement *awaitable* and *asynchronous iterator* protocols at the C-level. See *Async Object Structures* for details.

New in version 3.5: Formerly known as `tp_compare` and `tp_reserved`.

reprfunc **PyTypeObject.tp_repr**

An optional pointer to a function that implements the built-in function `repr()`.

The signature is the same as for *PyObject_Repr()*; it must return a string or a Unicode object. Ideally, this function should return a string that, when passed to `eval()`, given a suitable environment, returns an object with the same value. If this is not feasible, it should return a string starting with `'<'` and ending with `'>'` from which both the type and the value of the object can be deduced.

When this field is not set, a string of the form `<%s object at %p>` is returned, where `%s` is replaced by the type name, and `%p` by the object's memory address.

This field is inherited by subtypes.

*PyNumberMethods** **tp_as_number**

Pointer to an additional structure that contains fields relevant only to objects which implement the number protocol. These fields are documented in *Number Object Structures*.

The **tp_as_number** field is not inherited, but the contained fields are inherited individually.

*PySequenceMethods** **tp_as_sequence**

Pointer to an additional structure that contains fields relevant only to objects which implement the sequence protocol. These fields are documented in *Sequence Object Structures*.

The **tp_as_sequence** field is not inherited, but the contained fields are inherited individually.

*PyMappingMethods** **tp_as_mapping**

Pointer to an additional structure that contains fields relevant only to objects which implement the mapping protocol. These fields are documented in *Mapping Object Structures*.

The **tp_as_mapping** field is not inherited, but the contained fields are inherited individually.

hashfunc **PyTypeObject.tp_hash**

An optional pointer to a function that implements the built-in function `hash()`.

The signature is the same as for *PyObject_Hash()*; it must return a value of the type Py_hash_t. The value −1 should not be returned as a normal return value; when an error occurs during the computation of the hash value, the function should set an exception and return −1.

This field can be set explicitly to *PyObject_HashNotImplemented()* to block inheritance of the hash method from a parent type. This is interpreted as the equivalent of `__hash__` = None at the Python level, causing `isinstance(o, collections.Hashable)` to correctly return False. Note that the converse is also true - setting `__hash__` = None on a class at the Python level will result in the **tp_hash** slot being set to *PyObject_HashNotImplemented()*.

When this field is not set, an attempt to take the hash of the object raises **TypeError**.

This field is inherited by subtypes together with *tp_richcompare*: a subtype inherits both of *tp_richcompare* and *tp_hash*, when the subtype's *tp_richcompare* and *tp_hash* are both *NULL*.

ternaryfunc **PyTypeObject.tp_call**

An optional pointer to a function that implements calling the object. This should be *NULL* if the object is not callable. The signature is the same as for *PyObject_Call()*.

This field is inherited by subtypes.

reprfunc **PyTypeObject.tp_str**
> An optional pointer to a function that implements the built-in operation **str()**. (Note that **str** is a type now, and **str()** calls the constructor for that type. This constructor calls *PyObject_Str()* to do the actual work, and *PyObject_Str()* will call this handler.)
>
> The signature is the same as for *PyObject_Str()*; it must return a string or a Unicode object. This function should return a "friendly" string representation of the object, as this is the representation that will be used, among other things, by the **print()** function.
>
> When this field is not set, *PyObject_Repr()* is called to return a string representation.
>
> This field is inherited by subtypes.

getattrofunc **PyTypeObject.tp_getattro**
> An optional pointer to the get-attribute function.
>
> The signature is the same as for *PyObject_GetAttr()*. It is usually convenient to set this field to *PyObject_GenericGetAttr()*, which implements the normal way of looking for object attributes.
>
> This field is inherited by subtypes together with *tp_getattr*: a subtype inherits both *tp_getattr* and *tp_getattro* from its base type when the subtype's *tp_getattr* and *tp_getattro* are both *NULL*.

setattrofunc **PyTypeObject.tp_setattro**
> An optional pointer to the function for setting and deleting attributes.
>
> The signature is the same as for *PyObject_SetAttr()*, but setting *v* to *NULL* to delete an attribute must be supported. It is usually convenient to set this field to *PyObject_GenericSetAttr()*, which implements the normal way of setting object attributes.
>
> This field is inherited by subtypes together with *tp_setattr*: a subtype inherits both *tp_setattr* and *tp_setattro* from its base type when the subtype's *tp_setattr* and *tp_setattro* are both *NULL*.

*PyBufferProcs** **PyTypeObject.tp_as_buffer**
> Pointer to an additional structure that contains fields relevant only to objects which implement the buffer interface. These fields are documented in *Buffer Object Structures*.
>
> The *tp_as_buffer* field is not inherited, but the contained fields are inherited individually.

unsigned long **PyTypeObject.tp_flags**
> This field is a bit mask of various flags. Some flags indicate variant semantics for certain situations; others are used to indicate that certain fields in the type object (or in the extension structures referenced via **tp_as_number**, **tp_as_sequence**, **tp_as_mapping**, and *tp_as_buffer*) that were historically not always present are valid; if such a flag bit is clear, the type fields it guards must not be accessed and must be considered to have a zero or *NULL* value instead.
>
> Inheritance of this field is complicated. Most flag bits are inherited individually, i.e. if the base type has a flag bit set, the subtype inherits this flag bit. The flag bits that pertain to extension structures are strictly inherited if the extension structure is inherited, i.e. the base type's value of the flag bit is copied into the subtype together with a pointer to the extension structure. The *Py_TPFLAGS_HAVE_GC* flag bit is inherited together with the *tp_traverse* and *tp_clear* fields, i.e. if the *Py_TPFLAGS_HAVE_GC* flag bit is clear in the subtype and the *tp_traverse* and *tp_clear* fields in the subtype exist and have *NULL* values.
>
> The following bit masks are currently defined; these can be ORed together using the | operator to form the value of the *tp_flags* field. The macro *PyType_HasFeature()* takes a type and a flags value, *tp* and *f*, and checks whether **tp->tp_flags & f** is non-zero.
>
> **Py_TPFLAGS_HEAPTYPE**
>> This bit is set when the type object itself is allocated on the heap. In this case, the **ob_type** field of its instances is considered a reference to the type, and the type object is INCREF'ed when a new instance is created, and DECREF'ed when an instance is destroyed (this does not apply to instances of subtypes; only the type referenced by the instance's ob_type gets INCREF'ed or DECREF'ed).

Py_TPFLAGS_BASETYPE

This bit is set when the type can be used as the base type of another type. If this bit is clear, the type cannot be subtyped (similar to a "final" class in Java).

Py_TPFLAGS_READY

This bit is set when the type object has been fully initialized by *PyType_Ready()*.

Py_TPFLAGS_READYING

This bit is set while *PyType_Ready()* is in the process of initializing the type object.

Py_TPFLAGS_HAVE_GC

This bit is set when the object supports garbage collection. If this bit is set, instances must be created using *PyObject_GC_New()* and destroyed using *PyObject_GC_Del()*. More information in section *Supporting Cyclic Garbage Collection*. This bit also implies that the GC-related fields *tp_traverse* and *tp_clear* are present in the type object.

Py_TPFLAGS_DEFAULT

This is a bitmask of all the bits that pertain to the existence of certain fields in the type object and its extension structures. Currently, it includes the following bits: Py_TPFLAGS_HAVE_STACKLESS_EXTENSION, Py_TPFLAGS_HAVE_VERSION_TAG.

Py_TPFLAGS_LONG_SUBCLASS

Py_TPFLAGS_LIST_SUBCLASS

Py_TPFLAGS_TUPLE_SUBCLASS

Py_TPFLAGS_BYTES_SUBCLASS

Py_TPFLAGS_UNICODE_SUBCLASS

Py_TPFLAGS_DICT_SUBCLASS

Py_TPFLAGS_BASE_EXC_SUBCLASS

Py_TPFLAGS_TYPE_SUBCLASS

These flags are used by functions such as *PyLong_Check()* to quickly determine if a type is a subclass of a built-in type; such specific checks are faster than a generic check, like *PyObject_IsInstance()*. Custom types that inherit from built-ins should have their *tp_flags* set appropriately, or the code that interacts with such types will behave differently depending on what kind of check is used.

Py_TPFLAGS_HAVE_FINALIZE

This bit is set when the *tp_finalize* slot is present in the type structure.

New in version 3.4.

const char* **PyTypeObject.tp_doc**

An optional pointer to a NUL-terminated C string giving the docstring for this type object. This is exposed as the __doc__ attribute on the type and instances of the type.

This field is *not* inherited by subtypes.

traverseproc **PyTypeObject.tp_traverse**

An optional pointer to a traversal function for the garbage collector. This is only used if the *Py_TPFLAGS_HAVE_GC* flag bit is set. More information about Python's garbage collection scheme can be found in section *Supporting Cyclic Garbage Collection*.

The *tp_traverse* pointer is used by the garbage collector to detect reference cycles. A typical implementation of a *tp_traverse* function simply calls *Py_VISIT()* on each of the instance's members that are Python objects. For example, this is function **local_traverse()** from the _thread extension module:

```
static int
local_traverse(localobject *self, visitproc visit, void *arg)
{
    Py_VISIT(self->args);
    Py_VISIT(self->kw);
    Py_VISIT(self->dict);
    return 0;
}
```

Note that *Py_VISIT()* is called only on those members that can participate in reference cycles. Although there is also a **self->key** member, it can only be *NULL* or a Python string and therefore cannot be part of a reference cycle.

On the other hand, even if you know a member can never be part of a cycle, as a debugging aid you may want to visit it anyway just so the **gc** module's **get_referents()** function will include it.

Note that *Py_VISIT()* requires the *visit* and *arg* parameters to **local_traverse()** to have these specific names; don't name them just anything.

This field is inherited by subtypes together with *tp_clear* and the *Py_TPFLAGS_HAVE_GC* flag bit: the flag bit, *tp_traverse*, and *tp_clear* are all inherited from the base type if they are all zero in the subtype.

inquiry **PyTypeObject.tp_clear**

An optional pointer to a clear function for the garbage collector. This is only used if the *Py_TPFLAGS_HAVE_GC* flag bit is set.

The *tp_clear* member function is used to break reference cycles in cyclic garbage detected by the garbage collector. Taken together, all *tp_clear* functions in the system must combine to break all reference cycles. This is subtle, and if in any doubt supply a *tp_clear* function. For example, the tuple type does not implement a *tp_clear* function, because it's possible to prove that no reference cycle can be composed entirely of tuples. Therefore the *tp_clear* functions of other types must be sufficient to break any cycle containing a tuple. This isn't immediately obvious, and there's rarely a good reason to avoid implementing *tp_clear*.

Implementations of *tp_clear* should drop the instance's references to those of its members that may be Python objects, and set its pointers to those members to *NULL*, as in the following example:

```
static int
local_clear(localobject *self)
{
    Py_CLEAR(self->key);
    Py_CLEAR(self->args);
    Py_CLEAR(self->kw);
    Py_CLEAR(self->dict);
    return 0;
}
```

The *Py_CLEAR()* macro should be used, because clearing references is delicate: the reference to the contained object must not be decremented until after the pointer to the contained object is set to *NULL*. This is because decrementing the reference count may cause the contained object to become trash, triggering a chain of reclamation activity that may include invoking arbitrary Python code (due to finalizers, or weakref callbacks, associated with the contained object). If it's possible for such code to reference *self* again, it's important that the pointer to the contained object be *NULL* at that time, so that *self* knows the contained object can no longer be used. The *Py_CLEAR()* macro performs the operations in a safe order.

Because the goal of *tp_clear* functions is to break reference cycles, it's not necessary to clear contained objects like Python strings or Python integers, which can't participate in reference cycles. On the other hand, it may be convenient to clear all contained Python objects, and write the type's *tp_dealloc* function to invoke *tp_clear*.

More information about Python's garbage collection scheme can be found in section *Supporting Cyclic Garbage Collection*.

This field is inherited by subtypes together with *tp_traverse* and the *Py_TPFLAGS_HAVE_GC* flag bit: the flag bit, *tp_traverse*, and *tp_clear* are all inherited from the base type if they are all zero in the subtype.

richcmpfunc **PyTypeObject.tp_richcompare**

An optional pointer to the rich comparison function, whose signature is **PyObject *tp_richcompare(PyObject *a, PyObject *b, int op)**. The first parameter is guaranteed to be an instance of the type that is defined by *PyTypeObject*.

The function should return the result of the comparison (usually **Py_True** or **Py_False**). If the comparison is undefined, it must return **Py_NotImplemented**, if another error occurred it must return **NULL** and set an exception condition.

Note: If you want to implement a type for which only a limited set of comparisons makes sense (e.g. == and !=, but not < and friends), directly raise **TypeError** in the rich comparison function.

This field is inherited by subtypes together with *tp_hash*: a subtype inherits *tp_richcompare* and *tp_hash* when the subtype's *tp_richcompare* and *tp_hash* are both *NULL*.

The following constants are defined to be used as the third argument for *tp_richcompare* and for *PyObject_RichCompare()*:

Constant	Comparison
Py_LT	<
Py_LE	<=
Py_EQ	==
Py_NE	!=
Py_GT	>
Py_GE	>=

Py_ssize_t **PyTypeObject.tp_weaklistoffset**

If the instances of this type are weakly referenceable, this field is greater than zero and contains the offset in the instance structure of the weak reference list head (ignoring the GC header, if present); this offset is used by **PyObject_ClearWeakRefs()** and the **PyWeakref_*()** functions. The instance structure needs to include a field of type *PyObject** which is initialized to *NULL*.

Do not confuse this field with *tp_weaklist*; that is the list head for weak references to the type object itself.

This field is inherited by subtypes, but see the rules listed below. A subtype may override this offset; this means that the subtype uses a different weak reference list head than the base type. Since the list head is always found via *tp_weaklistoffset*, this should not be a problem.

When a type defined by a class statement has no **__slots__** declaration, and none of its base types are weakly referenceable, the type is made weakly referenceable by adding a weak reference list head slot to the instance layout and setting the *tp_weaklistoffset* of that slot's offset.

When a type's **__slots__** declaration contains a slot named **__weakref__**, that slot becomes the weak reference list head for instances of the type, and the slot's offset is stored in the type's *tp_weaklistoffset*.

When a type's `__slots__` declaration does not contain a slot named `__weakref__`, the type inherits its *tp_weaklistoffset* from its base type.

getiterfunc **PyTypeObject.tp_iter**

An optional pointer to a function that returns an iterator for the object. Its presence normally signals that the instances of this type are iterable (although sequences may be iterable without this function).

This function has the same signature as *PyObject_GetIter()*.

This field is inherited by subtypes.

iternextfunc **PyTypeObject.tp_iternext**

An optional pointer to a function that returns the next item in an iterator. When the iterator is exhausted, it must return *NULL*; a `StopIteration` exception may or may not be set. When another error occurs, it must return *NULL* too. Its presence signals that the instances of this type are iterators.

Iterator types should also define the *tp_iter* function, and that function should return the iterator instance itself (not a new iterator instance).

This function has the same signature as *PyIter_Next()*.

This field is inherited by subtypes.

struct *PyMethodDef** **PyTypeObject.tp_methods**

An optional pointer to a static *NULL*-terminated array of *PyMethodDef* structures, declaring regular methods of this type.

For each entry in the array, an entry is added to the type's dictionary (see *tp_dict* below) containing a method descriptor.

This field is not inherited by subtypes (methods are inherited through a different mechanism).

struct *PyMemberDef** **PyTypeObject.tp_members**

An optional pointer to a static *NULL*-terminated array of *PyMemberDef* structures, declaring regular data members (fields or slots) of instances of this type.

For each entry in the array, an entry is added to the type's dictionary (see *tp_dict* below) containing a member descriptor.

This field is not inherited by subtypes (members are inherited through a different mechanism).

struct *PyGetSetDef** **PyTypeObject.tp_getset**

An optional pointer to a static *NULL*-terminated array of *PyGetSetDef* structures, declaring computed attributes of instances of this type.

For each entry in the array, an entry is added to the type's dictionary (see *tp_dict* below) containing a getset descriptor.

This field is not inherited by subtypes (computed attributes are inherited through a different mechanism).

PyTypeObject* **PyTypeObject.tp_base**

An optional pointer to a base type from which type properties are inherited. At this level, only single inheritance is supported; multiple inheritance require dynamically creating a type object by calling the metatype.

This field is not inherited by subtypes (obviously), but it defaults to &PyBaseObject_Type (which to Python programmers is known as the type `object`).

PyObject* **PyTypeObject.tp_dict**

The type's dictionary is stored here by *PyType_Ready()*.

This field should normally be initialized to *NULL* before PyType_Ready is called; it may also be initialized to a dictionary containing initial attributes for the type. Once *PyType_Ready()* has initialized the type, extra attributes for the type may be added to this dictionary only if they don't correspond to overloaded operations (like `__add__()`).

This field is not inherited by subtypes (though the attributes defined in here are inherited through a different mechanism).

> **Warning:** It is not safe to use *PyDict_SetItem()* on or otherwise modify *tp_dict* with the dictionary C-API.

descrgetfunc **PyTypeObject.tp_descr_get**
    An optional pointer to a "descriptor get" function.

    The function signature is

```
PyObject * tp_descr_get(PyObject *self, PyObject *obj, PyObject *type);
```

    This field is inherited by subtypes.

descrsetfunc **PyTypeObject.tp_descr_set**
    An optional pointer to a function for setting and deleting a descriptor's value.

    The function signature is

```
int tp_descr_set(PyObject *self, PyObject *obj, PyObject *value);
```

    The *value* argument is set to *NULL* to delete the value. This field is inherited by subtypes.

Py_ssize_t **PyTypeObject.tp_dictoffset**
    If the instances of this type have a dictionary containing instance variables, this field is non-zero and contains the offset in the instances of the type of the instance variable dictionary; this offset is used by *PyObject_GenericGetAttr()*.

    Do not confuse this field with *tp_dict*; that is the dictionary for attributes of the type object itself.

    If the value of this field is greater than zero, it specifies the offset from the start of the instance structure. If the value is less than zero, it specifies the offset from the *end* of the instance structure. A negative offset is more expensive to use, and should only be used when the instance structure contains a variable-length part. This is used for example to add an instance variable dictionary to subtypes of **str** or **tuple**. Note that the *tp_basicsize* field should account for the dictionary added to the end in that case, even though the dictionary is not included in the basic object layout. On a system with a pointer size of 4 bytes, *tp_dictoffset* should be set to −4 to indicate that the dictionary is at the very end of the structure.

    The real dictionary offset in an instance can be computed from a negative *tp_dictoffset* as follows:

```
dictoffset = tp_basicsize + abs(ob_size)*tp_itemsize + tp_dictoffset
if dictoffset is not aligned on sizeof(void*):
    round up to sizeof(void*)
```

    where *tp_basicsize*, *tp_itemsize* and *tp_dictoffset* are taken from the type object, and **ob_size** is taken from the instance. The absolute value is taken because ints use the sign of **ob_size** to store the sign of the number. (There's never a need to do this calculation yourself; it is done for you by _PyObject_GetDictPtr().)

    This field is inherited by subtypes, but see the rules listed below. A subtype may override this offset; this means that the subtype instances store the dictionary at a difference offset than the base type. Since the dictionary is always found via *tp_dictoffset*, this should not be a problem.

    When a type defined by a class statement has no **__slots__** declaration, and none of its base types has an instance variable dictionary, a dictionary slot is added to the instance layout and the *tp_dictoffset* is set to that slot's offset.

When a type defined by a class statement has a `__slots__` declaration, the type inherits its `tp_dictoffset` from its base type.

(Adding a slot named `__dict__` to the `__slots__` declaration does not have the expected effect, it just causes confusion. Maybe this should be added as a feature just like `__weakref__` though.)

initproc **PyTypeObject.tp_init**

An optional pointer to an instance initialization function.

This function corresponds to the `__init__()` method of classes. Like `__init__()`, it is possible to create an instance without calling `__init__()`, and it is possible to reinitialize an instance by calling its `__init__()` method again.

The function signature is

```
int tp_init(PyObject *self, PyObject *args, PyObject *kwds)
```

The self argument is the instance to be initialized; the *args* and *kwds* arguments represent positional and keyword arguments of the call to `__init__()`.

The *tp_init* function, if not *NULL*, is called when an instance is created normally by calling its type, after the type's *tp_new* function has returned an instance of the type. If the *tp_new* function returns an instance of some other type that is not a subtype of the original type, no *tp_init* function is called; if *tp_new* returns an instance of a subtype of the original type, the subtype's *tp_init* is called.

This field is inherited by subtypes.

allocfunc **PyTypeObject.tp_alloc**

An optional pointer to an instance allocation function.

The function signature is

```
PyObject *tp_alloc(PyTypeObject *self, Py_ssize_t nitems)
```

The purpose of this function is to separate memory allocation from memory initialization. It should return a pointer to a block of memory of adequate length for the instance, suitably aligned, and initialized to zeros, but with **ob_refcnt** set to 1 and **ob_type** set to the type argument. If the type's *tp_itemsize* is non-zero, the object's **ob_size** field should be initialized to *nitems* and the length of the allocated memory block should be **tp_basicsize + nitems*tp_itemsize**, rounded up to a multiple of **sizeof(void*)**; otherwise, *nitems* is not used and the length of the block should be *tp_basicsize*.

Do not use this function to do any other instance initialization, not even to allocate additional memory; that should be done by *tp_new*.

This field is inherited by static subtypes, but not by dynamic subtypes (subtypes created by a class statement); in the latter, this field is always set to *PyType_GenericAlloc()*, to force a standard heap allocation strategy. That is also the recommended value for statically defined types.

newfunc **PyTypeObject.tp_new**

An optional pointer to an instance creation function.

If this function is *NULL* for a particular type, that type cannot be called to create new instances; presumably there is some other way to create instances, like a factory function.

The function signature is

```
PyObject *tp_new(PyTypeObject *subtype, PyObject *args, PyObject *kwds)
```

The subtype argument is the type of the object being created; the *args* and *kwds* arguments represent positional and keyword arguments of the call to the type. Note that subtype doesn't have to equal the type whose *tp_new* function is called; it may be a subtype of that type (but not an unrelated type).

The *tp_new* function should call `subtype->tp_alloc(subtype, nitems)` to allocate space for the object, and then do only as much further initialization as is absolutely necessary. Initialization that can safely be ignored or repeated should be placed in the *tp_init* handler. A good rule of thumb is that for immutable types, all initialization should take place in *tp_new*, while for mutable types, most initialization should be deferred to *tp_init*.

This field is inherited by subtypes, except it is not inherited by static types whose *tp_base* is *NULL* or `&PyBaseObject_Type`.

destructor **PyTypeObject.tp_free**
An optional pointer to an instance deallocation function. Its signature is `freefunc`:

```
void tp_free(void *)
```

An initializer that is compatible with this signature is *PyObject_Free()*.

This field is inherited by static subtypes, but not by dynamic subtypes (subtypes created by a class statement); in the latter, this field is set to a deallocator suitable to match *PyType_GenericAlloc()* and the value of the *Py_TPFLAGS_HAVE_GC* flag bit.

inquiry **PyTypeObject.tp_is_gc**
An optional pointer to a function called by the garbage collector.

The garbage collector needs to know whether a particular object is collectible or not. Normally, it is sufficient to look at the object's type's *tp_flags* field, and check the *Py_TPFLAGS_HAVE_GC* flag bit. But some types have a mixture of statically and dynamically allocated instances, and the statically allocated instances are not collectible. Such types should define this function; it should return 1 for a collectible instance, and 0 for a non-collectible instance. The signature is

```
int tp_is_gc(PyObject *self)
```

(The only example of this are types themselves. The metatype, *PyType_Type*, defines this function to distinguish between statically and dynamically allocated types.)

This field is inherited by subtypes.

PyObject* **PyTypeObject.tp_bases**
Tuple of base types.

This is set for types created by a class statement. It should be *NULL* for statically defined types.

This field is not inherited.

PyObject* **PyTypeObject.tp_mro**
Tuple containing the expanded set of base types, starting with the type itself and ending with `object`, in Method Resolution Order.

This field is not inherited; it is calculated fresh by *PyType_Ready()*.

destructor **PyTypeObject.tp_finalize**
An optional pointer to an instance finalization function. Its signature is `destructor`:

```
void tp_finalize(PyObject *)
```

If *tp_finalize* is set, the interpreter calls it once when finalizing an instance. It is called either from the garbage collector (if the instance is part of an isolated reference cycle) or just before the object is deallocated. Either way, it is guaranteed to be called before attempting to break reference cycles, ensuring that it finds the object in a sane state.

tp_finalize should not mutate the current exception status; therefore, a recommended way to write a non-trivial finalizer is:

```
static void
local_finalize(PyObject *self)
{
    PyObject *error_type, *error_value, *error_traceback;

    /* Save the current exception, if any. */
    PyErr_Fetch(&error_type, &error_value, &error_traceback);

    /* ... */

    /* Restore the saved exception. */
    PyErr_Restore(error_type, error_value, error_traceback);
}
```

For this field to be taken into account (even through inheritance), you must also set the *Py_TPFLAGS_HAVE_FINALIZE* flags bit.

This field is inherited by subtypes.

New in version 3.4.

See also:

"Safe object finalization" (PEP 442)

PyObject* **PyTypeObject.tp_cache**
    Unused. Not inherited. Internal use only.

PyObject* **PyTypeObject.tp_subclasses**
    List of weak references to subclasses. Not inherited. Internal use only.

PyObject* **PyTypeObject.tp_weaklist**
    Weak reference list head, for weak references to this type object. Not inherited. Internal use only.

The remaining fields are only defined if the feature test macro `COUNT_ALLOCS` is defined, and are for internal use only. They are documented here for completeness. None of these fields are inherited by subtypes.

Py_ssize_t **PyTypeObject.tp_allocs**
    Number of allocations.

Py_ssize_t **PyTypeObject.tp_frees**
    Number of frees.

Py_ssize_t **PyTypeObject.tp_maxalloc**
    Maximum simultaneously allocated objects.

PyTypeObject* **PyTypeObject.tp_next**
    Pointer to the next type object with a non-zero *tp_allocs* field.

Also, note that, in a garbage collected Python, tp_dealloc may be called from any Python thread, not just the thread which created the object (if the object becomes part of a refcount cycle, that cycle might be collected by a garbage collection on any thread). This is not a problem for Python API calls, since the thread on which tp_dealloc is called will own the Global Interpreter Lock (GIL). However, if the object being destroyed in turn destroys objects from some other C or C++ library, care should be taken to ensure that destroying those objects on the thread which called tp_dealloc will not violate any assumptions of the library.

11.4 Number Object Structures

PyNumberMethods
    This structure holds pointers to the functions which an object uses to implement the number protocol.

Each function is used by the function of similar name documented in the *Number Protocol* section.

Here is the structure definition:

```
typedef struct {
    binaryfunc nb_add;
    binaryfunc nb_subtract;
    binaryfunc nb_multiply;
    binaryfunc nb_remainder;
    binaryfunc nb_divmod;
    ternaryfunc nb_power;
    unaryfunc nb_negative;
    unaryfunc nb_positive;
    unaryfunc nb_absolute;
    inquiry nb_bool;
    unaryfunc nb_invert;
    binaryfunc nb_lshift;
    binaryfunc nb_rshift;
    binaryfunc nb_and;
    binaryfunc nb_xor;
    binaryfunc nb_or;
    unaryfunc nb_int;
    void *nb_reserved;
    unaryfunc nb_float;

    binaryfunc nb_inplace_add;
    binaryfunc nb_inplace_subtract;
    binaryfunc nb_inplace_multiply;
    binaryfunc nb_inplace_remainder;
    ternaryfunc nb_inplace_power;
    binaryfunc nb_inplace_lshift;
    binaryfunc nb_inplace_rshift;
    binaryfunc nb_inplace_and;
    binaryfunc nb_inplace_xor;
    binaryfunc nb_inplace_or;

    binaryfunc nb_floor_divide;
    binaryfunc nb_true_divide;
    binaryfunc nb_inplace_floor_divide;
    binaryfunc nb_inplace_true_divide;

    unaryfunc nb_index;

    binaryfunc nb_matrix_multiply;
    binaryfunc nb_inplace_matrix_multiply;
} PyNumberMethods;
```

Note: Binary and ternary functions must check the type of all their operands, and implement the necessary conversions (at least one of the operands is an instance of the defined type). If the operation is not defined for the given operands, binary and ternary functions must return Py_NotImplemented, if another error occurred they must return NULL and set an exception.

Note: The nb_reserved field should always be NULL. It was previously called nb_long, and was renamed in Python 3.0.1.

11.5 Mapping Object Structures

PyMappingMethods
> This structure holds pointers to the functions which an object uses to implement the mapping protocol. It has three members:

lenfunc **PyMappingMethods.mp_length**
> This function is used by *PyMapping_Length()* and *PyObject_Size()*, and has the same signature. This slot may be set to *NULL* if the object has no defined length.

binaryfunc **PyMappingMethods.mp_subscript**
> This function is used by *PyObject_GetItem()* and has the same signature. This slot must be filled for the *PyMapping_Check()* function to return 1, it can be *NULL* otherwise.

objobjargproc **PyMappingMethods.mp_ass_subscript**
> This function is used by *PyObject_SetItem()* and *PyObject_DelItem()*. It has the same signature as *PyObject_SetItem()*, but *v* can also be set to *NULL* to delete an item. If this slot is *NULL*, the object does not support item assignment and deletion.

11.6 Sequence Object Structures

PySequenceMethods
> This structure holds pointers to the functions which an object uses to implement the sequence protocol.

lenfunc **PySequenceMethods.sq_length**
> This function is used by *PySequence_Size()* and *PyObject_Size()*, and has the same signature.

binaryfunc **PySequenceMethods.sq_concat**
> This function is used by *PySequence_Concat()* and has the same signature. It is also used by the + operator, after trying the numeric addition via the **nb_add** slot.

ssizeargfunc **PySequenceMethods.sq_repeat**
> This function is used by *PySequence_Repeat()* and has the same signature. It is also used by the * operator, after trying numeric multiplication via the **nb_multiply** slot.

ssizeargfunc **PySequenceMethods.sq_item**
> This function is used by *PySequence_GetItem()* and has the same signature. This slot must be filled for the *PySequence_Check()* function to return 1, it can be *NULL* otherwise.
>
> Negative indexes are handled as follows: if the **sq_length** slot is filled, it is called and the sequence length is used to compute a positive index which is passed to **sq_item**. If **sq_length** is *NULL*, the index is passed as is to the function.

ssizeobjargproc **PySequenceMethods.sq_ass_item**
> This function is used by *PySequence_SetItem()* and has the same signature. This slot may be left to *NULL* if the object does not support item assignment and deletion.

objobjproc **PySequenceMethods.sq_contains**
> This function may be used by *PySequence_Contains()* and has the same signature. This slot may be left to *NULL*, in this case *PySequence_Contains()* simply traverses the sequence until it finds a match.

binaryfunc **PySequenceMethods.sq_inplace_concat**
> This function is used by *PySequence_InPlaceConcat()* and has the same signature. It should modify its first operand, and return it.

ssizeargfunc **PySequenceMethods.sq_inplace_repeat**
> This function is used by *PySequence_InPlaceRepeat()* and has the same signature. It should modify its first operand, and return it.

11.7 Buffer Object Structures

PyBufferProcs

This structure holds pointers to the functions required by the *Buffer protocol*. The protocol defines how an exporter object can expose its internal data to consumer objects.

getbufferproc **PyBufferProcs.bf_getbuffer**

The signature of this function is:

```
int (PyObject *exporter, Py_buffer *view, int flags);
```

Handle a request to *exporter* to fill in *view* as specified by *flags*. Except for point (3), an implementation of this function MUST take these steps:

1. Check if the request can be met. If not, raise `PyExc_BufferError`, set `view->obj` to *NULL* and return `-1`.

2. Fill in the requested fields.

3. Increment an internal counter for the number of exports.

4. Set `view->obj` to *exporter* and increment `view->obj`.

5. Return `0`.

If *exporter* is part of a chain or tree of buffer providers, two main schemes can be used:

- Re-export: Each member of the tree acts as the exporting object and sets `view->obj` to a new reference to itself.

- Redirect: The buffer request is redirected to the root object of the tree. Here, `view->obj` will be a new reference to the root object.

The individual fields of *view* are described in section *Buffer structure*, the rules how an exporter must react to specific requests are in section *Buffer request types*.

All memory pointed to in the *Py_buffer* structure belongs to the exporter and must remain valid until there are no consumers left. *format*, *shape*, *strides*, *suboffsets* and *internal* are read-only for the consumer.

PyBuffer_FillInfo() provides an easy way of exposing a simple bytes buffer while dealing correctly with all request types.

PyObject_GetBuffer() is the interface for the consumer that wraps this function.

releasebufferproc **PyBufferProcs.bf_releasebuffer**

The signature of this function is:

```
void (PyObject *exporter, Py_buffer *view);
```

Handle a request to release the resources of the buffer. If no resources need to be released, *PyBufferProcs.bf_releasebuffer* may be *NULL*. Otherwise, a standard implementation of this function will take these optional steps:

1. Decrement an internal counter for the number of exports.

2. If the counter is 0, free all memory associated with *view*.

The exporter MUST use the *internal* field to keep track of buffer-specific resources. This field is guaranteed to remain constant, while a consumer MAY pass a copy of the original buffer as the *view* argument.

This function MUST NOT decrement `view->obj`, since that is done automatically in *PyBuffer_Release()* (this scheme is useful for breaking reference cycles).

PyBuffer_Release() is the interface for the consumer that wraps this function.

11.8 Async Object Structures

New in version 3.5.

PyAsyncMethods
> This structure holds pointers to the functions required to implement *awaitable* and *asynchronous iterator* objects.
>
> Here is the structure definition:

```
typedef struct {
    unaryfunc am_await;
    unaryfunc am_aiter;
    unaryfunc am_anext;
} PyAsyncMethods;
```

unaryfunc **PyAsyncMethods.am_await**
> The signature of this function is:

```
PyObject *am_await(PyObject *self)
```

> The returned object must be an iterator, i.e. *PyIter_Check()* must return **1** for it.
>
> This slot may be set to *NULL* if an object is not an *awaitable*.

unaryfunc **PyAsyncMethods.am_aiter**
> The signature of this function is:

```
PyObject *am_aiter(PyObject *self)
```

> Must return an *awaitable* object. See __anext__() for details.
>
> This slot may be set to *NULL* if an object does not implement asynchronous iteration protocol.

unaryfunc **PyAsyncMethods.am_anext**
> The signature of this function is:

```
PyObject *am_anext(PyObject *self)
```

> Must return an *awaitable* object. See __anext__() for details. This slot may be set to *NULL*.

11.9 Supporting Cyclic Garbage Collection

Python's support for detecting and collecting garbage which involves circular references requires support from object types which are "containers" for other objects which may also be containers. Types which do not store references to other objects, or which only store references to atomic types (such as numbers or strings), do not need to provide any explicit support for garbage collection.

To create a container type, the *tp_flags* field of the type object must include the *Py_TPFLAGS_HAVE_GC* and provide an implementation of the *tp_traverse* handler. If instances of the type are mutable, a *tp_clear* implementation must also be provided.

Py_TPFLAGS_HAVE_GC
> Objects with a type with this flag set must conform with the rules documented here. For convenience these objects will be referred to as container objects.

Constructors for container types must conform to two rules:

1. The memory for the object must be allocated using *PyObject_GC_New()* or *PyObject_GC_NewVar()*.

2. Once all the fields which may contain references to other containers are initialized, it must call *PyObject_GC_Track()*.

TYPE* **PyObject_GC_New**(TYPE, *PyTypeObject *type*)
> Analogous to *PyObject_New()* but for container objects with the *Py_TPFLAGS_HAVE_GC* flag set.

TYPE* **PyObject_GC_NewVar**(TYPE, *PyTypeObject *type*, Py_ssize_t *size*)
> Analogous to *PyObject_NewVar()* but for container objects with the *Py_TPFLAGS_HAVE_GC* flag set.

TYPE* **PyObject_GC_Resize**(TYPE, *PyVarObject *op*, Py_ssize_t *newsize*)
> Resize an object allocated by *PyObject_NewVar()*. Returns the resized object or *NULL* on failure.

void **PyObject_GC_Track**(*PyObject *op*)
> Adds the object *op* to the set of container objects tracked by the collector. The collector can run at unexpected times so objects must be valid while being tracked. This should be called once all the fields followed by the *tp_traverse* handler become valid, usually near the end of the constructor.

void **_PyObject_GC_TRACK**(*PyObject *op*)
> A macro version of *PyObject_GC_Track()*. It should not be used for extension modules.

Similarly, the deallocator for the object must conform to a similar pair of rules:

1. Before fields which refer to other containers are invalidated, *PyObject_GC_UnTrack()* must be called.

2. The object's memory must be deallocated using *PyObject_GC_Del()*.

void **PyObject_GC_Del**(void *op*)
> Releases memory allocated to an object using *PyObject_GC_New()* or *PyObject_GC_NewVar()*.

void **PyObject_GC_UnTrack**(void *op*)
> Remove the object *op* from the set of container objects tracked by the collector. Note that *PyObject_GC_Track()* can be called again on this object to add it back to the set of tracked objects. The deallocator (*tp_dealloc* handler) should call this for the object before any of the fields used by the *tp_traverse* handler become invalid.

void **_PyObject_GC_UNTRACK**(*PyObject *op*)
> A macro version of *PyObject_GC_UnTrack()*. It should not be used for extension modules.

The *tp_traverse* handler accepts a function parameter of this type:

int **(*visitproc)**(*PyObject *object*, void *arg*)
> Type of the visitor function passed to the *tp_traverse* handler. The function should be called with an object to traverse as *object* and the third parameter to the *tp_traverse* handler as *arg*. The Python core uses several visitor functions to implement cyclic garbage detection; it's not expected that users will need to write their own visitor functions.

The *tp_traverse* handler must have the following type:

int **(*traverseproc)**(*PyObject *self*, *visitproc visit*, void *arg*)
> Traversal function for a container object. Implementations must call the *visit* function for each object directly contained by *self*, with the parameters to *visit* being the contained object and the *arg* value passed to the handler. The *visit* function must not be called with a *NULL* object argument. If *visit* returns a non-zero value that value should be returned immediately.

To simplify writing *tp_traverse* handlers, a *Py_VISIT()* macro is provided. In order to use this macro, the *tp_traverse* implementation must name its arguments exactly *visit* and *arg*:

void **Py_VISIT**(*PyObject *o*)
> If *o* is not *NULL*, call the *visit* callback, with arguments *o* and *arg*. If *visit* returns a non-zero value, then return it. Using this macro, *tp_traverse* handlers look like:

```
static int
my_traverse(Noddy *self, visitproc visit, void *arg)
{
    Py_VISIT(self->foo);
    Py_VISIT(self->bar);
    return 0;
}
```

The *tp_clear* handler must be of the *inquiry* type, or *NULL* if the object is immutable.

int (**inquiry**)(*PyObject *self*)

    Drop references that may have created reference cycles. Immutable objects do not have to define this method since they can never directly create reference cycles. Note that the object must still be valid after calling this method (don't just call *Py_DECREF()* on a reference). The collector will call this method if it detects that this object is involved in a reference cycle.

API AND ABI VERSIONING

PY_VERSION_HEX is the Python version number encoded in a single integer.

For example if the PY_VERSION_HEX is set to 0x030401a2, the underlying version information can be found by treating it as a 32 bit number in the following manner:

Bytes	Bits (big endian order)	Meaning
1	1-8	PY_MAJOR_VERSION (the 3 in 3.4.1a2)
2	9-16	PY_MINOR_VERSION (the 4 in 3.4.1a2)
3	17-24	PY_MICRO_VERSION (the 1 in 3.4.1a2)
4	25-28	PY_RELEASE_LEVEL (0xA for alpha, 0xB for beta, 0xC for release candidate and 0xF for final), in this case it is alpha.
	29-32	PY_RELEASE_SERIAL (the 2 in 3.4.1a2, zero for final releases)

Thus 3.4.1a2 is hexversion 0x030401a2.

All the given macros are defined in Include/patchlevel.h.

GLOSSARY

>>> The default Python prompt of the interactive shell. Often seen for code examples which can be executed interactively in the interpreter.

... The default Python prompt of the interactive shell when entering code for an indented code block or within a pair of matching left and right delimiters (parentheses, square brackets or curly braces).

2to3 A tool that tries to convert Python 2.x code to Python 3.x code by handling most of the incompatibilities which can be detected by parsing the source and traversing the parse tree.

2to3 is available in the standard library as `lib2to3`; a standalone entry point is provided as `Tools/scripts/2to3`. See 2to3-reference.

abstract base class Abstract base classes complement *duck-typing* by providing a way to define interfaces when other techniques like `hasattr()` would be clumsy or subtly wrong (for example with magic methods). ABCs introduce virtual subclasses, which are classes that don't inherit from a class but are still recognized by `isinstance()` and `issubclass()`; see the `abc` module documentation. Python comes with many built-in ABCs for data structures (in the `collections.abc` module), numbers (in the `numbers` module), streams (in the `io` module), import finders and loaders (in the `importlib.abc` module). You can create your own ABCs with the `abc` module.

argument A value passed to a *function* (or *method*) when calling the function. There are two kinds of argument:

- *keyword argument*: an argument preceded by an identifier (e.g. `name=`) in a function call or passed as a value in a dictionary preceded by `**`. For example, 3 and 5 are both keyword arguments in the following calls to `complex()`:

```
complex(real=3, imag=5)
complex(**{'real': 3, 'imag': 5})
```

- *positional argument*: an argument that is not a keyword argument. Positional arguments can appear at the beginning of an argument list and/or be passed as elements of an *iterable* preceded by `*`. For example, 3 and 5 are both positional arguments in the following calls:

```
complex(3, 5)
complex(*(3, 5))
```

Arguments are assigned to the named local variables in a function body. See the calls section for the rules governing this assignment. Syntactically, any expression can be used to represent an argument; the evaluated value is assigned to the local variable.

See also the *parameter* glossary entry, the FAQ question on the difference between arguments and parameters, and PEP 362.

asynchronous context manager An object which controls the environment seen in an `async with` statement by defining `__aenter__()` and `__aexit__()` methods. Introduced by PEP 492.

asynchronous generator A function which returns an *asynchronous generator iterator*. It looks like a coroutine function defined with `async def` except that it contains `yield` expressions for producing a series of values usable in an `async for` loop.

Usually refers to a asynchronous generator function, but may refer to an *asynchronous generator iterator* in some contexts. In cases where the intended meaning isn't clear, using the full terms avoids ambiguity.

An asynchronous generator function may contain `await` expressions as well as `async for`, and `async with` statements.

asynchronous generator iterator An object created by a *asynchronous generator* function.

This is an *asynchronous iterator* which when called using the `__anext__()` method returns an awaitable object which will execute that the body of the asynchronous generator function until the next `yield` expression.

Each `yield` temporarily suspends processing, remembering the location execution state (including local variables and pending try-statements). When the *asynchronous generator iterator* effectively resumes with another awaitable returned by `__anext__()`, it picks-up where it left-off. See PEP 492 and PEP 525.

asynchronous iterable An object, that can be used in an `async for` statement. Must return an *asynchronous iterator* from its `__aiter__()` method. Introduced by PEP 492.

asynchronous iterator An object that implements `__aiter__()` and `__anext__()` methods. `__anext__` must return an *awaitable* object. `async for` resolves awaitable returned from asynchronous iterator's `__anext__()` method until it raises `StopAsyncIteration` exception. Introduced by PEP 492.

attribute A value associated with an object which is referenced by name using dotted expressions. For example, if an object *o* has an attribute *a* it would be referenced as *o.a*.

awaitable An object that can be used in an `await` expression. Can be a *coroutine* or an object with an `__await__()` method. See also PEP 492.

BDFL Benevolent Dictator For Life, a.k.a. Guido van Rossum, Python's creator.

binary file A *file object* able to read and write *bytes-like objects*. Examples of binary files are files opened in binary mode (`'rb'`, `'wb'` or `'rb+'`), `sys.stdin.buffer`, `sys.stdout.buffer`, and instances of `io.BytesIO` and `gzip.GzipFile`.

See also:

A *text file* reads and writes `str` objects.

bytes-like object An object that supports the *Buffer Protocol* and can export a C-*contiguous* buffer. This includes all `bytes`, `bytearray`, and `array.array` objects, as well as many common `memoryview` objects. Bytes-like objects can be used for various operations that work with binary data; these include compression, saving to a binary file, and sending over a socket.

Some operations need the binary data to be mutable. The documentation often refers to these as "read-write bytes-like objects". Example mutable buffer objects include `bytearray` and a `memoryview` of a `bytearray`. Other operations require the binary data to be stored in immutable objects ("read-only bytes-like objects"); examples of these include `bytes` and a `memoryview` of a `bytes` object.

bytecode Python source code is compiled into bytecode, the internal representation of a Python program in the CPython interpreter. The bytecode is also cached in `.pyc` files so that executing the same file is faster the second time (recompilation from source to bytecode can be avoided). This "intermediate language" is said to run on a *virtual machine* that executes the machine code corresponding to each bytecode. Do note that bytecodes are not expected to work between different Python virtual machines, nor to be stable between Python releases.

A list of bytecode instructions can be found in the documentation for the dis module.

class A template for creating user-defined objects. Class definitions normally contain method definitions which operate on instances of the class.

coercion The implicit conversion of an instance of one type to another during an operation which involves two arguments of the same type. For example, `int(3.15)` converts the floating point number to the integer 3, but in `3+4.5`, each argument is of a different type (one int, one float), and both must be converted to the same type before they can be added or it will raise a `TypeError`. Without coercion, all arguments of even compatible types would have to be normalized to the same value by the programmer, e.g., `float(3)+4.5` rather than just `3+4.5`.

complex number An extension of the familiar real number system in which all numbers are expressed as a sum of a real part and an imaginary part. Imaginary numbers are real multiples of the imaginary unit (the square root of `-1`), often written i in mathematics or j in engineering. Python has built-in support for complex numbers, which are written with this latter notation; the imaginary part is written with a `j` suffix, e.g., `3+1j`. To get access to complex equivalents of the `math` module, use `cmath`. Use of complex numbers is a fairly advanced mathematical feature. If you're not aware of a need for them, it's almost certain you can safely ignore them.

context manager An object which controls the environment seen in a `with` statement by defining `__enter__()` and `__exit__()` methods. See PEP 343.

contiguous A buffer is considered contiguous exactly if it is either *C-contiguous* or *Fortran contiguous*. Zero-dimensional buffers are C and Fortran contiguous. In one-dimensional arrays, the items must be laid out in memory next to each other, in order of increasing indexes starting from zero. In multidimensional C-contiguous arrays, the last index varies the fastest when visiting items in order of memory address. However, in Fortran contiguous arrays, the first index varies the fastest.

coroutine Coroutines is a more generalized form of subroutines. Subroutines are entered at one point and exited at another point. Coroutines can be entered, exited, and resumed at many different points. They can be implemented with the `async def` statement. See also PEP 492.

coroutine function A function which returns a *coroutine* object. A coroutine function may be defined with the `async def` statement, and may contain `await`, `async for`, and `async with` keywords. These were introduced by PEP 492.

CPython The canonical implementation of the Python programming language, as distributed on python.org. The term "CPython" is used when necessary to distinguish this implementation from others such as Jython or IronPython.

decorator A function returning another function, usually applied as a function transformation using the `@wrapper` syntax. Common examples for decorators are `classmethod()` and `staticmethod()`.

The decorator syntax is merely syntactic sugar, the following two function definitions are semantically equivalent:

```
def f(...):
    ...
f = staticmethod(f)

@staticmethod
def f(...):
    ...
```

The same concept exists for classes, but is less commonly used there. See the documentation for function definitions and class definitions for more about decorators.

descriptor Any object which defines the methods `__get__()`, `__set__()`, or `__delete__()`. When a class attribute is a descriptor, its special binding behavior is triggered upon attribute lookup. Normally, using $a.b$ to get, set or delete an attribute looks up the object named b in the class dictionary for a, but if b is a descriptor, the respective descriptor method gets called. Understanding descriptors is a key to a deep understanding of Python because they are the basis for many features including functions, methods, properties, class methods, static methods, and reference to super classes.

For more information about descriptors' methods, see descriptors.

dictionary An associative array, where arbitrary keys are mapped to values. The keys can be any object with `__hash__()` and `__eq__()` methods. Called a hash in Perl.

dictionary view The objects returned from `dict.keys()`, `dict.values()`, and `dict.items()` are called dictionary views. They provide a dynamic view on the dictionary's entries, which means that when the dictionary changes, the view reflects these changes. To force the dictionary view to become a full list use `list(dictview)`. See dict-views.

docstring A string literal which appears as the first expression in a class, function or module. While ignored when the suite is executed, it is recognized by the compiler and put into the `__doc__` attribute of the enclosing class, function or module. Since it is available via introspection, it is the canonical place for documentation of the object.

duck-typing A programming style which does not look at an object's type to determine if it has the right interface; instead, the method or attribute is simply called or used ("If it looks like a duck and quacks like a duck, it must be a duck.") By emphasizing interfaces rather than specific types, well-designed code improves its flexibility by allowing polymorphic substitution. Duck-typing avoids tests using `type()` or `isinstance()`. (Note, however, that duck-typing can be complemented with *abstract base classes*.) Instead, it typically employs `hasattr()` tests or *EAFP* programming.

EAFP Easier to ask for forgiveness than permission. This common Python coding style assumes the existence of valid keys or attributes and catches exceptions if the assumption proves false. This clean and fast style is characterized by the presence of many `try` and `except` statements. The technique contrasts with the *LBYL* style common to many other languages such as C.

expression A piece of syntax which can be evaluated to some value. In other words, an expression is an accumulation of expression elements like literals, names, attribute access, operators or function calls which all return a value. In contrast to many other languages, not all language constructs are expressions. There are also *statements* which cannot be used as expressions, such as `if`. Assignments are also statements, not expressions.

extension module A module written in C or C++, using Python's C API to interact with the core and with user code.

f-string String literals prefixed with `'f'` or `'F'` are commonly called "f-strings" which is short for formatted string literals. See also PEP 498.

file object An object exposing a file-oriented API (with methods such as `read()` or `write()`) to an underlying resource. Depending on the way it was created, a file object can mediate access to a real on-disk file or to another type of storage or communication device (for example standard input/output, in-memory buffers, sockets, pipes, etc.). File objects are also called *file-like objects* or *streams*.

There are actually three categories of file objects: raw *binary files*, buffered *binary files* and *text files*. Their interfaces are defined in the `io` module. The canonical way to create a file object is by using the `open()` function.

file-like object A synonym for *file object*.

finder An object that tries to find the *loader* for a module that is being imported.

Since Python 3.3, there are two types of finder: *meta path finders* for use with `sys.meta_path`, and *path entry finders* for use with `sys.path_hooks`.

See PEP 302, PEP 420 and PEP 451 for much more detail.

floor division Mathematical division that rounds down to nearest integer. The floor division operator is `//`. For example, the expression `11 // 4` evaluates to `2` in contrast to the `2.75` returned by float true division. Note that `(-11) // 4` is `-3` because that is `-2.75` rounded *downward*. See PEP 238.

function A series of statements which returns some value to a caller. It can also be passed zero or more *arguments* which may be used in the execution of the body. See also *parameter*, *method*, and the function section.

function annotation An arbitrary metadata value associated with a function parameter or return value. Its syntax is explained in section function. Annotations may be accessed via the `__annotations__` special attribute of a function object.

Python itself does not assign any particular meaning to function annotations. They are intended to be interpreted by third-party libraries or tools. See PEP 3107, which describes some of their potential uses.

__future__ A pseudo-module which programmers can use to enable new language features which are not compatible with the current interpreter.

By importing the `__future__` module and evaluating its variables, you can see when a new feature was first added to the language and when it becomes the default:

```
>>> import __future__
>>> __future__.division
_Feature((2, 2, 0, 'alpha', 2), (3, 0, 0, 'alpha', 0), 8192)
```

garbage collection The process of freeing memory when it is not used anymore. Python performs garbage collection via reference counting and a cyclic garbage collector that is able to detect and break reference cycles. The garbage collector can be controlled using the `gc` module.

generator A function which returns a *generator iterator*. It looks like a normal function except that it contains `yield` expressions for producing a series of values usable in a for-loop or that can be retrieved one at a time with the `next()` function.

Usually refers to a generator function, but may refer to a *generator iterator* in some contexts. In cases where the intended meaning isn't clear, using the full terms avoids ambiguity.

generator iterator An object created by a *generator* function.

Each `yield` temporarily suspends processing, remembering the location execution state (including local variables and pending try-statements). When the *generator iterator* resumes, it picks-up where it left-off (in contrast to functions which start fresh on every invocation).

generator expression An expression that returns an iterator. It looks like a normal expression followed by a `for` expression defining a loop variable, range, and an optional `if` expression. The combined expression generates values for an enclosing function:

```
>>> sum(i*i for i in range(10))        # sum of squares 0, 1, 4, ... 81
285
```

generic function A function composed of multiple functions implementing the same operation for different types. Which implementation should be used during a call is determined by the dispatch algorithm.

See also the *single dispatch* glossary entry, the `functools.singledispatch()` decorator, and PEP 443.

GIL See *global interpreter lock*.

global interpreter lock The mechanism used by the *CPython* interpreter to assure that only one thread executes Python *bytecode* at a time. This simplifies the CPython implementation by making the object model (including critical built-in types such as `dict`) implicitly safe against concurrent access. Locking the entire interpreter makes it easier for the interpreter to be multi-threaded, at the expense of much of the parallelism afforded by multi-processor machines.

However, some extension modules, either standard or third-party, are designed so as to release the GIL when doing computationally-intensive tasks such as compression or hashing. Also, the GIL is always released when doing I/O.

Past efforts to create a "free-threaded" interpreter (one which locks shared data at a much finer granularity) have not been successful because performance suffered in the common single-processor case. It is believed that overcoming this performance issue would make the implementation much more complicated and therefore costlier to maintain.

hashable An object is *hashable* if it has a hash value which never changes during its lifetime (it needs a __hash__() method), and can be compared to other objects (it needs an __eq__() method). Hashable objects which compare equal must have the same hash value.

Hashability makes an object usable as a dictionary key and a set member, because these data structures use the hash value internally.

All of Python's immutable built-in objects are hashable; mutable containers (such as lists or dictionaries) are not. Objects which are instances of user-defined classes are hashable by default. They all compare unequal (except with themselves), and their hash value is derived from their id().

IDLE An Integrated Development Environment for Python. IDLE is a basic editor and interpreter environment which ships with the standard distribution of Python.

immutable An object with a fixed value. Immutable objects include numbers, strings and tuples. Such an object cannot be altered. A new object has to be created if a different value has to be stored. They play an important role in places where a constant hash value is needed, for example as a key in a dictionary.

import path A list of locations (or *path entries*) that are searched by the *path based finder* for modules to import. During import, this list of locations usually comes from sys.path, but for subpackages it may also come from the parent package's __path__ attribute.

importing The process by which Python code in one module is made available to Python code in another module.

importer An object that both finds and loads a module; both a *finder* and *loader* object.

interactive Python has an interactive interpreter which means you can enter statements and expressions at the interpreter prompt, immediately execute them and see their results. Just launch python with no arguments (possibly by selecting it from your computer's main menu). It is a very powerful way to test out new ideas or inspect modules and packages (remember help(x)).

interpreted Python is an interpreted language, as opposed to a compiled one, though the distinction can be blurry because of the presence of the bytecode compiler. This means that source files can be run directly without explicitly creating an executable which is then run. Interpreted languages typically have a shorter development/debug cycle than compiled ones, though their programs generally also run more slowly. See also *interactive*.

interpreter shutdown When asked to shut down, the Python interpreter enters a special phase where it gradually releases all allocated resources, such as modules and various critical internal structures. It also makes several calls to the *garbage collector*. This can trigger the execution of code in user-defined destructors or weakref callbacks. Code executed during the shutdown phase can encounter various exceptions as the resources it relies on may not function anymore (common examples are library modules or the warnings machinery).

The main reason for interpreter shutdown is that the __main__ module or the script being run has finished executing.

iterable An object capable of returning its members one at a time. Examples of iterables include all sequence types (such as list, str, and tuple) and some non-sequence types like dict, *file objects*, and objects of any classes you define with an __iter__() method or with a __getitem__() method that implements *Sequence* semantics.

Iterables can be used in a for loop and in many other places where a sequence is needed (zip(), map(), ...). When an iterable object is passed as an argument to the built-in function iter(), it returns an iterator for the object. This iterator is good for one pass over the set of values. When using iterables, it is usually not necessary to call `iter()` or deal with iterator objects yourself. The `for` statement does that automatically for you, creating a temporary unnamed variable to hold the iterator for the duration of the loop. See also *iterator*, *sequence*, and *generator*.

iterator An object representing a stream of data. Repeated calls to the iterator's `__next__()` method (or passing it to the built-in function `next()`) return successive items in the stream. When no more data are available a `StopIteration` exception is raised instead. At this point, the iterator object is exhausted and any further calls to its `__next__()` method just raise `StopIteration` again. Iterators are required to have an `__iter__()` method that returns the iterator object itself so every iterator is also iterable and may be used in most places where other iterables are accepted. One notable exception is code which attempts multiple iteration passes. A container object (such as a `list`) produces a fresh new iterator each time you pass it to the `iter()` function or use it in a `for` loop. Attempting this with an iterator will just return the same exhausted iterator object used in the previous iteration pass, making it appear like an empty container.

More information can be found in typeiter.

key function A key function or collation function is a callable that returns a value used for sorting or ordering. For example, `locale.strxfrm()` is used to produce a sort key that is aware of locale specific sort conventions.

A number of tools in Python accept key functions to control how elements are ordered or grouped. They include `min()`, `max()`, `sorted()`, `list.sort()`, `heapq.merge()`, `heapq.nsmallest()`, `heapq.nlargest()`, and `itertools.groupby()`.

There are several ways to create a key function. For example. the `str.lower()` method can serve as a key function for case insensitive sorts. Alternatively, a key function can be built from a `lambda` expression such as `lambda r: (r[0], r[2])`. Also, the `operator` module provides three key function constructors: `attrgetter()`, `itemgetter()`, and `methodcaller()`. See the Sorting HOW TO for examples of how to create and use key functions.

keyword argument See *argument*.

lambda An anonymous inline function consisting of a single *expression* which is evaluated when the function is called. The syntax to create a lambda function is `lambda [arguments]: expression`

LBYL Look before you leap. This coding style explicitly tests for pre-conditions before making calls or lookups. This style contrasts with the *EAFP* approach and is characterized by the presence of many `if` statements.

In a multi-threaded environment, the LBYL approach can risk introducing a race condition between "the looking" and "the leaping". For example, the code, `if key in mapping: return mapping[key]` can fail if another thread removes *key* from *mapping* after the test, but before the lookup. This issue can be solved with locks or by using the EAFP approach.

list A built-in Python *sequence*. Despite its name it is more akin to an array in other languages than to a linked list since access to elements are O(1).

list comprehension A compact way to process all or part of the elements in a sequence and return a list with the results. `result = ['{:#04x}'.format(x) for x in range(256) if x % 2 == 0]` generates a list of strings containing even hex numbers (0x..) in the range from 0 to 255. The `if` clause is optional. If omitted, all elements in `range(256)` are processed.

loader An object that loads a module. It must define a method named `load_module()`. A loader is typically returned by a *finder*. See PEP 302 for details and `importlib.abc.Loader` for an *abstract base class*.

mapping A container object that supports arbitrary key lookups and implements the methods specified in the `Mapping` or `MutableMapping` abstract base classes. Examples include `dict`, `collections.defaultdict`, `collections.OrderedDict` and `collections.Counter`.

meta path finder A *finder* returned by a search of `sys.meta_path`. Meta path finders are related to, but different from *path entry finders*.

See `importlib.abc.MetaPathFinder` for the methods that meta path finders implement.

metaclass The class of a class. Class definitions create a class name, a class dictionary, and a list of base classes. The metaclass is responsible for taking those three arguments and creating the class. Most object oriented programming languages provide a default implementation. What makes Python special is that it is possible to create custom metaclasses. Most users never need this tool, but when the need arises, metaclasses can provide powerful, elegant solutions. They have been used for logging attribute access, adding thread-safety, tracking object creation, implementing singletons, and many other tasks.

More information can be found in metaclasses.

method A function which is defined inside a class body. If called as an attribute of an instance of that class, the method will get the instance object as its first *argument* (which is usually called `self`). See *function* and *nested scope*.

method resolution order Method Resolution Order is the order in which base classes are searched for a member during lookup. See The Python 2.3 Method Resolution Order for details of the algorithm used by the Python interpreter since the 2.3 release.

module An object that serves as an organizational unit of Python code. Modules have a namespace containing arbitrary Python objects. Modules are loaded into Python by the process of *importing*.

See also *package*.

module spec A namespace containing the import-related information used to load a module. An instance of `importlib.machinery.ModuleSpec`.

MRO See *method resolution order*.

mutable Mutable objects can change their value but keep their `id()`. See also *immutable*.

named tuple Any tuple-like class whose indexable elements are also accessible using named attributes (for example, `time.localtime()` returns a tuple-like object where the *year* is accessible either with an index such as `t[0]` or with a named attribute like `t.tm_year`).

A named tuple can be a built-in type such as `time.struct_time`, or it can be created with a regular class definition. A full featured named tuple can also be created with the factory function `collections.namedtuple()`. The latter approach automatically provides extra features such as a self-documenting representation like `Employee(name='jones', title='programmer')`.

namespace The place where a variable is stored. Namespaces are implemented as dictionaries. There are the local, global and built-in namespaces as well as nested namespaces in objects (in methods). Namespaces support modularity by preventing naming conflicts. For instance, the functions `builtins.open` and `os.open()` are distinguished by their namespaces. Namespaces also aid readability and maintainability by making it clear which module implements a function. For instance, writing `random.seed()` or `itertools.islice()` makes it clear that those functions are implemented by the `random` and `itertools` modules, respectively.

namespace package A PEP 420 *package* which serves only as a container for subpackages. Namespace packages may have no physical representation, and specifically are not like a *regular package* because they have no `__init__.py` file.

See also *module*.

nested scope The ability to refer to a variable in an enclosing definition. For instance, a function defined inside another function can refer to variables in the outer function. Note that nested scopes by default work only for reference and not for assignment. Local variables both read and write in the innermost scope. Likewise, global variables read and write to the global namespace. The `nonlocal` allows writing to outer scopes.

new-style class Old name for the flavor of classes now used for all class objects. In earlier Python versions, only new-style classes could use Python's newer, versatile features like __slots__, descriptors, properties, __getattribute__(), class methods, and static methods.

object Any data with state (attributes or value) and defined behavior (methods). Also the ultimate base class of any *new-style class*.

package A Python *module* which can contain submodules or recursively, subpackages. Technically, a package is a Python module with an __path__ attribute.

See also *regular package* and *namespace package*.

parameter A named entity in a *function* (or method) definition that specifies an *argument* (or in some cases, arguments) that the function can accept. There are five kinds of parameter:

- *positional-or-keyword*: specifies an argument that can be passed either *positionally* or as a *keyword argument*. This is the default kind of parameter, for example *foo* and *bar* in the following:

```
def func(foo, bar=None): ...
```

- *positional-only*: specifies an argument that can be supplied only by position. Python has no syntax for defining positional-only parameters. However, some built-in functions have positional-only parameters (e.g. abs()).

- *keyword-only*: specifies an argument that can be supplied only by keyword. Keyword-only parameters can be defined by including a single var-positional parameter or bare * in the parameter list of the function definition before them, for example *kw_only1* and *kw_only2* in the following:

```
def func(arg, *, kw_only1, kw_only2): ...
```

- *var-positional*: specifies that an arbitrary sequence of positional arguments can be provided (in addition to any positional arguments already accepted by other parameters). Such a parameter can be defined by prepending the parameter name with *, for example *args* in the following:

```
def func(*args, **kwargs): ...
```

- *var-keyword*: specifies that arbitrarily many keyword arguments can be provided (in addition to any keyword arguments already accepted by other parameters). Such a parameter can be defined by prepending the parameter name with **, for example *kwargs* in the example above.

Parameters can specify both optional and required arguments, as well as default values for some optional arguments.

See also the *argument* glossary entry, the FAQ question on the difference between arguments and parameters, the inspect.Parameter class, the function section, and PEP 362.

path entry A single location on the *import path* which the *path based finder* consults to find modules for importing.

path entry finder A *finder* returned by a callable on sys.path_hooks (i.e. a *path entry hook*) which knows how to locate modules given a *path entry*.

See importlib.abc.PathEntryFinder for the methods that path entry finders implement.

path entry hook A callable on the sys.path_hook list which returns a *path entry finder* if it knows how to find modules on a specific *path entry*.

path based finder One of the default *meta path finders* which searches an *import path* for modules.

path-like object An object representing a file system path. A path-like object is either a str or bytes object representing a path, or an object implementing the os.PathLike protocol. An object that supports the os.PathLike protocol can be converted to a str or bytes file system path by calling the `os.fspath()` function; `os.fsdecode()` and `os.fsencode()` can be used to guarantee a `str` or `bytes` result instead, respectively. Introduced by PEP 519.

portion   A set of files in a single directory (possibly stored in a zip file) that contribute to a namespace package, as defined in PEP 420.

positional argument   See *argument*.

provisional API   A provisional API is one which has been deliberately excluded from the standard library's backwards compatibility guarantees. While major changes to such interfaces are not expected, as long as they are marked provisional, backwards incompatible changes (up to and including removal of the interface) may occur if deemed necessary by core developers. Such changes will not be made gratuitously – they will occur only if serious fundamental flaws are uncovered that were missed prior to the inclusion of the API.

Even for provisional APIs, backwards incompatible changes are seen as a "solution of last resort" - every attempt will still be made to find a backwards compatible resolution to any identified problems.

This process allows the standard library to continue to evolve over time, without locking in problematic design errors for extended periods of time. See PEP 411 for more details.

provisional package   See *provisional API*.

Python 3000   Nickname for the Python 3.x release line (coined long ago when the release of version 3 was something in the distant future.) This is also abbreviated "Py3k".

Pythonic   An idea or piece of code which closely follows the most common idioms of the Python language, rather than implementing code using concepts common to other languages. For example, a common idiom in Python is to loop over all elements of an iterable using a `for` statement. Many other languages don't have this type of construct, so people unfamiliar with Python sometimes use a numerical counter instead:

```
for i in range(len(food)):
    print(food[i])
```

As opposed to the cleaner, Pythonic method:

```
for piece in food:
    print(piece)
```

qualified name   A dotted name showing the "path" from a module's global scope to a class, function or method defined in that module, as defined in PEP 3155. For top-level functions and classes, the qualified name is the same as the object's name:

```
>>> class C:
...     class D:
...         def meth(self):
...             pass
...
>>> C.__qualname__
'C'
>>> C.D.__qualname__
'C.D'
>>> C.D.meth.__qualname__
'C.D.meth'
```

When used to refer to modules, the *fully qualified name* means the entire dotted path to the module, including any parent packages, e.g. `email.mime.text`:

```
>>> import email.mime.text
>>> email.mime.text.__name__
'email.mime.text'
```

reference count The number of references to an object. When the reference count of an object drops to zero, it is deallocated. Reference counting is generally not visible to Python code, but it is a key element of the *CPython* implementation. The `sys` module defines a `getrefcount()` function that programmers can call to return the reference count for a particular object.

regular package A traditional *package*, such as a directory containing an `__init__.py` file.

See also *namespace package*.

__slots__ A declaration inside a class that saves memory by pre-declaring space for instance attributes and eliminating instance dictionaries. Though popular, the technique is somewhat tricky to get right and is best reserved for rare cases where there are large numbers of instances in a memory-critical application.

sequence An *iterable* which supports efficient element access using integer indices via the `__getitem__()` special method and defines a `__len__()` method that returns the length of the sequence. Some built-in sequence types are `list`, `str`, `tuple`, and `bytes`. Note that `dict` also supports `__getitem__()` and `__len__()`, but is considered a mapping rather than a sequence because the lookups use arbitrary *immutable* keys rather than integers.

The `collections.abc.Sequence` abstract base class defines a much richer interface that goes beyond just `__getitem__()` and `__len__()`, adding `count()`, `index()`, `__contains__()`, and `__reversed__()`. Types that implement this expanded interface can be registered explicitly using `register()`.

single dispatch A form of *generic function* dispatch where the implementation is chosen based on the type of a single argument.

slice An object usually containing a portion of a *sequence*. A slice is created using the subscript notation, `[]` with colons between numbers when several are given, such as in `variable_name[1:3:5]`. The bracket (subscript) notation uses `slice` objects internally.

special method A method that is called implicitly by Python to execute a certain operation on a type, such as addition. Such methods have names starting and ending with double underscores. Special methods are documented in specialnames.

statement A statement is part of a suite (a "block" of code). A statement is either an *expression* or one of several constructs with a keyword, such as `if`, `while` or `for`.

struct sequence A tuple with named elements. Struct sequences expose an interface similar to *named tuple* in that elements can either be accessed either by index or as an attribute. However, they do not have any of the named tuple methods like `_make()` or `_asdict()`. Examples of struct sequences include `sys.float_info` and the return value of `os.stat()`.

text encoding A codec which encodes Unicode strings to bytes.

text file A *file object* able to read and write `str` objects. Often, a text file actually accesses a byte-oriented datastream and handles the *text encoding* automatically. Examples of text files are files opened in text mode (`'r'` or `'w'`), `sys.stdin`, `sys.stdout`, and instances of `io.StringIO`.

See also:

A *binary file* reads and write `bytes` objects.

triple-quoted string A string which is bound by three instances of either a quotation mark (") or an apostrophe ('). While they don't provide any functionality not available with single-quoted strings, they are useful for a number of reasons. They allow you to include unescaped single and double quotes within a string and they can span multiple lines without the use of the continuation character, making them especially useful when writing docstrings.

type   The type of a Python object determines what kind of object it is; every object has a type. An object's type is accessible as its `__class__` attribute or can be retrieved with `type(obj)`.

universal newlines   A manner of interpreting text streams in which all of the following are recognized as ending a line: the Unix end-of-line convention `'\n'`, the Windows convention `'\r\n'`, and the old Macintosh convention `'\r'`. See PEP 278 and PEP 3116, as well as `bytes.splitlines()` for an additional use.

variable annotation   A type metadata value associated with a module global variable or a class attribute. Its syntax is explained in section annassign. Annotations are stored in the `__annotations__` special attribute of a class or module object and can be accessed using `typing.get_type_hints()`.

Python itself does not assign any particular meaning to variable annotations. They are intended to be interpreted by third-party libraries or type checking tools. See PEP 526, PEP 484 which describe some of their potential uses.

virtual environment   A cooperatively isolated runtime environment that allows Python users and applications to install and upgrade Python distribution packages without interfering with the behaviour of other Python applications running on the same system.

See also `venv`.

virtual machine   A computer defined entirely in software. Python's virtual machine executes the *bytecode* emitted by the bytecode compiler.

Zen of Python   Listing of Python design principles and philosophies that are helpful in understanding and using the language. The listing can be found by typing "`import this`" at the interactive prompt.

ABOUT THESE DOCUMENTS

These documents are generated from reStructuredText sources by Sphinx, a document processor specifically written for the Python documentation.

Development of the documentation and its toolchain is an entirely volunteer effort, just like Python itself. If you want to contribute, please take a look at the reporting-bugs page for information on how to do so. New volunteers are always welcome!

Many thanks go to:

- Fred L. Drake, Jr., the creator of the original Python documentation toolset and writer of much of the content;

- the Docutils project for creating reStructuredText and the Docutils suite;

- Fredrik Lundh for his Alternative Python Reference project from which Sphinx got many good ideas.

B.1 Contributors to the Python Documentation

Many people have contributed to the Python language, the Python standard library, and the Python documentation. See Misc/ACKS in the Python source distribution for a partial list of contributors.

It is only with the input and contributions of the Python community that Python has such wonderful documentation – Thank You!

HISTORY AND LICENSE

C.1 History of the software

Python was created in the early 1990s by Guido van Rossum at Stichting Mathematisch Centrum (CWI, see https://www.cwi.nl/) in the Netherlands as a successor of a language called ABC. Guido remains Python's principal author, although it includes many contributions from others.

In 1995, Guido continued his work on Python at the Corporation for National Research Initiatives (CNRI, see https://www.cnri.reston.va.us/) in Reston, Virginia where he released several versions of the software.

In May 2000, Guido and the Python core development team moved to BeOpen.com to form the BeOpen PythonLabs team. In October of the same year, the PythonLabs team moved to Digital Creations (now Zope Corporation; see http://www.zope.com/). In 2001, the Python Software Foundation (PSF, see https://www.python.org/psf/) was formed, a non-profit organization created specifically to own Python-related Intellectual Property. Zope Corporation is a sponsoring member of the PSF.

All Python releases are Open Source (see https://opensource.org/ for the Open Source Definition). Historically, most, but not all, Python releases have also been GPL-compatible; the table below summarizes the various releases.

Release	Derived from	Year	Owner	GPL compatible?
0.9.0 thru 1.2	n/a	1991-1995	CWI	yes
1.3 thru 1.5.2	1.2	1995-1999	CNRI	yes
1.6	1.5.2	2000	CNRI	no
2.0	1.6	2000	BeOpen.com	no
1.6.1	1.6	2001	CNRI	no
2.1	2.0+1.6.1	2001	PSF	no
2.0.1	2.0+1.6.1	2001	PSF	yes
2.1.1	2.1+2.0.1	2001	PSF	yes
2.1.2	2.1.1	2002	PSF	yes
2.1.3	2.1.2	2002	PSF	yes
2.2 and above	2.1.1	2001-now	PSF	yes

Note: GPL-compatible doesn't mean that we're distributing Python under the GPL. All Python licenses, unlike the GPL, let you distribute a modified version without making your changes open source. The GPL-compatible licenses make it possible to combine Python with other software that is released under the GPL; the others don't.

Thanks to the many outside volunteers who have worked under Guido's direction to make these releases possible.

C.2 Terms and conditions for accessing or otherwise using Python

C.2.1 PSF LICENSE AGREEMENT FOR PYTHON 3.6.4

1. This LICENSE AGREEMENT is between the Python Software Foundation ("PSF"), and the Individual or Organization ("Licensee") accessing and otherwise using Python 3.6.4 software in source or binary form and its associated documentation.

2. Subject to the terms and conditions of this License Agreement, PSF hereby grants Licensee a nonexclusive, royalty-free, world-wide license to reproduce, analyze, test, perform and/or display publicly, prepare derivative works, distribute, and otherwise use Python 3.6.4 alone or in any derivative version, provided, however, that PSF's License Agreement and PSF's notice of copyright, i.e., "Copyright © 2001-2018 Python Software Foundation; All Rights Reserved" are retained in Python 3.6.4 alone or in any derivative version prepared by Licensee.

3. In the event Licensee prepares a derivative work that is based on or incorporates Python 3.6.4 or any part thereof, and wants to make the derivative work available to others as provided herein, then Licensee hereby agrees to include in any such work a brief summary of the changes made to Python 3.6.4.

4. PSF is making Python 3.6.4 available to Licensee on an "AS IS" basis. PSF MAKES NO REPRESENTATIONS OR WARRANTIES, EXPRESS OR IMPLIED. BY WAY OF EXAMPLE, BUT NOT LIMITATION, PSF MAKES NO AND DISCLAIMS ANY REPRESENTATION OR WARRANTY OF MERCHANTABILITY OR FITNESS FOR ANY PARTICULAR PURPOSE OR THAT THE USE OF PYTHON 3.6.4 WILL NOT INFRINGE ANY THIRD PARTY RIGHTS.

5. PSF SHALL NOT BE LIABLE TO LICENSEE OR ANY OTHER USERS OF PYTHON 3.6.4 FOR ANY INCIDENTAL, SPECIAL, OR CONSEQUENTIAL DAMAGES OR LOSS AS A RESULT OF MODIFYING, DISTRIBUTING, OR OTHERWISE USING PYTHON 3.6.4, OR ANY DERIVATIVE THEREOF, EVEN IF ADVISED OF THE POSSIBILITY THEREOF.

6. This License Agreement will automatically terminate upon a material breach of its terms and conditions.

7. Nothing in this License Agreement shall be deemed to create any relationship of agency, partnership, or joint venture between PSF and Licensee. This License Agreement does not grant permission to use PSF trademarks or trade name in a trademark sense to endorse or promote products or services of Licensee, or any third party.

8. By copying, installing or otherwise using Python 3.6.4, Licensee agrees to be bound by the terms and conditions of this License Agreement.

C.2.2 BEOPEN.COM LICENSE AGREEMENT FOR PYTHON 2.0

BEOPEN PYTHON OPEN SOURCE LICENSE AGREEMENT VERSION 1

```
1. This LICENSE AGREEMENT is between BeOpen.com ("BeOpen"), having an office at
   160 Saratoga Avenue, Santa Clara, CA 95051, and the Individual or Organization
   ("Licensee") accessing and otherwise using this software in source or binary
```

```
form and its associated documentation ("the Software").

2. Subject to the terms and conditions of this BeOpen Python License Agreement,
   BeOpen hereby grants Licensee a non-exclusive, royalty-free, world-wide license
   to reproduce, analyze, test, perform and/or display publicly, prepare derivative
   works, distribute, and otherwise use the Software alone or in any derivative
   version, provided, however, that the BeOpen Python License is retained in the
   Software, alone or in any derivative version prepared by Licensee.

3. BeOpen is making the Software available to Licensee on an "AS IS" basis.
   BEOPEN MAKES NO REPRESENTATIONS OR WARRANTIES, EXPRESS OR IMPLIED.  BY WAY OF
   EXAMPLE, BUT NOT LIMITATION, BEOPEN MAKES NO AND DISCLAIMS ANY REPRESENTATION OR
   WARRANTY OF MERCHANTABILITY OR FITNESS FOR ANY PARTICULAR PURPOSE OR THAT THE
   USE OF THE SOFTWARE WILL NOT INFRINGE ANY THIRD PARTY RIGHTS.

4. BEOPEN SHALL NOT BE LIABLE TO LICENSEE OR ANY OTHER USERS OF THE SOFTWARE FOR
   ANY INCIDENTAL, SPECIAL, OR CONSEQUENTIAL DAMAGES OR LOSS AS A RESULT OF USING,
   MODIFYING OR DISTRIBUTING THE SOFTWARE, OR ANY DERIVATIVE THEREOF, EVEN IF
   ADVISED OF THE POSSIBILITY THEREOF.

5. This License Agreement will automatically terminate upon a material breach of
   its terms and conditions.

6. This License Agreement shall be governed by and interpreted in all respects
   by the law of the State of California, excluding conflict of law provisions.
   Nothing in this License Agreement shall be deemed to create any relationship of
   agency, partnership, or joint venture between BeOpen and Licensee.  This License
   Agreement does not grant permission to use BeOpen trademarks or trade names in a
   trademark sense to endorse or promote products or services of Licensee, or any
   third party.  As an exception, the "BeOpen Python" logos available at
   http://www.pythonlabs.com/logos.html may be used according to the permissions
   granted on that web page.

7. By copying, installing or otherwise using the software, Licensee agrees to be
   bound by the terms and conditions of this License Agreement.
```

C.2.3 CNRI LICENSE AGREEMENT FOR PYTHON 1.6.1

```
1. This LICENSE AGREEMENT is between the Corporation for National Research
   Initiatives, having an office at 1895 Preston White Drive, Reston, VA 20191
   ("CNRI"), and the Individual or Organization ("Licensee") accessing and
   otherwise using Python 1.6.1 software in source or binary form and its
   associated documentation.

2. Subject to the terms and conditions of this License Agreement, CNRI hereby
   grants Licensee a nonexclusive, royalty-free, world-wide license to reproduce,
   analyze, test, perform and/or display publicly, prepare derivative works,
   distribute, and otherwise use Python 1.6.1 alone or in any derivative version,
   provided, however, that CNRI's License Agreement and CNRI's notice of copyright,
   i.e., "Copyright © 1995-2001 Corporation for National Research Initiatives; All
   Rights Reserved" are retained in Python 1.6.1 alone or in any derivative version
   prepared by Licensee.  Alternately, in lieu of CNRI's License Agreement,
   Licensee may substitute the following text (omitting the quotes): "Python 1.6.1
   is made available subject to the terms and conditions in CNRI's License
   Agreement.  This Agreement together with Python 1.6.1 may be located on the
   Internet using the following unique, persistent identifier (known as a handle):
```

1895.22/1013. This Agreement may also be obtained from a proxy server on the
Internet using the following URL: http://hdl.handle.net/1895.22/1013."

3. In the event Licensee prepares a derivative work that is based on or
   incorporates Python 1.6.1 or any part thereof, and wants to make the derivative
   work available to others as provided herein, then Licensee hereby agrees to
   include in any such work a brief summary of the changes made to Python 1.6.1.

4. CNRI is making Python 1.6.1 available to Licensee on an "AS IS" basis. CNRI
   MAKES NO REPRESENTATIONS OR WARRANTIES, EXPRESS OR IMPLIED. BY WAY OF EXAMPLE,
   BUT NOT LIMITATION, CNRI MAKES NO AND DISCLAIMS ANY REPRESENTATION OR WARRANTY
   OF MERCHANTABILITY OR FITNESS FOR ANY PARTICULAR PURPOSE OR THAT THE USE OF
   PYTHON 1.6.1 WILL NOT INFRINGE ANY THIRD PARTY RIGHTS.

5. CNRI SHALL NOT BE LIABLE TO LICENSEE OR ANY OTHER USERS OF PYTHON 1.6.1 FOR
   ANY INCIDENTAL, SPECIAL, OR CONSEQUENTIAL DAMAGES OR LOSS AS A RESULT OF
   MODIFYING, DISTRIBUTING, OR OTHERWISE USING PYTHON 1.6.1, OR ANY DERIVATIVE
   THEREOF, EVEN IF ADVISED OF THE POSSIBILITY THEREOF.

6. This License Agreement will automatically terminate upon a material breach of
   its terms and conditions.

7. This License Agreement shall be governed by the federal intellectual property
   law of the United States, including without limitation the federal copyright
   law, and, to the extent such U.S. federal law does not apply, by the law of the
   Commonwealth of Virginia, excluding Virginia's conflict of law provisions.
   Notwithstanding the foregoing, with regard to derivative works based on Python
   1.6.1 that incorporate non-separable material that was previously distributed
   under the GNU General Public License (GPL), the law of the Commonwealth of
   Virginia shall govern this License Agreement only as to issues arising under or
   with respect to Paragraphs 4, 5, and 7 of this License Agreement. Nothing in
   this License Agreement shall be deemed to create any relationship of agency,
   partnership, or joint venture between CNRI and Licensee. This License Agreement
   does not grant permission to use CNRI trademarks or trade name in a trademark
   sense to endorse or promote products or services of Licensee, or any third
   party.

8. By clicking on the "ACCEPT" button where indicated, or by copying, installing
   or otherwise using Python 1.6.1, Licensee agrees to be bound by the terms and
   conditions of this License Agreement.

C.2.4 CWI LICENSE AGREEMENT FOR PYTHON 0.9.0 THROUGH 1.2

```
EVENT SHALL STICHTING MATHEMATISCH CENTRUM BE LIABLE FOR ANY SPECIAL, INDIRECT
OR CONSEQUENTIAL DAMAGES OR ANY DAMAGES WHATSOEVER RESULTING FROM LOSS OF USE,
DATA OR PROFITS, WHETHER IN AN ACTION OF CONTRACT, NEGLIGENCE OR OTHER TORTIOUS
ACTION, ARISING OUT OF OR IN CONNECTION WITH THE USE OR PERFORMANCE OF THIS
SOFTWARE.
```

C.3 Licenses and Acknowledgements for Incorporated Software

This section is an incomplete, but growing list of licenses and acknowledgements for third-party software
incorporated in the Python distribution.

C.3.1 Mersenne Twister

The _random module includes code based on a download from http://www.math.sci.hiroshima-u.ac.jp/
~m-mat/MT/MT2002/emt19937ar.html. The following are the verbatim comments from the original code:

```
A C-program for MT19937, with initialization improved 2002/1/26.
Coded by Takuji Nishimura and Makoto Matsumoto.

Before using, initialize the state by using init_genrand(seed)
or init_by_array(init_key, key_length).

Copyright (C) 1997 - 2002, Makoto Matsumoto and Takuji Nishimura,
All rights reserved.

Redistribution and use in source and binary forms, with or without
modification, are permitted provided that the following conditions
are met:

  1. Redistributions of source code must retain the above copyright
     notice, this list of conditions and the following disclaimer.

  2. Redistributions in binary form must reproduce the above copyright
     notice, this list of conditions and the following disclaimer in the
     documentation and/or other materials provided with the distribution.

  3. The names of its contributors may not be used to endorse or promote
     products derived from this software without specific prior written
     permission.

THIS SOFTWARE IS PROVIDED BY THE COPYRIGHT HOLDERS AND CONTRIBUTORS
"AS IS" AND ANY EXPRESS OR IMPLIED WARRANTIES, INCLUDING, BUT NOT
LIMITED TO, THE IMPLIED WARRANTIES OF MERCHANTABILITY AND FITNESS FOR
A PARTICULAR PURPOSE ARE DISCLAIMED.  IN NO EVENT SHALL THE COPYRIGHT OWNER OR
CONTRIBUTORS BE LIABLE FOR ANY DIRECT, INDIRECT, INCIDENTAL, SPECIAL,
EXEMPLARY, OR CONSEQUENTIAL DAMAGES (INCLUDING, BUT NOT LIMITED TO,
PROCUREMENT OF SUBSTITUTE GOODS OR SERVICES; LOSS OF USE, DATA, OR
PROFITS; OR BUSINESS INTERRUPTION) HOWEVER CAUSED AND ON ANY THEORY OF
LIABILITY, WHETHER IN CONTRACT, STRICT LIABILITY, OR TORT (INCLUDING
NEGLIGENCE OR OTHERWISE) ARISING IN ANY WAY OUT OF THE USE OF THIS
SOFTWARE, EVEN IF ADVISED OF THE POSSIBILITY OF SUCH DAMAGE.


Any feedback is very welcome.
```

```
http://www.math.sci.hiroshima-u.ac.jp/~m-mat/MT/emt.html
email: m-mat @ math.sci.hiroshima-u.ac.jp (remove space)
```

C.3.2 Sockets

The `socket` module uses the functions, `getaddrinfo()`, and `getnameinfo()`, which are coded in separate source files from the WIDE Project, http://www.wide.ad.jp/.

```
Copyright (C) 1995, 1996, 1997, and 1998 WIDE Project.
All rights reserved.

Redistribution and use in source and binary forms, with or without
modification, are permitted provided that the following conditions
are met:
1. Redistributions of source code must retain the above copyright
   notice, this list of conditions and the following disclaimer.
2. Redistributions in binary form must reproduce the above copyright
   notice, this list of conditions and the following disclaimer in the
   documentation and/or other materials provided with the distribution.
3. Neither the name of the project nor the names of its contributors
   may be used to endorse or promote products derived from this software
   without specific prior written permission.

THIS SOFTWARE IS PROVIDED BY THE PROJECT AND CONTRIBUTORS ``AS IS'' AND
ANY EXPRESS OR IMPLIED WARRANTIES, INCLUDING, BUT NOT LIMITED TO, THE
IMPLIED WARRANTIES OF MERCHANTABILITY AND FITNESS FOR A PARTICULAR PURPOSE
ARE DISCLAIMED.  IN NO EVENT SHALL THE PROJECT OR CONTRIBUTORS BE LIABLE
FOR ANY DIRECT, INDIRECT, INCIDENTAL, SPECIAL, EXEMPLARY, OR CONSEQUENTIAL
DAMAGES (INCLUDING, BUT NOT LIMITED TO, PROCUREMENT OF SUBSTITUTE GOODS
OR SERVICES; LOSS OF USE, DATA, OR PROFITS; OR BUSINESS INTERRUPTION)
HOWEVER CAUSED AND ON ANY THEORY OF LIABILITY, WHETHER IN CONTRACT, STRICT
LIABILITY, OR TORT (INCLUDING NEGLIGENCE OR OTHERWISE) ARISING IN ANY WAY
OUT OF THE USE OF THIS SOFTWARE, EVEN IF ADVISED OF THE POSSIBILITY OF
SUCH DAMAGE.
```

C.3.3 Floating point exception control

The source for the `fpectl` module includes the following notice:

```
  ---------------------------------------------------------------------
 /                       Copyright (c) 1996.                          \
 |          The Regents of the University of California.              |
 |                       All rights reserved.                         |
 |                                                                    |
 |   Permission to use, copy, modify, and distribute this software for|
 |   any purpose without fee is hereby granted, provided that this en-|
 |   tire notice is included in all copies of any software which is or|
 |   includes  a  copy  or  modification  of  this software and in all|
 |   copies of the supporting documentation for such software.        |
 |                                                                    |
 |   This  work was produced at the University of California, Lawrence|
 |   Livermore National Laboratory under  contract  no.  W-7405-ENG-48|
 |   between  the  U.S.  Department  of  Energy and The Regents of the|
 |   University of California for the operation of UC LLNL.            |
 |                                                                    |
```

```
|                            DISCLAIMER                             |
|                                                                   |
|   This  software was prepared as an account of work sponsored by an |
|   agency of the United States Government. Neither the United States |
|   Government  nor the University of California nor any of their em- |
|   ployees, makes any warranty, express or implied, or  assumes  any |
|   liability  or responsibility  for the accuracy, completeness, or |
|   usefulness of any information, apparatus,  product,  or  process |
|   disclosed,   or  represents  that  its  use  would  not  infringe |
|   privately-owned rights. Reference herein to any specific  commer- |
|   cial  products,  process,  or  service  by trade name, trademark, |
|   manufacturer, or otherwise, does  not  necessarily  constitute  or |
|   imply  its endorsement, recommendation, or favoring by the United |
|   States Government or the University of California. The views  and |
|   opinions  of authors expressed herein do not necessarily state or |
|   reflect those of the United States Government or  the  University |
|   of  California,  and shall not be used for advertising or product |
\   endorsement purposes.                                           /
   ----------------------------------------------------------------
```

C.3.4 Asynchronous socket services

The asynchat and asyncore modules contain the following notice:

```
Copyright 1996 by Sam Rushing

                All Rights Reserved

Permission to use, copy, modify, and distribute this software and
its documentation for any purpose and without fee is hereby
granted, provided that the above copyright notice appear in all
copies and that both that copyright notice and this permission
notice appear in supporting documentation, and that the name of Sam
Rushing not be used in advertising or publicity pertaining to
distribution of the software without specific, written prior
permission.

SAM RUSHING DISCLAIMS ALL WARRANTIES WITH REGARD TO THIS SOFTWARE,
INCLUDING ALL IMPLIED WARRANTIES OF MERCHANTABILITY AND FITNESS, IN
NO EVENT SHALL SAM RUSHING BE LIABLE FOR ANY SPECIAL, INDIRECT OR
CONSEQUENTIAL DAMAGES OR ANY DAMAGES WHATSOEVER RESULTING FROM LOSS
OF USE, DATA OR PROFITS, WHETHER IN AN ACTION OF CONTRACT,
NEGLIGENCE OR OTHER TORTIOUS ACTION, ARISING OUT OF OR IN
CONNECTION WITH THE USE OR PERFORMANCE OF THIS SOFTWARE.
```

C.3.5 Cookie management

The http.cookies module contains the following notice:

```
Copyright 2000 by Timothy O'Malley <timo@alum.mit.edu>

                All Rights Reserved

Permission to use, copy, modify, and distribute this software
and its documentation for any purpose and without fee is hereby
```

```
granted, provided that the above copyright notice appear in all
copies and that both that copyright notice and this permission
notice appear in supporting documentation, and that the name of
Timothy O'Malley  not be used in advertising or publicity
pertaining to distribution of the software without specific, written
prior permission.

Timothy O'Malley DISCLAIMS ALL WARRANTIES WITH REGARD TO THIS
SOFTWARE, INCLUDING ALL IMPLIED WARRANTIES OF MERCHANTABILITY
AND FITNESS, IN NO EVENT SHALL Timothy O'Malley BE LIABLE FOR
ANY SPECIAL, INDIRECT OR CONSEQUENTIAL DAMAGES OR ANY DAMAGES
WHATSOEVER RESULTING FROM LOSS OF USE, DATA OR PROFITS,
WHETHER IN AN ACTION OF CONTRACT, NEGLIGENCE OR OTHER TORTIOUS
ACTION, ARISING OUT OF OR IN CONNECTION WITH THE USE OR
PERFORMANCE OF THIS SOFTWARE.
```

C.3.6 Execution tracing

The trace module contains the following notice:

```
portions copyright 2001, Autonomous Zones Industries, Inc., all rights...
err...  reserved and offered to the public under the terms of the
Python 2.2 license.
Author: Zooko O'Whielacronx
http://zooko.com/
mailto:zooko@zooko.com

Copyright 2000, Mojam Media, Inc., all rights reserved.
Author: Skip Montanaro

Copyright 1999, Bioreason, Inc., all rights reserved.
Author: Andrew Dalke

Copyright 1995-1997, Automatrix, Inc., all rights reserved.
Author: Skip Montanaro

Copyright 1991-1995, Stichting Mathematisch Centrum, all rights reserved.


Permission to use, copy, modify, and distribute this Python software and
its associated documentation for any purpose without fee is hereby
granted, provided that the above copyright notice appears in all copies,
and that both that copyright notice and this permission notice appear in
supporting documentation, and that the name of neither Automatrix,
Bioreason or Mojam Media be used in advertising or publicity pertaining to
distribution of the software without specific, written prior permission.
```

C.3.7 UUencode and UUdecode functions

The uu module contains the following notice:

```
Copyright 1994 by Lance Ellinghouse
Cathedral City, California Republic, United States of America.
                    All Rights Reserved
Permission to use, copy, modify, and distribute this software and its
```

```
documentation for any purpose and without fee is hereby granted,
provided that the above copyright notice appear in all copies and that
both that copyright notice and this permission notice appear in
supporting documentation, and that the name of Lance Ellinghouse
not be used in advertising or publicity pertaining to distribution
of the software without specific, written prior permission.
LANCE ELLINGHOUSE DISCLAIMS ALL WARRANTIES WITH REGARD TO
THIS SOFTWARE, INCLUDING ALL IMPLIED WARRANTIES OF MERCHANTABILITY AND
FITNESS, IN NO EVENT SHALL LANCE ELLINGHOUSE CENTRUM BE LIABLE
FOR ANY SPECIAL, INDIRECT OR CONSEQUENTIAL DAMAGES OR ANY DAMAGES
WHATSOEVER RESULTING FROM LOSS OF USE, DATA OR PROFITS, WHETHER IN AN
ACTION OF CONTRACT, NEGLIGENCE OR OTHER TORTIOUS ACTION, ARISING OUT
OF OR IN CONNECTION WITH THE USE OR PERFORMANCE OF THIS SOFTWARE.

Modified by Jack Jansen, CWI, July 1995:
- Use binascii module to do the actual line-by-line conversion
  between ascii and binary. This results in a 1000-fold speedup. The C
  version is still 5 times faster, though.
- Arguments more compliant with Python standard
```

C.3.8 XML Remote Procedure Calls

The `xmlrpc.client` module contains the following notice:

```
    The XML-RPC client interface is

Copyright (c) 1999-2002 by Secret Labs AB
Copyright (c) 1999-2002 by Fredrik Lundh

By obtaining, using, and/or copying this software and/or its
associated documentation, you agree that you have read, understood,
and will comply with the following terms and conditions:

Permission to use, copy, modify, and distribute this software and
its associated documentation for any purpose and without fee is
hereby granted, provided that the above copyright notice appears in
all copies, and that both that copyright notice and this permission
notice appear in supporting documentation, and that the name of
Secret Labs AB or the author not be used in advertising or publicity
pertaining to distribution of the software without specific, written
prior permission.

SECRET LABS AB AND THE AUTHOR DISCLAIMS ALL WARRANTIES WITH REGARD
TO THIS SOFTWARE, INCLUDING ALL IMPLIED WARRANTIES OF MERCHANT-
ABILITY AND FITNESS.  IN NO EVENT SHALL SECRET LABS AB OR THE AUTHOR
BE LIABLE FOR ANY SPECIAL, INDIRECT OR CONSEQUENTIAL DAMAGES OR ANY
DAMAGES WHATSOEVER RESULTING FROM LOSS OF USE, DATA OR PROFITS,
WHETHER IN AN ACTION OF CONTRACT, NEGLIGENCE OR OTHER TORTIOUS
ACTION, ARISING OUT OF OR IN CONNECTION WITH THE USE OR PERFORMANCE
OF THIS SOFTWARE.
```

C.3.9 test_epoll

The `test_epoll` module contains the following notice:

C.3.11 SipHash24

The file `Python/pyhash.c` contains Marek Majkowski' implementation of Dan Bernstein's SipHash24 algorithm. The contains the following note:

```
<MIT License>
Copyright (c) 2013  Marek Majkowski <marek@popcount.org>

Permission is hereby granted, free of charge, to any person obtaining a copy
of this software and associated documentation files (the "Software"), to deal
in the Software without restriction, including without limitation the rights
to use, copy, modify, merge, publish, distribute, sublicense, and/or sell
copies of the Software, and to permit persons to whom the Software is
furnished to do so, subject to the following conditions:

The above copyright notice and this permission notice shall be included in
all copies or substantial portions of the Software.
</MIT License>

Original location:
  https://github.com/majek/csiphash/

Solution inspired by code from:
  Samuel Neves (supercop/crypto_auth/siphash24/little)
  djb (supercop/crypto_auth/siphash24/little2)
  Jean-Philippe Aumasson (https://131002.net/siphash/siphash24.c)
```

C.3.12 strtod and dtoa

The file `Python/dtoa.c`, which supplies C functions dtoa and strtod for conversion of C doubles to and from strings, is derived from the file of the same name by David M. Gay, currently available from http://www.netlib.org/fp/. The original file, as retrieved on March 16, 2009, contains the following copyright and licensing notice:

```
/****************************************************************
 *
 * The author of this software is David M. Gay.
 *
 * Copyright (c) 1991, 2000, 2001 by Lucent Technologies.
 *
 * Permission to use, copy, modify, and distribute this software for any
 * purpose without fee is hereby granted, provided that this entire notice
 * is included in all copies of any software which is or includes a copy
 * or modification of this software and in all copies of the supporting
 * documentation for such software.
 *
 * THIS SOFTWARE IS BEING PROVIDED "AS IS", WITHOUT ANY EXPRESS OR IMPLIED
 * WARRANTY.  IN PARTICULAR, NEITHER THE AUTHOR NOR LUCENT MAKES ANY
 * REPRESENTATION OR WARRANTY OF ANY KIND CONCERNING THE MERCHANTABILITY
 * OF THIS SOFTWARE OR ITS FITNESS FOR ANY PARTICULAR PURPOSE.
 *
 ****************************************************************/
```

C.3.13 OpenSSL

The modules `hashlib`, `posix`, `ssl`, `crypt` use the OpenSSL library for added performance if made available by the operating system. Additionally, the Windows and Mac OS X installers for Python may include a copy of the OpenSSL libraries, so we include a copy of the OpenSSL license here:

```
LICENSE ISSUES
==============

The OpenSSL toolkit stays under a dual license, i.e. both the conditions of
the OpenSSL License and the original SSLeay license apply to the toolkit.
See below for the actual license texts. Actually both licenses are BSD-style
Open Source licenses. In case of any license issues related to OpenSSL
please contact openssl-core@openssl.org.

OpenSSL License
---------------

/* ====================================================================
 * Copyright (c) 1998-2008 The OpenSSL Project.  All rights reserved.
 *
 * Redistribution and use in source and binary forms, with or without
 * modification, are permitted provided that the following conditions
 * are met:
 *
 * 1. Redistributions of source code must retain the above copyright
 *    notice, this list of conditions and the following disclaimer.
 *
 * 2. Redistributions in binary form must reproduce the above copyright
 *    notice, this list of conditions and the following disclaimer in
 *    the documentation and/or other materials provided with the
 *    distribution.
 *
 * 3. All advertising materials mentioning features or use of this
 *    software must display the following acknowledgment:
 *    "This product includes software developed by the OpenSSL Project
 *    for use in the OpenSSL Toolkit. (http://www.openssl.org/)"
 *
 * 4. The names "OpenSSL Toolkit" and "OpenSSL Project" must not be used to
 *    endorse or promote products derived from this software without
 *    prior written permission. For written permission, please contact
 *    openssl-core@openssl.org.
 *
 * 5. Products derived from this software may not be called "OpenSSL"
 *    nor may "OpenSSL" appear in their names without prior written
 *    permission of the OpenSSL Project.
 *
 * 6. Redistributions of any form whatsoever must retain the following
 *    acknowledgment:
 *    "This product includes software developed by the OpenSSL Project
 *    for use in the OpenSSL Toolkit (http://www.openssl.org/)"
 *
 * THIS SOFTWARE IS PROVIDED BY THE OpenSSL PROJECT ``AS IS'' AND ANY
 * EXPRESSED OR IMPLIED WARRANTIES, INCLUDING, BUT NOT LIMITED TO, THE
 * IMPLIED WARRANTIES OF MERCHANTABILITY AND FITNESS FOR A PARTICULAR
 * PURPOSE ARE DISCLAIMED.  IN NO EVENT SHALL THE OpenSSL PROJECT OR
 * ITS CONTRIBUTORS BE LIABLE FOR ANY DIRECT, INDIRECT, INCIDENTAL,
 * SPECIAL, EXEMPLARY, OR CONSEQUENTIAL DAMAGES (INCLUDING, BUT
 * NOT LIMITED TO, PROCUREMENT OF SUBSTITUTE GOODS OR SERVICES;
 * LOSS OF USE, DATA, OR PROFITS; OR BUSINESS INTERRUPTION)
 * HOWEVER CAUSED AND ON ANY THEORY OF LIABILITY, WHETHER IN CONTRACT,
 * STRICT LIABILITY, OR TORT (INCLUDING NEGLIGENCE OR OTHERWISE)
 * ARISING IN ANY WAY OUT OF THE USE OF THIS SOFTWARE, EVEN IF ADVISED
 * OF THE POSSIBILITY OF SUCH DAMAGE.
```

```
 *  ====================================================================
 *
 *  This product includes cryptographic software written by Eric Young
 *  (eay@cryptsoft.com).  This product includes software written by Tim
 *  Hudson (tjh@cryptsoft.com).
 *
 */

Original SSLeay License
-----------------------

 /* Copyright (C) 1995-1998 Eric Young (eay@cryptsoft.com)
  * All rights reserved.
  *
  * This package is an SSL implementation written
  * by Eric Young (eay@cryptsoft.com).
  * The implementation was written so as to conform with Netscapes SSL.
  *
  * This library is free for commercial and non-commercial use as long as
  * the following conditions are aheared to.  The following conditions
  * apply to all code found in this distribution, be it the RC4, RSA,
  * lhash, DES, etc., code; not just the SSL code.  The SSL documentation
  * included with this distribution is covered by the same copyright terms
  * except that the holder is Tim Hudson (tjh@cryptsoft.com).
  *
  * Copyright remains Eric Young's, and as such any Copyright notices in
  * the code are not to be removed.
  * If this package is used in a product, Eric Young should be given attribution
  * as the author of the parts of the library used.
  * This can be in the form of a textual message at program startup or
  * in documentation (online or textual) provided with the package.
  *
  * Redistribution and use in source and binary forms, with or without
  * modification, are permitted provided that the following conditions
  * are met:
  * 1. Redistributions of source code must retain the copyright
  *    notice, this list of conditions and the following disclaimer.
  * 2. Redistributions in binary form must reproduce the above copyright
  *    notice, this list of conditions and the following disclaimer in the
  *    documentation and/or other materials provided with the distribution.
  * 3. All advertising materials mentioning features or use of this software
  *    must display the following acknowledgement:
  *    "This product includes cryptographic software written by
  *     Eric Young (eay@cryptsoft.com)"
  *    The word 'cryptographic' can be left out if the rouines from the library
  *    being used are not cryptographic related :-).
  * 4. If you include any Windows specific code (or a derivative thereof) from
  *    the apps directory (application code) you must include an acknowledgement:
  *    "This product includes software written by Tim Hudson (tjh@cryptsoft.com)"
  *
  * THIS SOFTWARE IS PROVIDED BY ERIC YOUNG ``AS IS'' AND
  * ANY EXPRESS OR IMPLIED WARRANTIES, INCLUDING, BUT NOT LIMITED TO, THE
  * IMPLIED WARRANTIES OF MERCHANTABILITY AND FITNESS FOR A PARTICULAR PURPOSE
  * ARE DISCLAIMED.  IN NO EVENT SHALL THE AUTHOR OR CONTRIBUTORS BE LIABLE
  * FOR ANY DIRECT, INDIRECT, INCIDENTAL, SPECIAL, EXEMPLARY, OR CONSEQUENTIAL
  * DAMAGES (INCLUDING, BUT NOT LIMITED TO, PROCUREMENT OF SUBSTITUTE GOODS
  * OR SERVICES; LOSS OF USE, DATA, OR PROFITS; OR BUSINESS INTERRUPTION)
  * HOWEVER CAUSED AND ON ANY THEORY OF LIABILITY, WHETHER IN CONTRACT, STRICT
```

```
 * LIABILITY, OR TORT (INCLUDING NEGLIGENCE OR OTHERWISE) ARISING IN ANY WAY
 * OUT OF THE USE OF THIS SOFTWARE, EVEN IF ADVISED OF THE POSSIBILITY OF
 * SUCH DAMAGE.
 *
 * The licence and distribution terms for any publically available version or
 * derivative of this code cannot be changed.  i.e. this code cannot simply be
 * copied and put under another distribution licence
 * [including the GNU Public Licence.]
 */
```

C.3.14 expat

The pyexpat extension is built using an included copy of the expat sources unless the build is configured
--with-system-expat:

```
Copyright (c) 1998, 1999, 2000 Thai Open Source Software Center Ltd
                    and Clark Cooper

Permission is hereby granted, free of charge, to any person obtaining
a copy of this software and associated documentation files (the
"Software"), to deal in the Software without restriction, including
without limitation the rights to use, copy, modify, merge, publish,
distribute, sublicense, and/or sell copies of the Software, and to
permit persons to whom the Software is furnished to do so, subject to
the following conditions:

The above copyright notice and this permission notice shall be included
in all copies or substantial portions of the Software.

THE SOFTWARE IS PROVIDED "AS IS", WITHOUT WARRANTY OF ANY KIND,
EXPRESS OR IMPLIED, INCLUDING BUT NOT LIMITED TO THE WARRANTIES OF
MERCHANTABILITY, FITNESS FOR A PARTICULAR PURPOSE AND NONINFRINGEMENT.
IN NO EVENT SHALL THE AUTHORS OR COPYRIGHT HOLDERS BE LIABLE FOR ANY
CLAIM, DAMAGES OR OTHER LIABILITY, WHETHER IN AN ACTION OF CONTRACT,
TORT OR OTHERWISE, ARISING FROM, OUT OF OR IN CONNECTION WITH THE
SOFTWARE OR THE USE OR OTHER DEALINGS IN THE SOFTWARE.
```

C.3.15 libffi

The _ctypes extension is built using an included copy of the libffi sources unless the build is configured
--with-system-libffi:

```
Copyright (c) 1996-2008  Red Hat, Inc and others.

Permission is hereby granted, free of charge, to any person obtaining
a copy of this software and associated documentation files (the
``Software''), to deal in the Software without restriction, including
without limitation the rights to use, copy, modify, merge, publish,
distribute, sublicense, and/or sell copies of the Software, and to
permit persons to whom the Software is furnished to do so, subject to
the following conditions:

The above copyright notice and this permission notice shall be included
in all copies or substantial portions of the Software.
```

```
THE SOFTWARE IS PROVIDED ``AS IS'', WITHOUT WARRANTY OF ANY KIND,
EXPRESS OR IMPLIED, INCLUDING BUT NOT LIMITED TO THE WARRANTIES OF
MERCHANTABILITY, FITNESS FOR A PARTICULAR PURPOSE AND
NONINFRINGEMENT.  IN NO EVENT SHALL THE AUTHORS OR COPYRIGHT
HOLDERS BE LIABLE FOR ANY CLAIM, DAMAGES OR OTHER LIABILITY,
WHETHER IN AN ACTION OF CONTRACT, TORT OR OTHERWISE, ARISING FROM,
OUT OF OR IN CONNECTION WITH THE SOFTWARE OR THE USE OR OTHER
DEALINGS IN THE SOFTWARE.
```

C.3.16 zlib

The `zlib` extension is built using an included copy of the zlib sources if the zlib version found on the system is too old to be used for the build:

```
Copyright (C) 1995-2011 Jean-loup Gailly and Mark Adler

This software is provided 'as-is', without any express or implied
warranty.  In no event will the authors be held liable for any damages
arising from the use of this software.

Permission is granted to anyone to use this software for any purpose,
including commercial applications, and to alter it and redistribute it
freely, subject to the following restrictions:

1. The origin of this software must not be misrepresented; you must not
   claim that you wrote the original software. If you use this software
   in a product, an acknowledgment in the product documentation would be
   appreciated but is not required.

2. Altered source versions must be plainly marked as such, and must not be
   misrepresented as being the original software.

3. This notice may not be removed or altered from any source distribution.

Jean-loup Gailly        Mark Adler
jloup@gzip.org          madler@alumni.caltech.edu
```

C.3.17 cfuhash

The implementation of the hash table used by the `tracemalloc` is based on the cfuhash project:

```
Copyright (c) 2005 Don Owens
All rights reserved.

This code is released under the BSD license:

Redistribution and use in source and binary forms, with or without
modification, are permitted provided that the following conditions
are met:

  * Redistributions of source code must retain the above copyright
    notice, this list of conditions and the following disclaimer.

  * Redistributions in binary form must reproduce the above
    copyright notice, this list of conditions and the following
```

```
    disclaimer in the documentation and/or other materials provided
    with the distribution.

  * Neither the name of the author nor the names of its
    contributors may be used to endorse or promote products derived
    from this software without specific prior written permission.

THIS SOFTWARE IS PROVIDED BY THE COPYRIGHT HOLDERS AND CONTRIBUTORS
"AS IS" AND ANY EXPRESS OR IMPLIED WARRANTIES, INCLUDING, BUT NOT
LIMITED TO, THE IMPLIED WARRANTIES OF MERCHANTABILITY AND FITNESS
FOR A PARTICULAR PURPOSE ARE DISCLAIMED. IN NO EVENT SHALL THE
COPYRIGHT OWNER OR CONTRIBUTORS BE LIABLE FOR ANY DIRECT, INDIRECT,
INCIDENTAL, SPECIAL, EXEMPLARY, OR CONSEQUENTIAL DAMAGES
(INCLUDING, BUT NOT LIMITED TO, PROCUREMENT OF SUBSTITUTE GOODS OR
SERVICES; LOSS OF USE, DATA, OR PROFITS; OR BUSINESS INTERRUPTION)
HOWEVER CAUSED AND ON ANY THEORY OF LIABILITY, WHETHER IN CONTRACT,
STRICT LIABILITY, OR TORT (INCLUDING NEGLIGENCE OR OTHERWISE)
ARISING IN ANY WAY OUT OF THE USE OF THIS SOFTWARE, EVEN IF ADVISED
OF THE POSSIBILITY OF SUCH DAMAGE.
```

C.3.18 libmpdec

The `_decimal` module is built using an included copy of the libmpdec library unless the build is configured `--with-system-libmpdec`:

```
Copyright (c) 2008-2016 Stefan Krah. All rights reserved.

Redistribution and use in source and binary forms, with or without
modification, are permitted provided that the following conditions
are met:

1. Redistributions of source code must retain the above copyright
   notice, this list of conditions and the following disclaimer.

2. Redistributions in binary form must reproduce the above copyright
   notice, this list of conditions and the following disclaimer in the
   documentation and/or other materials provided with the distribution.

THIS SOFTWARE IS PROVIDED BY THE AUTHOR AND CONTRIBUTORS "AS IS" AND
ANY EXPRESS OR IMPLIED WARRANTIES, INCLUDING, BUT NOT LIMITED TO, THE
IMPLIED WARRANTIES OF MERCHANTABILITY AND FITNESS FOR A PARTICULAR PURPOSE
ARE DISCLAIMED.  IN NO EVENT SHALL THE AUTHOR OR CONTRIBUTORS BE LIABLE
FOR ANY DIRECT, INDIRECT, INCIDENTAL, SPECIAL, EXEMPLARY, OR CONSEQUENTIAL
DAMAGES (INCLUDING, BUT NOT LIMITED TO, PROCUREMENT OF SUBSTITUTE GOODS
OR SERVICES; LOSS OF USE, DATA, OR PROFITS; OR BUSINESS INTERRUPTION)
HOWEVER CAUSED AND ON ANY THEORY OF LIABILITY, WHETHER IN CONTRACT, STRICT
LIABILITY, OR TORT (INCLUDING NEGLIGENCE OR OTHERWISE) ARISING IN ANY WAY
OUT OF THE USE OF THIS SOFTWARE, EVEN IF ADVISED OF THE POSSIBILITY OF
SUCH DAMAGE.
```

COPYRIGHT